God's Words
vs
Lucifer's
either/or - a simple choice

V. R. Richardson

I Am First

God's Words vs Lucifer's either/or - a Simple Choice

Copyright © 2024

Scriptures taken from the Holy Bible, New International Version®, NIV®. Copyright © 1973, 1978, 1984, 2011 by Biblica, Inc.™ Used by permission of Zondervan. All rights reserved worldwide. www.zondervan.com The "NIV" and "New International Version" are trademarks registered in the United States Patent and Trademark Office by Biblica, Inc.™

First Printing June 2024-06-22

ISBN 978-1-928116-80-6

Contents

- Preface 7
  - Jesus refers to God's Word "It is Written" 8
  - Relying on God's Word 8
- Collected Manuscripts of ONA 9
  - The XXI Satanic Points 9
  - I - What is Satanism? 14
  - IV The Black Mass 15
  - V Ceremony of Birth 16
  - VI Death Rite 16
  - VII - The Pledging 17
  - VIII - The Rite of Initiation 17
  - IX - Consecration of the Temple 18
  - X - The Dying time 19
  - XI - The Ceremony of Recalling 20
  - XII - Satanic Orders 20
  - XIII - Sinister Chant 21
  - XIV - Self-Initiation 23
  - XV - Organising and running Satanic Temples 25
  - XVI - Invokation to the Dark Gods 26
  - Sinister Creed 26
  - III - Initiate Names 30
  - I: The Sinister Calling 31
  - Sinister Chants 32
  - II: The Black Mass of Life 33
  - IV: The Black Mass – Gay Version 39
  - V: Synestry: A Sinister Ceremony 41
  - VI: The Rite of Nine Angles 43
  - VII: The Ceremony of Recalling 45
  - Order of Nine Angles 49

A Basic Introduction For Prospective Adherents 49
I - The Satanic Game 49
3. The Alchemy Of Magick 66
4- A Complete Guide To The Seven-Fold Sinister Way 68
I Neophyte 70
II Initiate 71
6. Guide To Black Magick 78
7- Darkness Is My Friend 87
8. An Introduction To Traditional Satanism 96
9- The Tradition Of The Sinister Way 111
10- The Meaning Of Sinister Initiation 112
11- The Seven-Fold Way : Training And Grades 117
13- Dark Pathworking: Satanas 122
15. Magickal Mastery - A Novice's Guide 124
16. Magick With Tears 125
17. Sinister Shadow Magick 127
19. The Aims Of The ONA 131
20. Ritual Magick: Dure And Sedue Ceremonial 132
21. Adeptship - Its Real Meaning And Purpose 133
23. The Left Handed Path - An Analysis 134
26. The Practical Esoteric Aims Of Satanism 142
27. Satanism, Blasphemy And The Black Mass 149
29- Satanism And Satanic Influence 154
30. Makrokosmos 158
32- Manipulation II 161
34- The Morality Of Satanism 164
35- Notes On Study And Practice In Modern Satanism 165
36. The Satanic Way Of Living 167
37- Thernn - An Introduction To Natural Septenary Magick 168
46 Esoteric Tradition - Synistry 169

- 52 Adeptship - Its Real Meaning And Significance 171
- 56 Way The Means, The End 173
- 60. A Gift For The Prince (A Guide To Human Sacrifice) 174
- 62 The Abyss 174
- 64. In Praise Of War 175
- 65 To Presence The Dark 176
- 66. Culling 177
- 71 Victims - A Sinister Expose 177
- 72 Revenge 178
- 82* The Creative Dialectic, Aeonic Strategy and National-Socialism 179
- 85 Aeonics And Manipulation II 180
- 98. Aeonic Insight Roles 181

The Satanic Bible 182
- Prelude 182
- The Nine Satanic Statements 183
- The Book of Satan II 184
- The Book of Satan III 185
- The Book of Satan IV 188
- The Book of Satan V 189
- The Enlightenment 192
- The Three Types of Satanic Ritual 205
- The Ingredients Used In The Performance Of Satanic Magic 207
- The Satanic Ritual 212

Magick In Theory And Practice by The Master Therion Aleister Crowley 215
- Introduction 215
- The Principles Of Ritual 216
- The Formulae Of The Elemental Weapons 217
- The Formula of I.A.O. 220

The Magical Memory 224
Of Equilibrium 227
Of Silence And Secrecy: and of the Barbarous Names of Evocation
.... 229
Of the Gestures 230
Of Our Lady Babalon and of the Beast Whereon She Rideth 232
Of the Bloody Sacrifice 234
Of the Banishings: and of the Purifications 235
Of the Consecrations: with an account of the Nature and Nurture of
the Magical Link 238
Of the Oath 245
Of the Invocation 248
Of the Charge to The Spirit With Some Account of the Constraints
and Curses Occasionally Necessary 251
Of the License to Depart 254
Of Clairvoyance and the Body of Light 254
Of the Eucharist and of the Art Of Alchemy 261
Of Black Magic of the Main Types of the Operations of Magick Art
and of the Powers of the Sphinx 264

Subject Index 272

Preface

Today there are numerous books supporting Satanism as a religion. However, in a contemporary context there are primary texts that supply the rituals, teachings, applications, and organizational structures of Satanic groups – namely, the works by English occultist Aleister Crowley whose primary text "Magick in Theory and Practice" was published in 1929, secondly the "Satanic Bible" by Anton LaVey who founded the Church of Satan in 1966, and third the "Collection of Various Manuscripts" of the Order of the Nine Angles, which was allegedly founded by Anton Long in 1973 after being initiated in Wales, United Kingdom. Of note in terms of public numerical attendance is the group known as the Church of Satan, founded in San Franciso in 1966 by LaVey. Additionally there is the Satanic Temple which Lucien Greaves "has described the Temple as being a progressive and updated version of LaVey's Satanism." – [(2016). The Invention of Satanism. Oxford University Press. p. 220]

As a result the focus is on the three texts referred to previously.

Consequently, to avoid duplication given the numerous ideas replicating one another in both major groups, the demonic verses selected are perceived as unique and drawn first from the ONA's texts due to the worldwide influence inspiring terrorism and crimes, with the remaining from the Satanic Bible as religious source for both the Church of Satan and the Temple of Satan.

Thus this collection may be used for various crucial objectives. One may use the book for a retreat, or to counter diabolical objectives which one encounters in society or on a personal ideological level.

Please note that unless otherwise referenced in brackets, by default Bible quotes are from the New International Version also known as the NIV.

Jesus refers to God's Word "It is Written"

Matthew 4:3 The tempter came to him and said, "If you are the Son of God, tell these stones to become bread." 4 Jesus answered, "It is written: 'Man shall not live on bread alone, but on every word that comes from the mouth of God.'

Romans 14:11 It is written: "'As surely as I live,' says the Lord, 'every knee will bow before me; every tongue will acknowledge God.'"

Relying on God's Word

2 Timothy 3:16 All Scripture is God-breathed and is useful for teaching, rebuking, correcting and training in righteousness, 17 so that the servant of God may be thoroughly equipped for every good work. — correcting, rebuking

Matthew 4:4 Jesus answered, "It is written: 'Man shall not live on bread alone, but on every word that comes from the mouth of God.'

Ephesians 5:11 Have nothing to do with the fruitless deeds of darkness, but rather expose them. 12 It is shameful even to mention what the disobedient do in secret. — expose evil

1 Corinthians 10:20 No, but the sacrifices of pagans are offered to demons, not to God, and I do not want you to be participants with demons. 21 You cannot drink the cup of the Lord and the cup of demons too; you cannot have a part in both the Lord's table and the table of demons. — either or

James 1:23 Anyone who listens to the word but does not do what it says is like someone who looks at his face in a mirror 24 and, after looking at himself, goes away and immediately forgets what he looks like. 25 But whoever looks intently into the perfect law that gives freedom, and continues in it—not forgetting what they have heard, but doing it—they will be blessed in what they do.

Collected Manuscripts of ONA
The XXI Satanic Points

1. Respect not pity or weakness, for they are a disease which makes sick the strong.   empathy
   2 Corinthians 12:9 But he said to me, "My   the strong
   grace is sufficient for you, for my power is made perfect in weakness." Therefore I will boast all the more gladly about my weaknesses, so that Christ's power may rest on me.
   Psalm 82:3 Defend the weak and the fatherless; uphold the cause of the poor and the oppressed..

2. Test always your strength, for therein lies success.   success
   Matthew 16:26 What good will it be for someone to gain the whole world, yet forfeit their soul? Or what can anyone give in exchange for their soul? 27 For the Son of Man is going to come in his Father's glory with his angels, and then he will reward each person according to what they have done.
   Isaiah 41:10 So do not fear, for I am with you; do not be dismayed, for I am your God. I will strengthen you and help you; I will uphold you with my righteous right hand.

3. Seek happiness in victory - but never in peace.   victory
   Matthew 5:9 Blessed are the peacemakers, for they will be called children of God.
   1 John 5:4 for everyone born of God overcomes the world. This is the victory that has overcome the world, even our faith.

4. Enjoy a short rest, better than a long.   rest
   Matthew 11:28 "Come to me, all you who are weary and burdened, and I will give you rest. 29 Take my yoke upon you and learn from me, for I am gentle and humble in heart, and you will find rest for your souls. 30 For my yoke is easy and my burden is light."

5. Come as a reaper, for thus you will sow.   success
   Hosea 10:12 Sow righteousness for yourselves, reap the fruit of unfailing love, and

break up your unplowed ground; for it is time to seek the Lord, until he comes and showers his righteousness on you.

   Galatians 6:7 Do not be deceived: God cannot be mocked. A man reaps what he sows. 8 Whoever sows to please their flesh, from the flesh will reap destruction; whoever sows to please the Spirit, from the Spirit will reap eternal life. 9 Let us not become weary in doing good, for at the proper time we will reap a harvest if we do not give up. 10 Therefore, as we have opportunity, let us do good to all people, especially to those who belong to the family of believers.

   Matthew 7:1 "Do not judge, or you too will be judged. 2 For in the same way you judge others, you will be judged, and with the measure you use, it will be measured to you. 3 "Why do you look at the speck of sawdust in your brother's eye and pay no attention to the plank in your own eye? 4 How can you say to your brother, 'Let me take the speck out of your eye,' when all the time there is a plank in your own eye? 5 You hypocrite, first take the plank out of your own eye, and then you will see clearly to remove the speck from your brother's eye.

6	Never love anything so much you cannot see it die.	love

   John 15:13 Greater love has no one than this: to lay down one's life for one's friends.

   1 John 4:8 Whoever does not love does not know God, because God is love.

7	Build not upon sand, but upon rock. And build not for today or yesterday but for all time.	success

   Luke 14:28 "Suppose one of you wants to build a tower. Won't you first sit down and estimate the cost to see if you have enough money to complete it? 29 For if you lay the foundation and are not able to finish it, everyone who sees it will ridicule you, 30 saying, 'This person began to build and wasn't able to finish.'

8	Strive ever for more, for conquest is never done.	success
	Matthew 5:9 Blessed are the peacemakers, for they will be called children of God.	war
	Romans 13:1 Let everyone be subject to the governing authorities, for there is no authority except that which God has established. The authorities that exist have been established by God. 2 Consequently, whoever rebels against the authority is rebelling against what God has instituted, and those who do so will bring judgment on themselves. 3 For rulers hold no terror for those who do right, but for those who do wrong. Do you want to be free from fear of the one in authority? Then do what is right and you will be commended. 4 For the one in authority is God's servant for your good. But if you do wrong, be afraid, for rulers do not bear the sword for no reason. They are God's servants, agents of wrath to bring punishment on the wrongdoer. 5 Therefore, it is necessary to submit to the authorities, not only because of possible punishment but also as a matter of conscience.	
9	And die rather than submit.	competition
	James 4:7 Submit yourselves, then, to God. Resist the devil, and he will flee from you.	elections
	Luke 22:42 Father, if you are willing, take this cup from me; yet not my will, but yours be done.	
10	Forge not works of art but swords of death, for therein lies great art.	love
	Matthew 26:52 "Put your sword back in its place," Jesus said to him, "for all who draw the sword will die by the sword. 53 Do you think I cannot call on my Father, and he will at once put at my disposal more than twelve legions of angels? 54 But how then would the Scriptures be fulfilled that say it must happen in this way?"	society
	Ephesians 2:10 For we are God's handiwork, created in Christ Jesus to do good works, which God prepared in advance for us to do.	
	1 Peter 4:10 Each of you should use whatever	

gift you have received to serve others, as faithful stewards of God's grace in its various forms.

Romans 12:17 Do not repay anyone evil for evil. Be careful to do what is right in the eyes of everyone.

1 Peter 3:8 Finally, all of you, be like-minded, be sympathetic, love one another, be compassionate and humble. 9 Do not repay evil with evil or insult with insult. On the contrary, repay evil with blessing, because to this you were called so that you may inherit a blessing.

11 Learn to raise yourself above yourself so you can triumph over all. self-development psychology

Philippians 2:3 Do nothing out of selfish ambition or vain conceit. Rather, in humility value others above yourselves, 4 not looking to your own interests but each of you to the interests of the others.

Luke 12:7 Indeed, the very hairs of your head are all numbered. Don't be afraid; you are worth more than many sparrows.

1 Peter 3:3 Your beauty should not come from outward adornment, such as elaborate hairstyles and the wearing of gold jewelry or fine clothes. 4 Rather, it should be that of your inner self, the unfading beauty of a gentle and quiet spirit, which is of great worth in God's sight.

12 The blood of the living makes good fertiliser for the seeds of the new. neighbour society

1 John 1:7 But if we walk in the light, as he is in the light, we have fellowship with one another, and the blood of Jesus, his Son, purifies us from all sin.

13 He who stands atop the highest pyramid of skulls can see the furthest. business competition

James 5:5 You have lived on earth in luxury and self-indulgence. You have fattened yourselves in the day of slaughter.

14 Discard not love but treat it as an impostor, but ever be just. love

1 Corinthians 16:14 Do everything in love.

Ephesians 4:2 Be completely humble and gentle; be patient, bearing with one another in love.

15. All that is great is built upon sorrow. — fame
    Philippians 4:13 I can do all this through him who gives me strength. — business
    Colossians 3:17 And whatever you do, whether in word or deed, do it all in the name of the Lord Jesus, giving thanks to God the Father through him.

16. Strive not only forwards, but upwards for greatness lies in the highest — celebrity
    Luke 9:48 Then he said to them, "Whoever welcomes this little child in my name welcomes me; and whoever welcomes me welcomes the one who sent me. For it is the one who is least among you all who is the greatest." — humility

17. Come as a fresh strong wind that breaks yet also creates — personality
    Matthew 6:33 But seek first his kingdom and his righteousness, and all these things will be given to you as well. — artist

18. Let love of life be a goal but let your highest goal be greatness. — goals
    Romans 8:28 And we know that in all things God works for the good of those who love him, who have been called according to his purpose.
    1 Corinthians 10:31 So whether you eat or drink or whatever you do, do it all for the glory of God.

19. Nothing is beautiful except man: but most beautiful of all is woman. — beauty
    1 Peter 3:3 Your beauty should not come from outward adornment, such as elaborate hairstyles and the wearing of gold jewelry or fine clothes. 4 Rather, it should be that of your inner self, the unfading beauty of a gentle and quiet spirit, which is of great worth in God's sight. — gender

20. Reject all illusion and lies, for they hinder the strong. — illusions
    1 Peter 5:8 Be alert and of sober mind. Your enemy the devil prowls around like a roaring — reality

lion looking for someone to devour.

21 What does not kill, makes stronger.   survival

Galatians 5:19 The acts of the flesh are obvious: sexual immorality, impurity and debauchery; 20 idolatry and witchcraft; hatred, discord, jealousy, fits of rage, selfish ambition, dissensions, factions 21 and envy; drunkenness, orgies, and the like. I warn you, as I did before, that those who live like this will not inherit the kingdom of God.

I - What is Satanism?

22 (a) Satanism is fundamentally a way of living -   Way of life
a practical philosophy of life. The essence of this way is the belief that we can all, as individuals, achieve far more with our lives than we realize. Most people waste the opportunities that life can, by magick, be made to bring.

Matthew 16:26 What good will it be for someone to gain the whole world, yet forfeit their soul? Or what can anyone give in exchange for their soul? 27 For the Son of Man is going to come in his Father's glory with his angels, and then he will reward each person according to what they have done.

Matthew 16:24 - Then Jesus said to his disciples, "Whoever wants to be my disciple must deny themselves and take up their cross and follow me.

23 (b) Satanism, in its beginnings, is all about   psychology
making conscious (or liberating) our dark or shadow nature

Romans 8:6 The mind governed by the flesh is death, but the mind governed by the Spirit is life and peace. 7 The mind governed by the flesh is hostile to God; it does not submit to God's law, nor can it do so.

24 The religion of Yeshua has inverted all natural   evolution
values, setting back the course of our conscious evolution. Satanism, on the contrary, is a natural expression of the evolutionary or 'Promethean' urge within us: and its magick is a means to make us gods upon Earth, to realize the potential that lies within us all.

Philippians 4:13 I can do everything through him who gives me strength.

IV The Black Mass

25   (a) The Black Mass is a ceremonial ritual with a threefold purpose. First, it is a positive inversion of the mass of the Nazarene church, and in this sense is a rite Black Magick ... Second it is a means of personal liberation from the chains of Nazarene dogma and thus a blasphemy: a ritual to liberate unconscious feelings. Third, it is a magickal rite in itself, that is, correct performance generates magickal energy which the celebrant can direct.   worship

Hebrews 12:28 Therefore, since we are receiving a kingdom that cannot be shaken, let us be thankful, and so worship God acceptably with reverence and awe,   ritual

Romans 12:1 Therefore, I urge you, brothers and sisters, in view of God's mercy, to offer your bodies as a living sacrifice, holy and pleasing to God—this is your true and proper worship. 2 Do not conform to the pattern of this world, but be transformed by the renewing of your mind. Then you will be able to test and approve what God's will is—his good, pleasing and perfect will.   worship

26   (b) Our Father which wert in heaven Hallowed be thy name In heaven as it is on Earth. Give us this day our ecstasy And deliver us to evil as well as temptation For we are your kingdom for aeons and aeons.   prayer

Matthew 6:9 "This, then, is how you should pray:

"'Our Father in heaven,
hallowed be your name,
10 your kingdom come,
your will be done,
   on earth as it is in heaven.
11 Give us today our daily bread.
12 And forgive us our debts,
   as we also have forgiven our debtors.
13 And lead us not into temptation,
   but deliver us from the evil one.

27	Blessed are the strong for they shall inherit the Earth.	strength
	Matthew 5:5 Blessed are the meek, for they will inherit the earth.	humility
28	(e) Hail Satan, Prince of life	praise
	2 Corinthians 1:3 Praise be to the God and Father of our Lord Jesus Christ, the Father of compassion and the God of all comfort, 4 who comforts us in all our troubles, so that we can comfort those in any trouble with the comfort we ourselves receive from God.	true king
29	(f) Let the church of the impostor Yeshua crumble into dust. Let all the scum who worship the rotting fish suffer and die in their misery and rejection! We trample on them and spit of their sin! Let there be ecstasy and darkness; let there be chaos and laughter, Let there be sacrifice and strife: but above all let us enjoy The gifts of life!	other religions
	Colossians 3:12 Therefore, as God's chosen people, holy and dearly loved, clothe yourselves with compassion, kindness, humility, gentleness and patience.	non-believers
	John 13:34 "A new command I give you: Love one another. As I have loved you, so you must love one another. 35 By this everyone will know that you are my disciples, if you love one another."	

V Ceremony of Birth

30	(a) Ad Satanas qui leatificat juventutem meam. translated - To Satan, who rejoices in my youth.	enemy
	1 Peter 5:8 Be alert and of sober mind. Your enemy the devil prowls around like a roaring lion looking for someone to devour.	youth

VI Death Rite

31	Priest: I will go down to the altars in Hell. All: To Satan, the giver of life. (The Priest then kisses the Priestess on the lips, turns toward the congregation and makes the sign of the inverted pentagram, saying:) Our Father which wert in heaven Hallowed be thy name In heaven as it is on Earth. Give us this day our ecstasy And deliver us to evil as well as temptation For we	afterlife

are your kingdom for aeons and aeons.
    John 11:25 Jesus said to her, "I am the   prayer
resurrection and the life. The one who believes
in me will live, even though they die;
    John 3:16 For God so loved the world that he
gave his one and only Son, that whoever
believes in him shall not perish but have eternal
life.

32 Provide us pleasure, Prince of Darkness, and   pleasure
help us fulfil our desires.
    Galatians 5:16 So I say, walk by the Spirit,   desires
and you will not gratify the desires of the flesh.

VII - The Pledging

33 We are gathered here to join in oath through our   matrimony
sinister magick this man and this woman.
Together they shall be as inner sanctuaries to
our gods!
    Eph 5:25 Husbands, love your wives, just as
Christ loved the church and gave himself up for
her 26 to make her holy, cleansing her by the
washing with water through the word, 27 and to
present her to himself as a radiant church,
without stain or wrinkle or any other blemish,
but holy and blameless. 28 In this same way,
husbands ought to love their wives as their own
bodies. He who loves his wife loves himself.

34 Thus in oath and magick they are joined.   matrimony
    Mark 10:9 Therefore what God has joined
together, let no one separate."
    2 Kings 17:17 They sacrificed their sons and   magic
daughters in the fire. They practiced divination
and sought omens and sold themselves to do
evil in the eyes of the Lord, arousing his anger.

VIII - The Rite of Initiation

35 The ritual takes place at sunset. A small phial   ritual
containing a civit-based oil is placed on the
altar. Black candles to be used, incense of the
Moon burnt (petriochor, if available, otherwise
hazel). Some symbolism appropriate to the
Moon should also be present - e.g. quartz
crystals. Chalices full of strong wine.
    1 Corinthians 10:16 Is not the cup of   Lord's supper
thanksgiving for which we give thanks a

participation in the blood of Christ? And is not the bread that we break a participation in the body of Christ?

John 3:5 Jesus answered, "Very truly I tell you, no one can enter the kingdom of God unless they are born of water and the Spirit.   baptism

36   Master: Do you renounce the Nazarene Yeshua the deceiver, and all his works ?   Jesus
R:I do renounce Yeshua the deceiver and all his works.

Acts 4:11 Jesus is "'the stone you builders rejected, which has become the cornerstone.' 12 Salvation is found in no one else, for there is no other name under heaven given to mankind by which we must be saved."   salvation

37   Master: Do you affirm Satan?   creed
R: I do affirm Satan.
Master: Satan, whose word is Chaos?
R: Satan, whose word is Chaos.
Master: Then break this symbol which we detest.
(The Mistress hands the candidate a suitably defiled wooden cross which the candidate breaks and thrown it to the ground.)

Matthew 10:38 Whoever does not take up their cross and follow me is not worthy of me. 39 Whoever finds their life will lose it, and whoever loses their life for my sake will find it.   cross

Mark 8:33 But when Jesus turned and looked at his disciples, he rebuked Peter. "Get behind me, Satan!" he said. "You do not have in mind the concerns of God, but merely human concerns."   devil

John 10:10 The thief comes only to steal and kill and destroy; I have come that they may have life, and have it to the full.   devil

IX - Consecration of the Temple

38   The Master enters the Temple before the congregation, and seal seals the dimensions according to the Rite of Sealing: For this, a crystal tetrahedron is required. It should be as large as possible and made of quartz.   crystals

Ezekiel 13:18 and say, 'This is what the

Sovereign Lord says: Woe to the women who sew magic charms on all their wrists and make veils of various lengths for their heads in order to ensnare people. Will you ensnare the lives of my people but preserve your own? 19 You have profaned me among my people for a few handfuls of barley and scraps of bread. By lying to my people, who listen to lies, you have killed those who should not have died and have spared those who should not live.20
"'Therefore this is what the Sovereign Lord says: I am against your magic charms with which you ensnare people like birds and I will tear them from your arms; I will set free the people that you ensnare like birds.

39 We gather here in this place at this Hour to dedicate this Temple to our sinister work. We Summon forth Satan, Prince of Darkness and Guardian of the Gate to the Dark Gods, to witness our rite of Dedication. For this shall be a Temple wherein we shall celebrate the Mysteries and the joys of life - wherein we and others Shall partake of the Elixir which is black to the blind. — temple dedication

Psalm 127:1 Unless the Lord builds the house, the builders labor in vain. Unless the Lord watches over the city, the guards stand watch in vain.

X - The Dying time

40 Agios o Satanas! We gather here to pay homage to our brother/sister who by his/her life and magick did deeds of glory to the honour of our name! Agios o Satanas! — magic

Deu 18:10 Let no one be found among you who sacrifices their son or daughter in the fire, who practices divination or sorcery, interprets omens, engages in witchcraft, 11 or casts spells, or who is a medium or spiritist or who consults the dead. — sorcery

Revelation 21:8 But the cowardly, the unbelieving, the vile, the murderers, the sexually immoral, those who practice magic arts, the idolaters and all liars—they will be

consigned to the fiery lake of burning sulfur. This is the second death."

XI - The Ceremony of Recalling

41 I pour my kisses at your feet and kneel before you Who crushes your enemies and who washes in a basin full of Their blood. — enemies

Luke 6:27 "But to you who are listening I say: Love your enemies, do good to those who hate you, 28 bless those who curse you, pray for those who mistreat you. 29 If someone slaps you on one cheek, turn to them the other also. If someone takes your coat, do not withhold your shirt from them. 30 Give to everyone who asks you, and if anyone takes what belongs to you, do not demand it back.

XII - Satanic Orders

42 In its initial stages, genuine Satanism is all about the Initiate experiencing the dark or shadow aspect of themselves — initiation

Ephesians 4:22 You were taught, with regard to your former way of life, to put off your old self, which is being corrupted by its deceitful desires; 23 to be made new in the attitude of your minds; 24 and to put on the new self, created to be like God in true righteousness and holiness.

43 Some of these experiences were unconventional and frowned on by 'conventional society' -and some would have been 'illegal' as well. — authority

Romans 13:1 Let everyone be subject to the governing authorities, for there is no authority except that which God has established. The authorities that exist have been established by God. 2 Consequently, whoever rebels against the authority is rebelling against what God has instituted, and those who do so will bring judgment on themselves. — crime

44 Associated with the Grade Rituals are other tasks and these form the basis of the training of the Satanic Initiate! By their very nature, they produce a specific type of individual: one, that is, imbued with the Satanist spirit. — ritual

Acts 1:8 But you will receive power when the

Holy Spirit comes on you; and you will be my witnesses in Jerusalem, and in all Judea and Samaria, and to the ends of the earth." .

45 In short, they exemplify the spirit of the Satanist: that life-affirming ecstasy which both conquers and defies. ecstasy defiance

1 Thessalonians 5:23 May God himself, the God of peace, sanctify you through and through. May your whole spirit, soul and body be kept blameless at the coming of our Lord Jesus Christ.

XIII - Sinister Chant

46 Sinister chant is divided into three distinct methods, all of which have the same general aim - to produce magickal energy. singing chanting

Psalm 147:7 Sing to the Lord with grateful praise; make music to our God on the harp.

Colossians 3:16 Let the message of Christ dwell among you richly as you teach and admonish one another with all wisdom through psalms, hymns, and songs from the Spirit, singing to God with gratitude in your hearts.

Ephesians 5:19 speaking to one another with psalms, hymns, and songs from the Spirit. Sing and make music from your heart to the Lord, 20 always giving thanks to God the Father for everything, in the name of our Lord Jesus Christ.

47 The first method is the vibration of words and phrases; the second is chanting, and the third is 'Esoteric Chant' - that is, the following of a specific text which is chanted in one of the esoteric modes. chanting

Matthew 6:7 But when ye pray, use not vain repetitions, as the heathen do: for they think that they shall be heard for their much speaking. (KJV)

Matthew 6:7 And when you pray, do not keep on babbling like pagans, for they think they will be heard because of their many words. 8 Do not be like them, for your Father knows what you need before you ask him.

48 Sanctus Satanas, Sanctus Dominus Diabolus this world

Sabaoth.
Satanas - venire!
Satanas - venire!
Ave, Satanas, ave Satanas.
Tui sunt caeli,
Tua est terra,
Ave Satanas!
<u>Translated</u>:
Holy Satan, Holy Lord the Devil Sabaoth.
Satan - come!
Satan - come!
Hail, Satan, Hail Satan.
the heavens are yours
the land is yours
Hail Satan!

 2 Corinthians 4:4 The god of this age has blinded the minds of unbelievers, so that they cannot see the light of the gospel that displays the glory of Christ, who is the image of God.

 John 12:31 Now is the time for judgment on this world; now the prince of this world will be driven out.

49	Invokation to Baphomet	
	We stand armed and dangerous before the bloody fields of history	history

 Romans 15:4 For everything that was written in the past was written to teach us, so that through the endurance taught in the Scriptures and the encouragement they provide we might have hope.

50	Devoid of dogma - but ready to carve, to defy the transient	dogma teachings

 Matthew 7:29 because he taught as one who had authority, and not as their teachers of the law.

51	Ready to stab forth with our penetrative will	man's will
		God's will

 John 6:38 For I have come down from heaven not to do my will but to do the will of him who sent me. 39 And this is the will of him who sent me, that I shall lose none of all those he has given me, but raise them up at the last day. 40 For my Father's will is that everyone who looks to the Son and believes in him shall have eternal

life, and I will raise them up at the last day."

XIV - Self-Initiation

52   To you, Satan, Prince of Darkness and Lord of the Earth, I dedicate this Temple: let it become, like my body, A vessel for your power and an expression of your glory!   *ritual*

     1 Corinthians 6:19 Do you not know that your bodies are temples of the Holy Spirit, who is in you, whom you have received from God? You are not your own; 20 you were bought at a price. Therefore honor God with your bodies.

53   Then vibrate 'Agios o Satanas' nine times. After this, take up the salt and sprinkle it over the altar and around the room, saying: With this salt I seal the power of Satan in!   *salt*

     Matthew 5:1 "You are the salt of the earth. But if the salt loses its saltiness, how can it be made salty again? It is no longer good for anything, except to be thrown out and trampled underfoot. 14 "You are the light of the world. A town built on a hill cannot be hidden. 15 Neither do people light a lamp and put it under a bowl. Instead they put it on its stand, and it gives light to everyone in the house. 16 In the same way, let your light shine before others, that they may see your good deeds and glorify your Father in heaven.

54   Once in the Temple, do the 'Sinister Blessing', then facing the altar, lightly prick your left forefinger with the knife. With the blood and using the pen inscribe on one parchment the Occult name you have chosen.
With my blood I dedicate the Temple of my life!   *blood*

     Romans 5:9 Since we have now been justified by his blood, how much more shall we be saved from God's wrath through him!   *justification*

55   Satan, may your power mingle with mine as my blood now mingles with fire!   *invocation*

     2 Thessalonians 2:9 The coming of the lawless one will be in accordance with how Satan works. He will use all sorts of displays of power through signs and wonders that serve the lie,   *power*

Ephesians 6:10 Finally, be strong in the Lord and in his mighty power. 11 Put on the full armor of God, so that you can take your stand against the devil's schemes. 12 For our struggle is not against flesh and blood, but against the rulers, against the authorities, against the powers of this dark world and against the spiritual forces of evil in the heavenly realms.

56   With this drink I seal my oath. I am yours and shall do works to the glory of your name!   chalice

John 6:55 For my flesh is real food and my blood is real drink. 56 Whoever eats my flesh and drinks my blood remains in me, and I in them. 57 Just as the living Father sent me and I live because of the Father, so the one who feeds on me will live because of me. 58 This is the bread that came down from heaven. Your ancestors ate manna and died, but whoever feeds on this bread will live forever."

57   With this drink I seal my oath. I am yours and shall do works to the glory of your name!   works

2 Corinthians 11:13 For such people are false apostles, deceitful workers, masquerading as apostles of Christ. 14 And no wonder, for Satan himself masquerades as an angel of light. 15 It is not surprising, then, if his servants also masquerade as servants of righteousness. Their end will be what their actions deserve.   servants of God

58   'I (state your Occult name) am here to begin my sinister quest. Prince of Darkness, hear me! Hear me, you Dark Gods waiting beyond the Abyss.'

Colossians 3:17 And whatever you do, whether in word or deed, do it all in the name of the Lord Jesus, giving thanks to God the Father through him.   name

59   'Satan, may your power mingle with mine as my blood now mingles with fire!'   unity

John 17:20 "My prayer is not for them alone. I pray also for those who will believe in me through their message, 21 that all of them may be one, Father, just as you are in me and I am in you. May they also be in us so that the world

may believe that you have sent me. 22 I have given them the glory that you gave me, that they may be one as we are one— 23 I in them and you in me—so that they may be brought to complete unity. Then the world will know that you sent me and have loved them even as you have loved me.

60   'With this drink I seal my oath. I am yours and shall do works to the glory of your name.'   oaths

Matthew 5:33 "Again, you have heard that it was said to the people long ago, 'Do not break your oath, but fulfill to the Lord the vows you have made.'

XV - Organising and running Satanic Temples

61   Once a month (at a new moon if possible) celebrate the Black Mass. This celebration should be followed by a feast where food and wine prepared and/or brought to the Temple by the members is consumed, this feast itself following on after the orgy that concludes the Black Mass.   meeting

1 Corinthians 11:23 For I received from the Lord what I also passed on to you: The Lord Jesus, on the night he was betrayed, took bread, 24 and when he had given thanks, he broke it and said, "This is my body, which is for you; do this in remembrance of me." 25 In the same way, after supper he took the cup, saying, "This cup is the new covenant in my blood; do this, whenever you drink it, in remembrance of me."   Lord's supper

Mark 2:27 Then he said to them, "The Sabbath was made for man, not man for the Sabbath.

62   Gaining Members: There are many ways of gaining members. For instance, you might infiltrate already existing groups (of either Left or Right Hand Paths) and seek out those interested in working sinister magick. You might also try and interest friends or the friends of your companion - using the bait of an 'orgy'.   membership marketing

Matthew 5:16 In the same way, let your light shine before others, that they may see your good deeds and glorify your Father in heaven.

Matthew 5:14 "You are the light of the world. A town built on a hill cannot be hidden. 15 Neither do people light a lamp and put it under a bowl. Instead they put it on its stand, and it gives light to everyone in the house. 16 In the same way, let your light shine before others, that they may see your good deeds and glorify your Father in heaven.

John 13:35 By this everyone will know that you are my disciples, if you love one another."

1 Peter 2:12 Live such good lives among the pagans that, though they accuse you of doing wrong, they may see your good deeds and glorify God on the day he visits us.

XVI - Invokation to the Dark Gods

63 However, if the ritual is undertaken correctly, the Dark Gods may become manifest. Should this occur, all the participants should exult. — demons

1 John 3:8 The one who does what is sinful is of the devil, because the devil has been sinning from the beginning. The reason the Son of God appeared was to destroy the devil's work.

2 Corinthians 4:4 The god of this age has blinded the minds of unbelievers, so that they cannot see the light of the gospel that displays the glory of Christ, who is the image of God.

1 Corinthians 10:20 No, but the sacrifices of pagans are offered to demons, not to God, and I do not want you to be participants with demons. 21 You cannot drink the cup of the Lord and the cup of demons too; you cannot have a part in both the Lord's table and the table of demons.

Sinister Creed

64 1. Satan in particular and the Dark Gods in general are a means to self-fulfilment and self understanding. — self-fulfillment

Matthew 6:25 "Therefore I tell you, do not worry about your life, what you will eat or drink; or about your body, what you will wear. Is not life more than food, and the body more than clothes? 26 Look at the birds of the air; they do not sow or reap or store away in barns, and yet your heavenly Father feeds them. Are you not much more valuable than they? 27 Can any one of you by worrying add a single hour to your life? 28 "And why do you worry about clothes? See how the flowers of the field grow. They do not labor or spin. 29 Yet I tell you that not even Solomon in all his splendor was dressed like one of these. 30 If that is how God clothes the grass of the field, which is here today and tomorrow is thrown into the fire, will he not much more clothe you—you of little faith? 31 So do not worry, saying, 'What shall we eat?' or 'What shall we drink?' or 'What shall we wear?' 32 For the pagans run after all these things, and your heavenly Father knows that you need them. 33 But seek first his kingdom and his righteousness, and all these things will be given to you as well.

65	2. Only by journeying through the darkness within us and without can we attain self-divinity and thus fulfil the potentiality of our existence.	self-actualization

2 Corinthians 3:18 And we all, who with unveiled faces contemplate the Lord's glory, are being transformed into his image with ever-increasing glory, which comes from the Lord, who is the Spirit.

2 Corinthians 5:17 Therefore, if anyone is in Christ, the new creation has come: The old has gone, the new is here!

Colossians 3:10 and have put on the new self, which is being renewed in knowledge in the image of its Creator.

66	3. Our rites, ceremonies and practices are all life affirming, and show us the ecstasy of existence and the self-overcoming of the true Adept.	ceremony

Colossians 3:2 Set your minds on things above, not on earthly things.   worldliness

Psalm 37:4 Take delight in the Lord, and he will give you the desires of your heart.

John 15:10 If you keep my commands, you will remain in my love, just as I have kept my Father's commands and remain in his love. 11 I have told you this so that my joy may be in you and that your joy may be complete.

Romans 5:1 Therefore, since we have been justified through faith, we have peace with God through our Lord Jesus Christ, 2 through whom we have gained access by faith into this grace in which we now stand. And we boast in the hope of the glory of God.

67   4. We are feared because we defy and seek to know and thus understand. We rejoice in living in all its pleasures but most particularly in its possibilities. We thus extend the frontiers of evolution while others sleep or cry.   self-knowledge pleasures

Colossians 2:2 My goal is that they may be encouraged in heart and united in love, so that they may have the full riches of complete understanding, in order that they may know the mystery of God, namely, Christ, 3 in whom are hidden all the treasures of wisdom and knowledge.

2 Timothy 3:16 All Scripture is God-breathed and is useful for teaching, rebuking, correcting and training in righteousness, 17 so that the servant of God may be thoroughly equipped for every good work.

Colossians 3:10 and have put on the new self, which is being renewed in knowledge in the image of its Creator.

1 John 2:15 Do not love the world or anything in the world. If anyone loves the world, love for the Father is not in them. 16 For everything in the world—the lust of the flesh, the lust of the eyes, and the pride of life—comes not from the Father but from the world. 17 The world and its desires pass away, but whoever does the will of God lives forever.

68   5. We detest all that enervates and would rather die than submit to anyone or anything - this pride is the pride of Satan, and Satan is a symbol of our defiance and a sign of our life-enhancing energy. Others see our way of living and our way of dying and are afraid.   pride

Proverbs 11:2 When pride comes, then comes disgrace, but with humility comes wisdom.

James 4:6 But he gives us more grace. That is

why Scripture says: "God opposes the proud but shows favor to the humble.

Romans:13 Let everyone be subject to the governing authorities, for there is no authority except that which God has established. The authorities that exist have been established by God. 2 Consequently, whoever rebels against the authority is rebelling against what God has instituted, and those who do so will bring judgment on themselves."

69   6. When we hate we hate openly and with arrogance, and when we love, we love with a passion to match this arrogance: always mindful never to love anyone so much that we cannot see them die, for death is a natural changing of energies.   hatred

1 John 3:14 We know that we have passed from death to life, because we love each other. Anyone who does not love remains in death. 15 Anyone who hates a brother or sister is a murderer, and you know that no murderer has eternal life residing in him.   neighbour

Leviticus 19:17 "'Do not hate a fellow Israelite in your heart. Rebuke your neighbor frankly so you will not share in their guilt. 18 "'Do not seek revenge or bear a grudge against anyone among your people, but love your neighbor as yourself. I am the Lord.

1 John 4:19 We love because he first loved us. 20 Whoever claims to love God yet hates a brother or sister is a liar. For whoever does not love their brother and sister, whom they have seen, cannot love God, whom they have not seen.

70   7. We prepare - through our magick and our ways of living - for the Age of Fire (the Aeon of the Dark Gods) which is to come, when we elitist few shall reach out toward the stars and the galaxies and the new challenges they will bring.   future

Matthew 6:31 So do not worry, saying, 'What shall we eat?' or 'What shall we drink?' or 'What shall we wear?' 32 For the pagans run

after all these things, and your heavenly Father knows that you need them. 33 But seek first his kingdom and his righteousness, and all these things will be given to you as well.

Jeremiah 29:11 For I know the plans I have for you," declares the Lord, "plans to prosper you and not to harm you, plans to give you hope and a future.

71 8. Our way is difficult and dangerous and is for the few who can truly defy the matrix of illusions - of 'good' and 'evil' - that stifle the potentiality of our being.   illusions

James 1:13 When tempted, no one should say, "God is tempting me." For God cannot be tempted by evil, nor does he tempt anyone; 14 but each person is tempted when they are dragged away by their own evil desire and enticed. 15 Then, after desire has conceived, it gives birth to sin; and sin, when it is full-grown, gives birth to death.   temptation

Isaiah 5: Woe to those who call evil good and good evil, who put darkness for light and light for darkness, who put bitter for sweet and sweet for bitter.   delusions

71 9. What does not kill us, makes us stronger.

Philippians 4:12 I know what it is to be in need, and I know what it is to have plenty. I have learned the secret of being content in any and every situation, whether well fed or hungry, whether living in plenty or in want. 13 I can do all this through him who gives me strength.

Proverbs 18:10 The name of the Lord is a fortified tower; the righteous run to it and are safe.

Isaiah 40:29 He gives strength to the weary and increases the power of the weak. 30 Even youths grow tired and weary, and young men stumble and fall; 31 but those who hope in the Lord will renew their strength. They will soar on wings like eagles; they will run and not grow weary, they will walk and not be faint.   inner strength

III - Initiate Names

72 Find a demon form with whom you feel an   names

affinity, and use that name, either as it is or contracted/transposed.

Revelation 2:17 Whoever has ears, let them hear what the Spirit says to the churches. To the one who is victorious, I will give some of the hidden manna. I will also give that person a white stone with a new name written on it, known only to the one who receives it.

Isaiah 62:2 The nations will see your vindication, and all kings your glory; you will be called by a new name that the mouth of the Lord will bestow.   renaming

The Black Book Of Satan
I: The Sinister Calling

73 The aim of the following ceremonial ritual can   rituals
be either (a) returning to Earth those 'negative, chaotic, sinister' forms/energies dark legend knows as 'The Dark Gods';(b) drawing forth from acausal dimensions chaotic energies, directed towards a specific goal/aim/intent or channelled into a particular individual(s)/group/temporal form.

1 John 4 Dear friends, do not believe every spirit, but test the spirits to see whether they are from God, because many false prophets have gone out into the world. 2 This is how you can recognize the Spirit of God: Every spirit that acknowledges that Jesus Christ has come in the flesh is from God, 3 but every spirit that does not acknowledge Jesus is not from God. This is the spirit of the antichrist, which you have heard is coming and even now is already in the world.

Revelation 21:8 But the cowardly, the unbelieving, the vile, the murderers, the sexually immoral, those who practice magic arts, the idolaters and all liars—they will be consigned to the fiery lake of burning sulfur. This is the second death."

Ezekiel 13:18 and say, 'This is what the Sovereign Lord says: Woe to the women who sew magic charms on all their wrists and make veils of various lengths for their heads in order

to ensnare people. Will you ensnare the lives of my people but preserve your own?
Ezekiel 13:20 " 'Therefore this is what the Sovereign Lord says: I am against your magic charms with which you ensnare people like birds and I will tear them from your arms; I will set free the people that you ensnare like birds. 21 I will tear off your veils and save my people from your hands, and they will no longer fall prey to your power. Then you will know that I am the Lord.
Deuteronomy 18:10 Let no one be found among you who sacrifices their son or daughter in the fire, who practices divination or sorcery, interprets omens, engages in witchcraft,

Sinister Chants

74   Dies irae, dies illa Solvet Saeclum in favilla   chants
Teste Satan cum sibylla. Quantos tremor est futurus Quando Vindex est venturus Cuncta stricte discussurus. Dies irae, dies illa!
Translated:
The day of wrath, that day Will dissolve the century in a ember Witness Satan with the sibyl. How many tremors is it going to be? When the Avenger is to come, all will be strictly discussed. That day is a day of wrath!

Revelation 20:10 And the devil, who deceived   judgment
them, was thrown into the lake of burning sulfur, where the beast and the false prophet had been thrown. They will be tormented day and night for ever and ever.
Revelation 21:8 But the cowardly, the unbelieving, the vile, the murderers, the sexually immoral, those who practice magic arts, the idolaters and all liars—they will be consigned to the fiery lake of burning sulfur. This is the second death."

75   Sanctus Satanas, Sanctus Dominus Diabolus   chants
Sabaoth. Satanas - venire! Satanas - venire! Ave, Satanas, ave Satanas. Tui sunt caeli, Tua est terra, Ave Satanas!
Translated:
Holy Satan, Holy Lord the Devil Sabaoth. Satan

- come! Satan - come! Hail, Satan, Hail Satan. the heavens are yours the land is yours Hail Satan!

Matthew 24:30 "Then will appear the sign of the Son of Man in heaven. And then all the peoples of the earth will mourn when they see the Son of Man coming on the clouds of heaven, with power and great glory. 31 And he will send his angels with a loud trumpet call, and they will gather his elect from the four winds, from one end of the heavens to the other. 32 "Now learn this lesson from the fig tree: As soon as its twigs get tender and its leaves come out, you know that summer is near. 33 Even so, when you see all these things, you know that it is near, right at the door. 34 Truly I tell you, this generation will certainly not pass away until all these things have happened. 35 Heaven and earth will pass away, but my words will never pass away. heaven

1 Thessalonians 4:16 16 For the Lord himself will come down from heaven, with a loud command, with the voice of the archangel and with the trumpet call of God, and the dead in Christ will rise first. 17 After that, we who are still alive and are left will be caught up together with them in the clouds to meet the Lord in the air. And so we will be with the Lord forever.

Jeremiah 32:17 "Ah, Sovereign Lord, you have made the heavens and the earth by your great power and outstretched arm. Nothing is too hard for you.

Genesis 1: 1 In the beginning God created the heavens and the earth. 2 Now the earth was formless and empty, darkness was over the surface of the deep, and the Spirit of God was hovering over the waters.

II: The Black Mass of Life

76 Aperiatur terra, et germinet Vindex   vengeance
Translated:
Let the earth be opened, and the Avenger spring up

Romans 12:19 19 Do not take revenge, my

dear friends, but leave room for God's wrath, for it is written: "It is mine to avenge; I will repay," says the Lord.
1 Peter 3:9 Do not repay evil with evil or insult with insult. On the contrary, repay evil with blessing, because to this you were called so that you may inherit a blessing.

77 Agios o Baphomet O Oriens splendour lucis aeternae Et sol justitiae: Veni et illumina sedentes in tenebris Et umbra mortis Translated
Agios o Baphomet O East splendor of eternal light And the sun of justice: Come and give light to those who sit in darkness and the shadow of death

light

Matthew 5:16 In the same way, let your light shine before others, that they may see your good deeds and glorify your Father in heaven.
2 Corinthians 4:6 For God, who said, "Let light shine out of darkness," made his light shine in our hearts to give us the light of the knowledge of God's glory displayed in the face of Christ.
Isaiah 60:1 "Arise, shine, for your light has come, and the glory of the Lord rises upon you.

III: The Mass of Heresy

78 Behind the altar is a large swastika banner: black swastika on white circle against red background. Silver chalices containing strong wine; crystal tetrahedron and small altar bell on altar.

nazism
Israel

Genesis 12:3 I will bless those who bless you, and whoever curses you I will curse; and all peoples on earth will be blessed through you."
Revelation 7:1 After this I saw four angels standing at the four corners of the earth, holding back the four winds of the earth to prevent any wind from blowing on the land or on the sea or on any tree. 2 Then I saw another angel coming up from the east, having the seal of the living God. He called out in a loud voice to the four angels who had been given power to harm the land and the sea: 3 "Do not harm the

land or the sea or the trees until we put a seal on the foreheads of the servants of our God." 4 Then I heard the number of those who were sealed: 144,000 from all the tribes of Israel.

Ezekiel 25:6 For this is what the Sovereign Lord says: Because you have clapped your hands and stamped your feet, rejoicing with all the malice of your heart against the land of Israel, 7 therefore I will stretch out my hand against you and give you as plunder to the nations. I will wipe you out from among the nations and exterminate you from the countries. I will destroy you, and you will know that I am the Lord.'"

79   We believe - Congregation: Adolf Hitler was sent by our gods To guide us to greatness.   nazism

John 4:22 You Samaritans worship what you do not know; we worship what we do know, for salvation is from the Jews.

Romans 11:1 I ask then: Did God reject his people? By no means! I am an Israelite myself, a descendant of Romans 11Abraham, from the tribe of Benjamin. 2 God did not reject his people, whom he foreknew. Don't you know what Scripture says in the passage about Elijah—how he appealed to God against Israel: 3 "Lord, they have killed your prophets and torn down your altars; I am the only one left, and they are trying to kill me"? 4 And what was God's answer to him? "I have reserved for myself seven thousand who have not bowed the knee to Baal." 5 So too, at the present time there is a remnant chosen by grace. 6 And if by grace, then it cannot be based on works; if it were, grace would no longer be grace.

80   We believe in the inequality of races And in the right of the Aryan to live According to the laws of the folk.   racism ayranism

Galatians 3:28 There is neither Jew nor Gentile, neither slave nor free, nor is there male and female, for you are all one in Christ Jesus.   equality

Leviticus 19:34 The foreigner residing among you must be treated as your native-born. Love

them as yourself, for you were foreigners in Egypt. I am the Lord your God.

1 Corinthians 12:13 For we were all baptized by one Spirit so as to form one body—whether Jews or Gentiles, slave or free—and we were all given the one Spirit to drink.

81	We acknowledge that the story of the holocaust Is a lie to keep our race in chains And express our desire to see the truth revealed.	holocaust

Luke 21:23 How dreadful it will be in those days for pregnant women and nursing mothers! There will be great distress in the land and wrath against this people. 24 They will fall by the sword and will be taken as prisoners to all the nations. Jerusalem will be trampled on by the Gentiles until the times of the Gentiles are fulfilled.

81	And shall not cease from striving Since we believe the destiny Of our noble Aryan race lies among the stars!	aryan race

John 4:22 You Samaritans worship what you do not know; we worship what we do know, for salvation is from the Jews.

Deuteronomy 4:19 And when you look up to the sky and see the sun, the moon and the stars—all the heavenly array—do not be enticed into bowing down to them and worshiping things the Lord your God has apportioned to all the nations under heaven. — stars

82	I who am Mistress of Earth welcome you Who have dared to defy the dogmas That now holds our peoples in chains!	temptation

Jeremiah 17:9 The heart is deceitful above all things and beyond cure. Who can understand it?

Titus 2:12 It teaches us to say "No" to ungodliness and worldly passions, and to live self-controlled, upright and godly lives in this present age,

Numbers 15:30 "'But anyone who sins defiantly, whether native-born or foreigner, blasphemes the Lord and must be cut off from the people of Israel.

83   Behold the sign of the sun And the flag of he who was chosen By our gods!   gods

John 14:6 Jesus answered, "I am the way and the truth and the life. No one comes to the Father except through me.

Isaiah 44:6 "This is what the Lord says—Israel's King and Redeemer, the Lord Almighty: I am the first and I am the last; apart from me there is no God.

1 Corinthians 10:20 No, but the sacrifices of pagans are offered to demons, not to God, and I do not want you to be participants with demons.

Deuteronomy 32:17 They sacrificed to false gods, which are not God—gods they had not known, gods that recently appeared, gods your ancestors did not fear.

84   Praised are you by the defiant: Through your courage we have The strength to dream!   defiance

Revelation 12:7 Then war broke out in heaven. Michael and his angels fought against the dragon, and the dragon and his angels fought back. 8 But he was not strong enough, and they lost their place in heaven. 9 The great dragon was hurled down—that ancient serpent called the devil, or Satan, who leads the whole world astray. He was hurled to the earth, and his angels with him.

Matthew 7:21 "Not everyone who says to me, 'Lord, Lord,' will enter the kingdom of heaven, but only the one who does the will of my Father who is in heaven. 22 Many will say to me on that day, 'Lord, Lord, did we not prophesy in your name and in your name drive out demons and in your name perform many miracles?' 23 Then I will tell them plainly, 'I never knew you. Away from me, you evildoers!'

Jeremiah 17:9 The heart is deceitful above all things and beyond cure. Who can understand it? 10 "I the Lord search the heart and examine the mind, to reward each person according to their conduct, according to what their deeds deserve."

1 Samuel 15:23 For rebellion is like the sin of

divination, and arrogance like the evil of idolatry. Because you have rejected the word of the Lord, he has rejected you as king."

Proverbs 17:11 Evildoers foster rebellion against God; the messenger of death will be sent against them.

85 To believe is easy, To defy is hard - But most difficult of all Is to die fighting for a noble cause.   obedience
defiance

1 Timothy 4:10 That is why we labor and strive, because we have put our hope in the living God, who is the Savior of all people, and especially of those who believe.

John 14:15 "If you love me, keep my commands.

Romans 5:19 For just as through the disobedience of the one man the many were made sinners, so also through the obedience of the one man the many will be made righteous.

Isaiah 1:19 If you are willing and obedient, you will eat the good things of the land;

Exodus 19:5 Now if you obey me fully and keep my covenant, then out of all nations you will be my treasured possession. Although the whole earth is mine, 6 you will be for me a kingdom of priests and a holy nation.' These are the words you are to speak to the Israelites."

86 Go now, and remember So that we few who survive Can gather again in secret At the appointed time To recall the greatness promised us By our gods!   gods

Romans 1:21 For although they knew God, they neither glorified him as God nor gave thanks to him, but their thinking became futile and their foolish hearts were darkened. 22 Although they claimed to be wise, they became fools 23 and exchanged the glory of the immortal God for images made to look like a mortal human being and birds and animals and reptiles.   idolatry

Galatians 4:6 Because you are his sons, God sent the Spirit of his Son into our hearts, the

Spirit who calls out, "Abba, Father." 7 So you are no longer a slave, but God's child; and since you are his child, God has made you also an heir. 8 Formerly, when you did not know God, you were slaves to those who by nature are not gods. 9 But now that you know God—or rather are known by God—how is it that you are turning back to those weak and miserable forces? Do you wish to be enslaved by them all over again?

   Exodus 20:3 "You shall have no other gods before "You shall have no other gods before me. 4 "You shall not make for yourself an image in the form of anything in heaven above or on the earth beneath or in the waters below. 5 You shall not bow down to them or worship them; for I, the Lord your God, am a jealous God, punishing the children for the sin of the parents to the third and fourth generation of those who hate me, 6 but showing love to a thousand generations of those who love me and keep my commandments.

   Jonah 2:8 "Those who cling to worthless idols turn away from God's love for them. 9 But I, with shouts of grateful praise, will sacrifice to you. What I have vowed I will make good. I will say, 'Salvation comes from the Lord.'"

IV: The Black Mass – Gay Version

87 My Prince, bringer of lust and fire. I greet you   lust
who cause us to struggle And seek the forbidden pleasure.

   Colossians 3:5 Put to death, therefore, whatever belongs to your earthly nature: sexual immorality, impurity, lust, evil desires and greed, which is idolatry.

   1 John 2:16 For everything in the world—the lust of the flesh, the lust of the eyes, and the pride of life—comes not from the Father but from the world.

   1 Corinthians 6:18 Flee from sexual immorality. All other sins a person commits are outside the body, but whoever sins sexually, sins against their own body. 19 Do you not know that your bodies are temples of the Holy Spirit, who is in you, whom you have received from God? You are not your own; 20 you were bought at a price. Therefore honor God with your bodies.

　　Exodus 20:17 "You shall not covet your neighbor's house. You shall not covet your neighbor's wife, or his male or female servant, his ox or donkey, or anything that belongs to your neighbor."

88　Blessed are the proud For they produce ecstasy.　　pride

　　Romans 12:16 proud, but be willing to associate with people of low position. Do not be conceited.

　　James 4:6 But he gives us more grace. That is why Scripture says: "God opposes the proud but shows favor to the humble."

　　Proverbs 8:13 To fear the Lord is to hate evil; I hate pride and arrogance, evil behavior and perverse speech.

　　Proverbs 11:2 When pride comes, then comes disgrace, but with humility comes wisdom.

89　Blessed are the strong For they shall bring delight.　　the strong

　　2 Corinthians 12:9 But he said to me, "My　　weakness
grace is sufficient for you, for my power is made perfect in weakness." Therefore I will boast all the more gladly about my weaknesses, so that Christ's power may rest on me.

　　Romans 15:1 We who are strong ought to bear with the failings of the weak and not to please ourselves.

　　Isaiah 40:29 He gives strength to the weary and increases the power of the weak.

　　Psalm 82:3 Defend the weak and the fatherless; uphold the cause of the poor and the oppressed. 4 Rescue the weak and the needy; deliver them from the hand of the wicked.

90　With pride in my heart I give praise To those　　enemies
who drove the nails And he who thrust the spear Into the body of Yeshua, the impostor. May his followers rot in filth!

　　Matthew 5:43 "You have heard that it was

said, 'Love your neighbor and hate your enemy.' 44 But I tell you, love your enemies and pray for those who persecute you,
   Luke 6:27 "But to you who are listening I say: Love your enemies, do good to those who hate you, 28 bless those who curse you, pray for those who mistreat you.
   Genesis 50:20 You intended to harm me, but God intended it for good to accomplish what is now being done, the saving of many lives.
   Proverbs 20:22 Do not say, "I'll pay you back for this wrong!" Wait for the Lord, and he will avenge you.

91   Hail and praise to Satan, the lord of life And provider of pleasure.   pleasure

   1 Corinthians 10:13 No temptation has overtaken you except what is common to mankind. And God is faithful; he will not let you be tempted beyond what you can bear. But when you are tempted, he will also provide a way out so that you can endure it.   temptation
   Colossians 3:5 Put to death, therefore, whatever belongs to your earthly nature: sexual immorality, impurity, lust, evil desires and greed, which is idolatry.
   Titus 3 At one time we too were foolish, disobedient, deceived and enslaved by all kinds of passions and pleasures. We lived in malice and envy, being hated and hating one another.
   Proverbs 21:17 Whoever loves pleasure will become poor; whoever loves wine and olive oil will never be rich.

V: Synestry: A Sinister Ceremony

92   I CAME, opened my body and Brought you lust!   lust

   Colossians 3:5 Put to death, therefore, whatever belongs to your earthly nature: sexual immorality, impurity, lust, evil desires and greed, which is idolatry.
   James 1:13 When tempted, no one should say, "God is tempting me." For God cannot be tempted by evil, nor does he tempt anyone; 14 but each person is tempted when they are

dragged away by their own evil desire and enticed. 15 Then, after desire has conceived, it gives birth to sin; and sin, when it is full-grown, gives birth to death.

93   But then the bastard came: Yeshua, the deceiver! Curse him! We curse him!   *deceiver*

Revelation 12:9 The great dragon was hurled down—that ancient serpent called the devil, or Satan, who leads the whole world astray. He was hurled to the earth, and his angels with him.

2 Corinthians 11:13 For such people are false apostles, deceitful workers, masquerading as apostles of Christ. 14 And no wonder, for Satan himself masquerades as an angel of light. 15 It is not surprising, then, if his servants also masquerade as servants of righteousness. Their end will be what their actions deserve.   *disguise*

John 8:44 You belong to your father, the devil, and you want to carry out your father's desires. He was a murderer from the beginning, not holding to the truth, for there is no truth in him. When he lies, he speaks his native language, for he is a liar and the father of lies.

Revelation 20:10 And the devil, who deceived them, was thrown into the lake of burning sulfur, where the beast and the false prophet had been thrown. They will be tormented day and night for ever and ever.

94   Curse him! We curse him!   *cursing*

1 John 4:7 Dear friends, let us love one another, for love comes from God. Everyone who loves has been born of God and knows God.

Romans 13:10 Love does no harm to a neighbor. Therefore love is the fulfillment of the law.

Proverbs 24:17 Do not gloat when your enemy falls; when they stumble, do not let your heart rejoice, 18 or the Lord will see and disapprove and turn his wrath away from them.

95   So we gather again to give praise to her Who rules our world. Agios o Baphomet! Agios o   *ruler of the world*

Baphomet!

John 14:6 Jesus answered, "I am the way and the truth and the life. No one comes to the Father except through me.

1 John 5:19 We know that we are children of God, and that the whole world is under the control of the evil one.

Matthew 4:10 Jesus said to him, "Away from me, Satan! For it is written: 'Worship the Lord your God, and serve him only.'

Exodus 20:3 3 "You shall have no other gods before me. 4 "You shall not make for yourself an image in the form of anything in heaven above or on the earth beneath or in the waters below.

false gods

96 The congregation repeat the chant seven times while the Amatrix takes up the crystal which she holds in her outstretched hands. The Priestess places her own hands over the crystal.

crystals

Deuteronomy 18:10 Let no one be found among you who sacrifices their son or daughter in the fire, who practices divination or sorcery, interprets omens, engages in witchcraft, 11 or casts spells, or who is a medium or spiritist or who consults the dead. 12 Anyone who does these things is detestable to the Lord; because of these same detestable practices the Lord your God will drive out those nations before you.

Ezekiel 13:20 "'Therefore this is what the Sovereign Lord says: I am against your magic charms with which you ensnare people like birds and I will tear them from your arms; I will set free the people that you ensnare like birds. 21 I will tear off your veils and save my people from your hands, and they will no longer fall prey to your power. Then you will know that I am the Lord.

VI: The Rite of Nine Angles

97 If desired (ie. sinister intent) this energy may be symbolised by Atazoth - a dark nebulous chaos issuing forth from a star strewn Space which changes into a 'Dagon' like entity before becoming chaos again. This visualisation

religious sex

43

continues until the sexual climax of the Priestess after which the Priest reaches his own climax

Ephesians 5:3 But among you there must not be even a hint of sexual immorality, or of any kind of impurity, or of greed, because these are improper for God's holy people.

1 Thessalonians 4:3 It is God's will that you should be sanctified: that you should avoid sexual immorality; 4 that each of you should learn to control your own body in a way that is holy and honorable, 5 not in passionate lust like the pagans, who do not know God; 6 and that in this matter no one should wrong or take advantage of a brother or sister. The Lord will punish all those who commit such sins, as we told you and warned you before. 7 For God did not call us to be impure, but to live a holy life. 8 Therefore, anyone who rejects this instruction does not reject a human being but God, the very God who gives you his Holy Spirit.

98 Aperiatur terra, et germinet Chaos — chaos
Translated:
Let the earth be opened, and Chaos will sprout

1 Corinthians 14:33 For God is not a God of disorder but of peace—as in all the congregations of the Lord's people. — order

Philippians 4:6 Do not be anxious about anything, but in every situation, by prayer and petition, with thanksgiving, present your requests to God. 7 And the peace of God, which transcends all understanding, will guard your hearts and your minds in Christ Jesus.

Isaiah 32:17 The fruit of that righteousness will be peace; its effect will be quietness and confidence forever. 18 My people will live in peaceful dwelling places, in secure homes, in undisturbed places of rest.

99 If only one Cantor is present, the "Atazoth" — dark gods
vibration is continued nine times and then the 'Atazoth chant' undertaken by the Cantor and the Priest, in fifths. The Dark Gods will then be manifest.

Ephesians 6:10 Finally, be strong in the Lord and in his mighty power. 11 Put on the full armor of God, so that you can take your stand against the devil's schemes. 12 For our struggle is not against flesh and blood, but against the rulers, against the authorities, against the powers of this dark world and against the spiritual forces of evil in the heavenly realms.

2 Corinthians 11:14 And no wonder, for Satan himself masquerades as an angel of light.

100 Note: This ritual should not be undertaken lightly. There must be a preparedness to exult in the energies.   energy

Colossians 1:29 To this end I strenuously contend with all the energy Christ so powerfully works in me.

Isaiah 40:28 Do you not know? Have you not heard? The LORD is the everlasting God, the Creator of the ends of the earth. He will not grow tired or weary, and his understanding no one can fathom. 29 He gives strength to the weary and increases the power of the weak. 30 Even youths grow tired and weary, and young men stumble and fall; 31 but those who hope in the LORD will renew their strength. They will soar on wings like eagles; they will run and not grow weary, they will walk and not be faint.

VII: The Ceremony of Recalling

101 The night before the ritual the Priestess bakes the consecrated cakes made from wheat, water, egg, honey, animal fat and marijuana.   communion

1 Thessalonians 5:6 So then, let us not be like others, who are asleep, but let us be awake and sober.

1 Corinthians 11:28 Everyone ought to examine themselves before they eat of the bread and drink from the cup. 29 For those who eat and drink without discerning the body of Christ eat and drink judgment on themselves. 30 That is why many among you are weak and sick, and a number of you have fallen asleep. 31 But if we were more discerning with regard to ourselves, we would not come under such judgment. 32

Nevertheless, when we are judged in this way by the Lord, we are being disciplined so that we will not be finally condemned with the world.

Exodus 12:15 For seven days you are to eat bread made without yeast. On the first day remove the yeast from your houses, for whoever eats anything with yeast in it from the first day through the seventh must be cut off from Israel.

102 Devil: The day of wrath, that day Will dissolve the century in a ember Witness Satan with the sibyl. How many tremors will there be When the Avenger is about to come He will discuss everything strictly. That day is a day of wrath! Translated:
Devil: The day of wrath, that day Will dissolve the century in a ember Witness Satan with the sibyl. How many tremors will there be When the Avenger is about to come He will discuss everything strictly. That day is a day of wrath!

last days

2 Timothy: 1 But mark this: There will be terrible times in the last days. 2 People will be lovers of themselves, lovers of money, boastful, proud, abusive, disobedient to their parents, ungrateful, unholy, 3 without love, unforgiving, slanderous, without self-control, brutal, not lovers of the good, 4 treacherous, rash, conceited, lovers of pleasure rather than lovers of God— 5 having a form of godliness but denying its power. Have nothing to do with such people.

Isaiah 2:2 In the last days the mountain of the LORD's temple will be established as the highest of the mountains; it will be exalted above the hills, and all nations will stream to it.

103 I put my kisses at your feet. And kneel before you who crushes Your enemies and who washes In a basin full of their blood.

enemies

Luke 6:27 "But to you who are listening I say: Love your enemies, do good to those who hate you, 28 bless those who curse you, pray for those who mistreat you. 29 If someone slaps you on one cheek, turn to them the other also. If someone takes your coat, do not withhold your shirt from them. 30 Give to everyone who asks you, and if anyone takes what belongs to you, do not demand it back. 31 Do to others as you would have them do to you.

Deuteronomy 31:6 Be strong and courageous. Do not be afraid or terrified because of them, for the Lord your God goes with you; he will never leave you nor forsake you."

Proverbs 25:21 If your enemy is hungry, give him food to eat; if he is thirsty, give him water to drink.

104 I lift up my eyes to gaze Upon your beauty of body: You who are the daughter and a Gate To our Dark Gods.   lust

Colossians 3:5 Put to death, therefore, whatever belongs to your earthly nature: sexual immorality, impurity, lust, evil desires and greed, which is idolatry.

James 1:14 but each person is tempted when they are dragged away by their own evil desire and enticed. 15 Then, after desire has conceived, it gives birth to sin; and sin, when it is full-grown, gives birth to death.

Romans 13:14 Rather, clothe yourselves with the Lord Jesus Christ, and do not think about how to gratify the desires of the flesh.

Galatians 5:17 For the flesh desires what is contrary to the Spirit, and the Spirit what is contrary to the flesh. They are in conflict with each other, so that you are not to do whatever you want.

105 Mistress: Kiss me and I shall make you As an eagle to its prey. Touch me and I shall make you As a strong sword that severs And stains my Earth with blood. Taste me and I shall make you As a seed of corn which grows Toward the sun, and never dies. Plough me and plant me With your seed and I shall make you
As a Gate that opens to our gods!   seduction

Matthew 5:28 But I tell you that anyone who looks at a woman lustfully has already committed adultery with her in his heart.

Proverbs 5:3 For the lips of the adulterous woman drip honey, and her speech is smoother than oil; 4 but in the end she is bitter as gall, sharp as a double-edged sword. 5 Her feet go down to death; her steps lead straight to the grave.

James 1:14 but each person is tempted when they are dragged away by their own evil desire and enticed. 15 Then, after desire has conceived, it gives birth to sin; and sin, when it is full-grown, gives birth to death.

106   I know you, my children, you are dark Yet none of you is as dark Or as deadly As I. I know you and the thoughts Within all your hearts: yet Not one of you is as hateful Or as loving as I. With a glance I can strike You dead.   threats

Matthew 26:52 "Put your sword back in its place," Jesus said to him, "for all who draw the sword will die by the sword. 53 Do you think I cannot call on my Father, and he will at once put at my disposal more than twelve legions of angels? 54 But how then would the Scriptures be fulfilled that say it must happen in this way?"

107   No guilt shall bind you No thought restrict! Feast then and enjoy The ecstasy of this life   this life

1 John 2:15 Do not love the world or anything in the world. If anyone loves the world, love for the Father is not in them. 16 For everything in the world—the lust of the flesh, the lust of the eyes, and the pride of life—comes not from the Father but from the world. 17 The world and its desires pass away, but whoever does the will of God lives forever. 18 Dear children, this is the last hour; and as you have heard that the antichrist is coming, even now many antichrists have come. This is how we know it is the last hour.

John 15:19 If you belonged to the world, it would love you as its own. As it is, you do not belong to the world, but I have chosen you out of the world. That is why the world hates you.

1 John 5:19 We know that we are children of

God, and that the whole world is under the control of the evil one.

108 But ever remember I as the wind that snatches Your soul!   soul

1 Peter 5:8 Be alert and of sober mind. Your enemy the devil prowls around like a roaring lion looking for someone to devour.

Order of Nine Angles
A Basic Introduction For Prospective Adherents

In consequence, some of the deeds a Satanic Adept may consciously decide undertake may be disruptive; some may involve 'culling' [ie. removing human dross or those who oppose the Destiny of the Satanist wishes to achieve];   culling
business
success

Matthew 25:44 "They also will answer, 'Lord, when did we see you hungry or thirsty or a stranger or needing clothes or sick or in prison, and did not help you?' 45 "He will reply, 'Truly I tell you, whatever you did not do for one of the least of these, you did not do for me.'

Matthew 25:40 "The King will reply, 'Truly I tell you, whatever you did for one of the least of these brothers and sisters of mine, you did for me.

Ephesians 4:32 Be kind and compassionate to one another, forgiving each other, just as in Christ God forgave you.

Romans 12:13 Share with the Lord's people who are in need. Practice hospitality.

Proverbs 3:27 Do not withhold good from those to whom it is due, when it is in your power to act.

109 1 - The Satanic Game

The specific path is a dark, sinister, or 'Left Hand Path' one, and the specific goal is the creation of a new type of individual.   new person

2 Corinthians 5:17 Therefore, if anyone is in Christ, the new creation has come: The old has gone, the new is here!

John 3:1 Now there was a Pharisee, a man named Nicodemus who was a member of the Jewish ruling council. 2 He came to Jesus at night and said, "Rabbi, we know that you are a

teacher who has come from God. For no one could perform the signs you are doing if God were not with him." 3 Jesus replied, "Very truly I tell you, no one can see the kingdom of God unless they are born again.

Ezekiel 36:26 I will give you a new heart and put a new spirit in you; I will remove from you your heart of stone and give you a heart of flesh.

110 On a more general level, Satanism is concerned with changing our evolution and the societies we live in - creating, in fact a new human species and a civilization appropriate to the new type of human being   evolution

Romans 1:19 since what may be known about God is plain to them, because God has made it plain to them. 20 For since the creation of the world God's invisible qualities—his eternal power and divine nature—have been clearly seen, being understood from what has been made, so that people are without excuse.

Genesis 2:1 Thus the heavens and the earth were completed in all their vast array.

Genesis 2:7 Then the Lord God formed a man from the dust of the ground and breathed into his nostrils the breath of life, and the man became a living being.

Genesis 1:26 Then God said, "Let us make mankind in our image, in our likeness, so that they may rule over the fish in the sea and the birds in the sky, over the livestock and all the wild animals, and over all the creatures that move along the ground." 27 So God created mankind in his own image, in the image of God he created them; male and female he created them.

111 The way of Satanism is the total opposite of this - it is the way of liberation, internally and externally. There is a desire to know based on personal experience.   experience

Colossians 3:16 Let the message of Christ dwell among you richly as you teach and admonish one another with all wisdom through

psalms, hymns, and songs from the Spirit, singing to God with gratitude in your hearts. 17 And whatever you do, whether in word or deed, do it all in the name of the Lord Jesus, giving thanks to God the Father through him.

James 1:5 If any of you lacks wisdom, you should ask God, who gives generously to all without finding fault, and it will be given to you. 6 But when you ask, you must believe and not doubt, because the one who doubts is like a wave of the sea, blown and tossed by the wind.

Galatians 5:1 It is for freedom that Christ has set us free. Stand firm, then, and do not let yourselves be burdened again by a yoke of slavery.

Job 5:7 Yet man is born to trouble as surely as sparks fly upward. 8 "But if I were you, I would appeal to God; I would lay my cause before him.

Proverbs 12:15 The way of fools seems right to them, but the wise listen to advice.

112 There is a desire to be proud - to exult and revel in life and so fulfil the possibilities that life offers.   pride

1 John 2:16 For everything in the world—the lust of the flesh, the lust of the eyes, and the pride of life—comes not from the Father but from the world. 17 The world and its desires pass away, but whoever does the will of God lives forever.

Philippians 2:3 Do nothing out of selfish ambition or vain conceit. Rather, in humility value others above yourselves, 4 not looking to your own interests but each of you to the interests of the others.

Proverbs 11:2 When pride comes, then comes disgrace, but with humility comes wisdom.

113 There is a desire to excel, to achieve, to set the standards for others to follow rather than follow the standards set by someone else.   following

2 John 1:9 Anyone who runs ahead and does not continue in the teaching of Christ does not have God; whoever continues in the teaching

has both the Father and the Son.

Romans 12:2 Do not conform to the pattern of this world, but be transformed by the renewing of your mind. Then you will be able to test and approve what God's will is—his good, pleasing and perfect will.

2 Timothy 3:16 All Scripture is God-breathed and is useful for teaching, rebuking, correcting and training in righteousness, 17 so that the servant of God may be thoroughly equipped for every good work.

114 This, of course, is not easy - it requires a certain type of person: someone imbued with spirit, with an urge to conquer and defy. Someone with character.   defiance

1 Peter 2:18 Slaves, in reverent fear of God submit yourselves to your masters, not only to those who are good and considerate, but also to those who are harsh. 19 For it is commendable if someone bears up under the pain of unjust suffering because they are conscious of God. 20 But how is it to your credit if you receive a beating for doing wrong and endure it? But if you suffer for doing good and you endure it, this is commendable before God. 21 To this you were called, because Christ suffered for you, leaving you an example, that you should follow in his steps.

Romans 8:7 The mind governed by the flesh is hostile to God; it does not submit to God's law, nor can it do so.   rebellion

1 Samuel 15:23 For rebellion is like the sin of divination, and arrogance like the evil of idolatry. Because you have rejected the word of the Lord, he has rejected you as king."

Exodus 23:21 Pay attention to him and listen to what he says. Do not rebel against him; he will not forgive your rebellion, since my Name is in him.

Isaiah 30:9 For these are rebellious people, deceitful children, children unwilling to listen to the Lord's instruction.

115 For it has been a fundamental principle of   moral code

genuine Satanism that each individual Satanist finds his or her own limits and thus lives, and if necessary dies, by their own morality or ethics.

1 Timothy 1:8 We know that the law is good if one uses it properly. 9 We also know that the law is made not for the righteous but for lawbreakers and rebels, the ungodly and sinful, the unholy and irreligious, for those who kill their fathers or mothers, for murderers,

Romans 6:15 What then? Shall we sin because we are not under the law but under grace? By no means! 16 Don't you know that when you offer yourselves to someone as obedient slaves, you are slaves of the one you obey—whether you are slaves to sin, which leads to death, or to obedience, which leads to righteousness? 17 But thanks be to God that, though you used to be slaves to sin, you have come to obey from your heart the pattern of teaching that has now claimed your allegiance. 18 You have been set free from sin and have become slaves to righteousness.

Romans 7:9 Once I was alive apart from the law; but when the commandment came, sin sprang to life and I died. 10 I found that the very commandment that was intended to bring life actually brought death. 11 For sin, seizing the opportunity afforded by the commandment, deceived me, and through the commandment put me to death. 12 So then, the law is holy, and the commandment is holy, righteous and good.

116 That is, a Satanist accepts no restrictions other morality than those they impose on themselves. They accept that it is they and only they who can find answers to their questions - and that these answers are derived from direct personal experience of living at the very edge.

Romans 13:1 Let everyone be subject to the governing authorities, for there is no authority except that which God has established. The authorities that exist have been established by God.

Romans 2:12 All who sin apart from the law

will also perish apart from the law, and all who sin under the law will be judged by the law. 13 For it is not those who hear the law who are righteous in God's sight, but it is those who obey the law who will be declared righteous. 14 (Indeed, when Gentiles, who do not have the law, do by nature things required by the law, they are a law for themselves, even though they do not have the law. 15 They show that the requirements of the law are written on their hearts, their consciences also bearing witness, and their thoughts sometimes accusing them and at other times even defending them.)

117 This means that Satanists are amoral in the conventional sense: there is not, never has been and never can be, any such thing as "Satanic ethics" or a "Satanic authority" which individual Satanists must are subservient to - for such things are contrary to genuine Satanism

amoral

2 Timothy 3:16 All Scripture is God-breathed and is useful for teaching, rebuking, correcting and training in righteousness, 17 so that the servant of God may be thoroughly equipped for every good work.

1 Corinthians 13:1 If I speak in the tongues of men or of angels, but do not have love, I am only a resounding gong or a clanging cymbal. 2 If I have the gift of prophecy and can fathom all mysteries and all knowledge, and if I have a faith that can move mountains, but do not have love, I am nothing. 3 If I give all I possess to the poor and give over my body to hardship that I may boast, but do not have love, I gain nothing.

118 Satanism applies the principle of evolution to human practice - the strong survive and win through, while the weak fail or perish.

strong vs weak

Romans 15:1 We who are strong ought to bear with the failings of the weak and not to please ourselves.

Romans 8:26 In the same way, the Spirit helps us in our weakness. We do not know what we ought to pray for, but the Spirit himself intercedes for us through wordless groans. 27

And he who searches our hearts knows the mind of the Spirit, because the Spirit intercedes for God's people in accordance with the will of God.

2 Corinthians 12:9 But he said to me, "My grace is sufficient for you, for my power is made perfect in weakness." Therefore I will boast all the more gladly about my weaknesses, so that Christ's power may rest on me.

119   A Satanist has a goal - an ulterior motive beyond the satisfaction of their own ego and beyond indulging in and giving way to, of unconscious impulses. This goal is to excel - to go beyond what one is. success

James 4:10 Humble yourselves before the Lord, and he will lift you up.

Romans 12:2 Do not conform to the pattern of this world, but be transformed by the renewing of your mind. Then you will be able to test and approve what God's will is—his good, pleasing and perfect will.

Proverbs 16:3 Commit to the Lord whatever you do, and he will establish your plans.

Psalms 37:4 Take delight in the LORD, and he will give you the desires of your heart.

Proverbs 3:1 My son, do not forget my teaching, but keep my commands in your heart, 2 for they will prolong your life many years and bring you peace and prosperity. 3 Let love and faithfulness never leave you; bind them around your neck, write them on the tablet of your heart. 4 Then you will win favor and a good name in the sight of God and man.

120   A Satanist desires to evolve - and this evolution this requires resolve and thus a certain strength of character. personal growth

2 Peter 3:18 But grow in the grace and knowledge of our Lord and Savior Jesus Christ. To him be glory both now and forever! Amen.

2 Corinthians 13:5 Examine yourselves to see whether you are in the faith; test yourselves. Do you not realize that Christ Jesus is in you— unless, of course, you fail the test? 6 And I trust

that you will discover that we have not failed the test. 7 Now we pray to God that you will not do anything wrong—not so that people will see that we have stood the test but so that you will do what is right even though we may seem to have failed.

1 Peter 2:1 Therefore, rid yourselves of all malice and all deceit, hypocrisy, envy, and slander of every kind. 2 Like newborn babies, crave pure spiritual milk, so that by it you may grow up in your salvation, 3 now that you have tasted that the Lord is good.

Job 8:5 But if you will seek God earnestly and plead with the Almighty, 6 if you are pure and upright, even now he will rouse himself on your behalf and restore you to your prosperous state. 7 Your beginnings will seem humble, so prosperous will your future be.

121 What a genuine Satanist does, in real-life or in the learning experiences that are magickal/Occult rituals, is to explore - to find the limits of themselves and the world; they experience and so grow, and so fulfill their latent, diabolical potential.   potential

Philippians 4:13 I can do all this through him who gives me strength.

Ephesians 2:10 For we are God's handiwork, created in Christ Jesus to do good works, which God prepared in advance for us to do

James 1:5 If any of you lacks wisdom, you should ask God, who gives generously to all without finding fault, and it will be given to you.

Ephesians 1:18 I pray that the eyes of your heart may be enlightened in order that you may know the hope to which he has called you, the riches of his glorious inheritance in his holy people, 19 and his incomparably great power for us who believe. That power is the same as the mighty strength

Genesis 1:28 God blessed them and said to them, "Be fruitful and increase in number; fill the earth and subdue it. Rule over the fish in the sea and the birds in the sky and over every

living creature that moves on the ground."

1 Samuel 16:7 But the Lord said to Samuel, "Do not consider his appearance or his height, for I have rejected him. The Lord does not look at the things people look at. People look at the outward appearance, but the Lord looks at the heart."

Psalm 37:4 Take delight in the Lord, and he will give you the desires of your heart.

122 The Satanist is strong, proud, defiant and in control of the experience and themselves; the failures, the pseuds are in thrall to their feelings/emotions/desires (both conscious and unconscious) and thus are without any real self-insight. — locus of control

Proverbs 19:21 Many are the plans in a person's heart, but it is the Lord's purpose that prevails.

Ephesians 1:11 In him we were also chosen, having been predestined according to the plan of him who works out everything in conformity with the purpose of his will, 12 in order that we, who were the first to put our hope in Christ, might be for the praise of his glory. 13 And you also were included in Christ when you heard the message of truth, the gospel of your salvation. When you believed, you were marked in him with a seal, the promised Holy Spirit, 14 who is a deposit guaranteeing our inheritance until the redemption of those who are God's possession—to the praise of his glory.

2 Chronicles 7:14 if my people, who are called by my name, will humble themselves and pray and seek my face and turn from their wicked ways, then I will hear from heaven, and I will forgive their sin and will heal their land.

Psalm 73:26 My flesh and my heart may fail, but God is the strength of my heart and my portion forever.

Isaiah 55:8 "For my thoughts are not your thoughts, neither are your ways my ways," declares the Lord. 9 "As the heavens are higher than the earth, so are my ways higher than your

ways and my thoughts than your thoughts.

123 This way is a practical one - a way of living - and in the early stages a part of this involves magickal practices and rituals. These specific experiences develop certain esoteric skills - and thus enable a learning of 'forbidden' Arts. They also enable indulgence in worldly pleasures - carnal, material and otherwise.   worldly pleasures

Ephesians 4:29 Do not let any unwholesome talk come out of your mouths, but only what is helpful for building others up according to their needs, that it may benefit those who listen. 30 And do not grieve the Holy Spirit of God, with whom you were sealed for the day of redemption. 31 Get rid of all bitterness, rage and anger, brawling and slander, along with every form of malice. 32 Be kind and compassionate to one another, forgiving each other, just as in Christ God forgave you.

124 For the novice Satanist always moves on - to new experiences, new challenges, and thus new insights.   insights

James 3:13 Who is wise and understanding among you? Let them show it by their good life, by deeds done in the humility that comes from wisdom. 14 But if you harbor bitter envy and selfish ambition in your hearts, do not boast about it or deny the truth. 15 Such "wisdom" does not come down from heaven but is earthly, unspiritual, demonic. 16 For where you have envy and selfish ambition, there you find disorder and every evil practice. 17 But the wisdom that comes from heaven is first of all pure; then peace-loving, considerate, submissive, full of mercy and good fruit, impartial and sincere. 18 Peacemakers who sow in peace reap a harvest of righteousness.

Matthew 7:13 "Enter through the narrow gate. For wide is the gate and broad is the road that leads to destruction, and many enter through it. 14 But small is the gate and narrow the road that leads to life, and only a few find it.

Philippians 1:6 being confident of this, that he

who began a good work in you will carry it on to completion until the day of Christ Jesus.
Proverbs 1:7 The fear of the Lord is the beginning of knowledge, but fools despise wisdom and instruction.
1 Chronicles 16:11 Look to the Lord and his strength; seek his face always.

125 That is, the Satanist has achieved the goals of a Satanic novice and moves further along the path, becoming a Satanic Adept. — spiritual growth

1 Peter 2:1 Therefore, rid yourselves of all malice and all deceit, hypocrisy, envy, and slander of every kind. 2 Like newborn babies, crave pure spiritual milk, so that by it you may grow up in your salvation, 3 now that you have tasted that the Lord is good.
2 Peter 3:18 But grow in the grace and knowledge of our Lord and Savior Jesus Christ. To him be glory both now and forever! Amen.
Colossians 1:9 For this reason, since the day we heard about you, we have not stopped praying for you. We continually ask God to fill you with the knowledge of his will through all the wisdom and understanding that the Spirit gives, 10 so that you may live a life worthy of the Lord and please him in every way: bearing fruit in every good work, growing in the knowledge of God,
Job 17:9 Nevertheless, the righteous will hold to their ways, and those with clean hands will grow stronger.

126 There are then more challenges to undertake, more ordeals to develop character and aid one's judgment and insight and self-mastery. Of course, there are also many rewards - some carnal, some material, some spiritual (in the sinister sense, naturally!). — rewards

Colossians 3:23 Whatever you do, work at it with all your heart, as working for the Lord, not for human masters, 24 since you know that you will receive an inheritance from the Lord as a reward. It is the Lord Christ you are serving.
Matthew 6:1 "Be careful not to practice your

righteousness in front of others to be seen by them. If you do, you will have no reward from your Father in heaven.2 "So when you give to the needy, do not announce it with trumpets, as the hypocrites do in the synagogues and on the streets, to be honored by others. Truly I tell you, they have received their reward in full. 3 But when you give to the needy, do not let your left hand know what your right hand is doing, 4 so that your giving may be in secret. Then your Father, who sees what is done in secret, will reward you.

Matthew 6:20 But store up for yourselves treasures in heaven, where moths and vermin do not destroy, and where thieves do not break in and steal. 21 For where your treasure is, there your heart will be also.

Proverbs 11:18 A wicked person earns deceptive wages, but the one who sows righteousness reaps a sure reward.

127 There develops an awareness of one's Destiny and an understanding of what is hidden from the majority by virtue of their rather rudimentary level of consciousness and knowledge. During all this, one is aiding the dark forces by the very act of doing Satanic things. That is, aiding evolution - of one's self, and existence in general. One is being significant; doing and achieving.   destiny

Galatians 6:7 Do not be deceived: God cannot be mocked. A man reaps what he sows. 8 Whoever sows to please their flesh, from the flesh will reap destruction; whoever sows to please the Spirit, from the Spirit will reap eternal life. 9 Let us not become weary in doing good, for at the proper time we will reap a harvest if we do not give up.

Romans 8:29 For those God foreknew he also predestined to be conformed to the image of his Son, that he might be the firstborn among many brothers and sisters. 30 And those he predestined, he also called; those he called, he also justified; those he justified, he also

glorified.

Jeremiah 29:11 For I know the plans I have for you," declares the Lord, "plans to prosper you and not to harm you, plans to give you hope and a future. 12 Then you will call on me and come and pray to me, and I will listen to you. 13 You will seek me and find me when you seek me with all your heart. 14 I will be found by you," declares the Lord, "and will bring you back from captivity. I will gather you from all the nations and places where I have banished you," declares the Lord, "and will bring you back to the place from which I carried you into exile."

Psalm 31:15 My times are in your hands; deliver me from the hands of my enemies, from those who pursue me.

Ephesians 1:11 In him we were also chosen, having been predestined according to the plan of him who works out everything in conformity with the purpose of his will,

128	What is important, is that one really lives; achieves things; works in and alters the real world; and learns and so develops - in character, insight, knowledge and so on.	development

Acts 20:24 However, I consider my life worth nothing to me; my only aim is to finish the race and complete the task the Lord Jesus has given me—the task of testifying to the good news of God's grace.

Ephesians 5:15 Be very careful, then, how you live—not as unwise but as wise, 16 making the most of every opportunity, because the days are evil. 17 Therefore do not be foolish, but understand what the Lord's will is.

John 10:27 My sheep listen to my voice; I know them, and they follow me. 28 I give them eternal life, and they shall never perish; no one will snatch them out of my hand.

Proverbs 21:21 Whoever pursues righteousness and love finds life, prosperity and honor.

129	Most people waste their lives. A Satanist wants to be a god - and is prepared to change the	wasting life

world to make their dreams a reality. Most people dream, but lack the courage to act.

Ephesians 5:11 Have nothing to do with the fruitless deeds of darkness, but rather expose them. 12 It is shameful even to mention what the disobedient do in secret. 13 But everything exposed by the light becomes visible—and everything that is illuminated becomes a light. 14 This is why it is said: "Wake up, sleeper, rise from the dead, and Christ will shine on you." 15 Be very careful, then, how you live—not as unwise but as wise, 16 making the most of every opportunity, because the days are evil.

James 4:15 Instead, you ought to say, "If it is the Lord's will, we will live and do this or that." 16 As it is, you boast in your arrogant schemes. All such boasting is evil.

Exodus 20:1 And God spoke all these words: 2 "I am the Lord your God, who brought you out of Egypt, out of the land of slavery. "You shall have no other gods before me. 4 "You shall not make for yourself an image in the form of anything in heaven above or on the earth beneath or in the waters below.

Isaiah 41:10 So do not fear, for I am with you; do not be dismayed, for I am your God. I will strengthen you and help you; I will uphold you with my righteous right hand.

130 And life does not even end with causal death - one can become Immortal! The form of life simply changes. But this immortality is not given - it is not a reward. It is achieved, it is a conscious act: a becoming-one with the dark force itself, with Satan.   afterlife

John 11:25 Jesus said to her, "I am the resurrection and the life. The one who believes in me will live, even though they die; 26 and whoever lives by believing in me will never die. Do you believe this?"

Romans 6:23 For the wages of sin is death, but the gift of God is eternal life in Christ Jesus our Lord.

Matthew 10:28 Do not be afraid of those who

kill the body but cannot kill the soul. Rather, be afraid of the One who can destroy both soul and body in hell.

Romans 14:7 For none of us lives for ourselves alone, and none of us dies for ourselves alone. 8 If we live, we live for the Lord; and if we die, we die for the Lord. So, whether we live or die, we belong to the Lord. 9 For this very reason, Christ died and returned to life so that he might be the Lord of both the dead and the living.

Revelation 20:10 And the devil, who deceived them, was thrown into the lake of burning sulfur, where the beast and the false prophet had been thrown. They will be tormented day and night for ever and ever.

131 There is much that is numinous, but nothing known surpasses Man in numinosity. — divine presence

Matthew 18:20 For where two or three gather in my name, there am I with them."

John 14:22 Then Judas (not Judas Iscariot) said, "But, Lord, why do you intend to show yourself to us and not to the world?" 23 Jesus replied, "Anyone who loves me will obey my teaching. My Father will love them, and we will come to them and make our home with them.

Acts 17:27 God did this so that they would seek him and perhaps reach out for him and find him, though he is not far from any one of us. 28 'For in him we live and move and have our being.' As some of your own poets have said, 'We are his offspring.

Isaiah 41:10 So do not fear, for I am with you; do not be dismayed, for I am your God. I will strengthen you and help you; I will uphold you with my righteous right hand.

Exodus 33:14 The Lord replied, "My Presence will go with you, and I will give you rest."

Ecclesiastes 5:2 Do not be quick with your mouth, do not be hasty in your heart to utter anything before God. God is in heaven and you are on earth, so let your words be few.

132   That is, of all life, we as individuals possess the   create
most potential - have the 'creative fire' of life
itself.

2 Corinthians 5:17 Therefore, if anyone is in Christ, the new creation has come: The old has gone, the new is here!

Hebrews 3:4 For every house is built by someone, but God is the builder of everything.

Job 12:7 "But ask the animals, and they will teach you, or the birds in the sky, and they will tell you; 8 or speak to the earth, and it will teach you, or let the fish in the sea inform you. 9 Which of all these does not know that the hand of the Lord has done this? 10 In his hand is the life of every creature and the breath of all mankind.

133   Satanism is a means to not only understand this,   potential
but to implement it - fulfil our divine (and
diabolic) potential.

Philippians 4:12 I know what it is to be in need, and I know what it is to have plenty. I have learned the secret of being content in any and every situation, whether well fed or hungry, whether living in plenty or in want. 13 I can do all this through him who gives me strength.

Matthew 7:12 So in everything, do to others what you would have them do to you, for this sums up the Law and the Prophets. 13 "Enter through the narrow gate. For wide is the gate and broad is the road that leads to destruction, and many enter through it. 14 But small is the gate and narrow the road that leads to life, and only a few find it.

Ephesians 2:10 For we are God's handiwork, created in Christ Jesus to do good works, which God prepared in advance for us to do.

Proverbs 3:5 Trust in the Lord with all your heart and lean not on your own understanding; 6 in all your ways submit to him, and he will make your paths straight.

Exodus 35:10 "All who are skilled among you are to come and make everything the Lord has commanded:

134 But Satanism is dangerous - it is testing. It defiance
requires a demonic desire, a strength of
character. It is genuine Heresy. It is for the few
who can really defy, who really wish to become
like gods and are prepared to take the risks
involved.

Galatians 6:7 Do not be deceived: God cannot be mocked. A man reaps what he sows. 8 Whoever sows to please their flesh, from the flesh will reap destruction; whoever sows to please the Spirit, from the Spirit will reap eternal life. 9 Let us not become weary in doing good, for at the proper time we will reap a harvest if we do not give up.

Revelation 20:10 And the devil, who deceived them, was thrown into the lake of burning sulfur, where the beast and the false prophet had been thrown. They will be tormented day and night for ever and ever.

Ephesians 6:10 Finally, be strong in the Lord and in his mighty power. 11 Put on the full armor of God, so that you can take your stand against the devil's schemes. 12 For our struggle is not against flesh and blood, but against the rulers, against the authorities, against the powers of this dark world and against the spiritual forces of evil in the heavenly realms.

2 Peter 1:21 For prophecy never had its origin in the human will, but prophets, though human, spoke from God as they were carried along by the Holy Spirit.

2. The Dark Forces

135 It has been said (by Nietzsche): "The more strength
mediocre, the weaker, the more submissive and
cowardly a man is, the more he will posit as
evil: it is with him that the realm of evil is most
comprehensive. The basest (most
dishonourable) man will see the realm of evil
that is, of that which is forbidden and hostile to
him - everywhere."

"The most powerful man, the creator, would
have to be the most evil, in as much as he
carries his ideal against the ideals of other men

and remakes them in his own image..."

2 Corinthians 12:8 Three times I pleaded with the Lord to take it away from me. 9 But he said to me, "My grace is sufficient for you, for my power is made perfect in weakness." Therefore I will boast all the more gladly about my weaknesses, so that Christ's power may rest on me.

Romans 1:20 For since the creation of the world God's invisible qualities—his eternal power and divine nature—have been clearly seen, being understood from what has been made, so that people are without excuse.

2 Samuel 22:32 For who is God besides the Lord? And who is the Rock except our God? 33 It is God who arms me with strength and keeps my way secure.

Colossians 2:12 having been buried with him in baptism, in which you were also raised with him through your faith in the working of God, who raised him from the dead.

Ephesians 3:20 Now to him who is able to do immeasurably more than all we ask or imagine, according to his power that is at work within us, 21 to him be glory in the church and in Christ Jesus throughout all generations, for ever and ever! Amen.

3. The Alchemy Of Magick

136   There is not and never has been any substitute for self-learning from experience.   learning

2 Timothy 3:16 All Scripture is God-breathed and is useful for teaching, rebuking, correcting and training in righteousness, 17 so that the servant of God may be thoroughly equipped for every good work.

Romans 15:4 For everything that was written in the past was written to teach us, so that through the endurance taught in the Scriptures and the encouragement they provide we might have hope.

Matthew 11:28 "Come to me, all you who are weary and burdened, and I will give you rest. 29 Take my yoke upon you and learn from me, for I

am gentle and humble in heart, and you will find rest for your souls. 30 For my yoke is easy and my burden is light."

Hebrews 4:12 For the word of God is alive and active. Sharper than any double-edged sword, it penetrates even to dividing soul and spirit, joints and marrow; it judges the thoughts and attitudes of the heart.

Matthew 5:19 Therefore anyone who sets aside one of the least of these commands and teaches others accordingly will be called least in the kingdom of heaven, but whoever practices and teaches these commands will be called great in the kingdom of heaven.

Proverbs 1:7 The fear of the Lord is the beginning of knowledge, but fools despise wisdom and instruction.

Psalm 86:11 Teach me your way, Lord, that I may rely on your faithfulness; give me an undivided heart, that I may fear your name.

137 The alchemy of magick is in learning this control in being able to access the energies, and being able to produce changes via the presencing of what is accessed: internally (within one's own psyche), externally (in others and the things of the everyday) and aeonically (within and beyond the confines of aeonics). energies

Ephesians 1:18 I pray that the eyes of your heart may be enlightened in order that you may know the hope to which he has called you, the riches of his glorious inheritance in his holy people, 19 and his incomparably great power for us who believe. That power is the same as the mighty strength 20 he exerted when he raised Christ from the dead and seated him at his right hand in the heavenly realms,

2 Timothy 1:6 For this reason I remind you to fan into flame the gift of God, which is in you through the laying on of my hands. 7 For the Spirit God gave us does not make us timid, but gives us power, love and self-discipline.

Joshua 1:8 Keep this Book of the Law always on your lips; meditate on it day and night, so

that you may be careful to do everything written in it. Then you will be prosperous and successful. 9 Have I not commanded you? Be strong and courageous. Do not be afraid; do not be discouraged, for the Lord your God will be with you wherever you go."

4- A Complete Guide To The Seven-Fold Sinister Way

138	The Way is an individual one - each stage, of the seven stages that make the Way, is achieved by the individual as a result of their own effort. To reach a particular stage, requires considerable effort by the individual, who works mostly on their own.	create

1 John 1:7 But if we walk in the light, as he is in the light, we have fellowship with one another, and the blood of Jesus, his Son, purifies us from all sin.

Hebrews 10:24 And let us consider how we may spur one another on toward love and good deeds, 25 not giving up meeting together, as some are in the habit of doing, but encouraging one another—and all the more as you see the Day approaching.

Matthew 18:19 "Again, truly I tell you that if two of you on earth agree about anything they ask for, it will be done for them by my Father in heaven. 20 For where two or three gather in my name, there am I with them."

1 Corinthians 12:12 Just as a body, though one, has many parts, but all its many parts form one body, so it is with Christ.

139	The individual also acquires genuine esoteric knowledge and a genuine understanding. The Way itself enables any individual to achieve genuine magickal Adeptship (and beyond) and thus fulfil the potential latent within them - thus they can and do enhance their life, and achieve their unique Destiny.	knowledge
		destiny

2 Peter 1:5 For this very reason, make every effort to add to your faith goodness; and to goodness, knowledge; 6 and to knowledge, self-control; and to self-control, perseverance; and to perseverance, godliness; 7 and to godliness, mutual affection; and to mutual affection, love.

James 3:17 But the wisdom that comes from heaven is first of all pure; then peace-loving, considerate, submissive, full of mercy and good fruit, impartial and sincere.

Ecclesiastes 2:26 To the person who pleases him, God gives wisdom, knowledge and happiness, but to the sinner he gives the task of gathering and storing up wealth to hand it over to the one who pleases God. This too is meaningless, a chasing after the wind.

Proverbs 1:7 The fear of the Lord is the beginning of knowledge, but fools despise wisdom and instruction.

140 The Way is essentially practical - involving experiences in the real world, and ordeals, as well as the completion of difficult, challenging tasks. It also involves a practical mastery of all forms of magick.   *witchcraft*

Revelation 21:8 But the cowardly, the unbelieving, the vile, the murderers, the sexually immoral, those who practice magic arts, the idolaters and all liars—they will be consigned to the fiery lake of burning sulfur. This is the second death."

Galatians 5:20 idolatry and witchcraft; hatred, discord, jealousy, fits of rage, selfish ambition, dissensions, factions 21 and envy; drunkenness, orgies, and the like. I warn you, as I did before, that those who live like this will not inherit the kingdom of God.

2 Chronicles 33:6 He sacrificed his children in the fire in the Valley of Ben Hinnom, practiced divination and witchcraft, sought omens, and consulted mediums and spiritists. He did much evil in the eyes of the Lord, arousing his anger.

2 Kings 21:6 He sacrificed his own son in the fire, practiced divination, sought omens, and consulted mediums and spiritists. He did much evil in the eyes of the Lord, arousing his anger.

Leviticus 19:31 "'Do not turn to mediums or

seek out spiritists, for you will be defiled by them. I am the Lord your God.

141 The Way is divided into seven stages, and these mark a specific level of individual achievement. ... Each stage represents a development of and in the individual - of their personality, their skills, their understanding, their knowledge and insight.

    achievement

1 John 5:4 for everyone born of God overcomes the world. This is the victory that has overcome the world, even our faith.

Mark 8:36 What good is it for someone to gain the whole world, yet forfeit their soul?

Joshua 1:8 Keep this Book of the Law always on your lips; meditate on it day and night, so that you may be careful to do everything written in it. Then you will be prosperous and successful.

Psalm 1:1 Blessed is the one who does not walk in step with the wicked or stand in the way that sinners take or sit in the company of mockers, 2 but whose delight is in the law of the Lord, and who meditates on his law day and night. 3 That person is like a tree planted by streams of water, which yields its fruit in season and whose leaf does not wither—whatever they do prospers.

142 1 Neophyte

The first task of a neophyte [the word means "a beginner; a new convert"] is to obtain copies of the various Order MSS

    book

2 Timothy 3:16 All Scripture is God-breathed and is useful for teaching, rebuking, correcting and training in righteousness, 17 so that the servant of God may be thoroughly equipped for every good work.

Romans 15:4 For everything that was written in the past was written to teach us, so that through the endurance taught in the Scriptures and the encouragement they provide we might have hope.

Colossians 3:16 Let the message of Christ dwell among you richly as you teach and admonish one another with all wisdom through psalms, hymns, and songs from the Spirit, singing to God with gratitude in your hearts.

Psalm 119:105 Your word is a lamp for my feet, a light on my path.

Joshua 1:8 Keep this Book of the Law always on your lips; meditate on it day and night, so that you may be careful to do everything written in it. Then you will be prosperous and successful.

143	II Initiate Write a personal "magickal diary" about these workings. Study and begin to use the Sinister Tarot	tarot

Leviticus 20:6 "'I will set my face against anyone who turns to mediums and spiritists to prostitute themselves by following them, and I will cut them off from their people.

Leviticus 19:26 "'Do not practice divination or seek omens.

Deuteronomy 18:10 Let no one be found among you who sacrifices their son or daughter in the fire, who practices divination or sorcery, interprets omens, engages in witchcraft, 11 or casts spells, or who is a medium or spiritist or who consults the dead.

144	Undertake hermetic workings/rituals for specific personal desires/personal requests of your own choosing, as described in Naos.	desires

Colossians 3:5 Put to death, therefore, whatever belongs to your earthly nature: sexual immorality, impurity, lust, evil desires and greed, which is idolatry. 6 Because of these, the wrath of God is coming.

James 4:2 You desire but do not have, so you kill. You covet but you cannot get what you want, so you quarrel and fight. You do not have because you do not ask God. 3 When you ask, you do not receive, because you ask with wrong motives, that you may spend what you get on your pleasures.

145	Set yourself one very demanding physical goal, train and achieve or surpass that goal.	goals

Philippians 2:3 Do nothing out of selfish ambition or vain conceit. Rather, in humility value others above yourselves, 4 not looking to your own interests but each of you to the interests of the others.

Romans 8:28 And we know that in all things God works for the good of those who love him, who have been called according to his purpose. 29 For those God foreknew he also predestined to be conformed to the image of his Son, that he might be the firstborn among many brothers and sisters.

Proverbs 16:3 Commit to the Lord whatever you do, and he will establish your plans.

Jeremiah 29:11 For I know the plans I have for you," declares the Lord, "plans to prosper you and not to harm you, plans to give you hope and a future.

145 Seek and find someone of the opposite sex to be partner your 'magickal' companion and sexual partner, and introduce this person to Satanism. Initiate them according to the rite in The Black Book of Satan. Undertake the path and sphere workings with this partner.

1 Corinthians 7:8 Now to the unmarried and the widows I say: It is good for them to stay unmarried, as I do. 9 But if they cannot control themselves, they should marry, for it is better to marry than to burn with passion.

Hebrews 13:4 Marriage should be honored by all, and the marriage bed kept pure, for God will judge the adulterer and all the sexually immoral.

2 Corinthians 6:14 Do not be yoked together with unbelievers. For what do righteousness and wickedness have in common? Or what fellowship can light have with darkness?

1 John 4:7 Dear friends, let us love one another, for love comes from God. Everyone who loves has been born of God and knows God. 8 Whoever does not love does not know God, because God is love.

1 Peter 3:7 Husbands, in the same way be

considerate as you live with your wives, and treat them with respect as the weaker partner and as heirs with you of the gracious gift of life, so that nothing will hinder your prayers.

Psalm 85:10 Love and faithfulness meet together; righteousness and peace kiss each other.

146   Undertake an 'Insight Role'   insight

2 Timothy 3:13 while evildoers and impostors will go from bad to worse, deceiving and being deceived.

2 Corinthians 11:14 And no wonder, for Satan himself masquerades as an angel of light. 15 It is not surprising, then, if his servants also masquerade as servants of righteousness. Their end will be what their actions deserve.

Proverbs 26:25 Though their speech is charming, do not believe them, for seven abominations fill their hearts.

Romans 12:9 Love must be sincere. Hate what is evil; cling to what is good. 10 Be devoted to one another in love. Honor one another above yourselves.

Psalm 26:4 I do not sit with the deceitful, nor do I associate with hypocrites.

Luke 6:46 "Why do you call me, 'Lord, Lord,' and do not do what I say? 47 As for everyone who comes to me and hears my words and puts them into practice, I will show you what they are like. 48 They are like a man building a house, who dug down deep and laid the foundation on rock. When a flood came, the torrent struck that house but could not shake it, because it was well built.

147   After completion of your Insight Role,   initiation
undertake the Grade Ritual of External Adept, given in Naos. The stage of Initiation can last - depending on the commitment of the Initiate - from six months to a year. Occasionally, it lasts two years.

John 3:16 For God so loved the world that he   salvation
gave his one and only Son, that whoever believes in him shall not perish but have eternal

life.

Matthew 7:21 "Not everyone who says to me, 'Lord, Lord,' will enter the kingdom of heaven, but only the one who does the will of my Father who is in heaven.

Acts 16:30 He then brought them out and asked, "Sirs, what must I do to be saved?" 31 They replied, "Believe in the Lord Jesus, and you will be saved—you and your household." 32 Then they spoke the word of the Lord to him and to all the others in his house. 33 At that hour of the night the jailer took them and washed their wounds; then immediately he and all his household were baptized.

148	Satanic Initiation is the awakening of the darker/sinister/unconscious aspects of the psyche, and of the inner (often repressed) and latent personality/character of the Initiate.	initiation

John 6:35 Then Jesus declared, "I am the bread of life. Whoever comes to me will never go hungry, and whoever believes in me will never be thirsty.

2 Corinthians 5:17 Therefore, if anyone is in Christ, the new creation has come: The old has gone, the new is here! 18 All this is from God, who reconciled us to himself through Christ and gave us the ministry of reconciliation: 19 that God was reconciling the world to himself in Christ, not counting people's sins against them. And he has committed to us the message of reconciliation.

Ezekiel 36:26 I will give you a new heart and put a new spirit in you; I will remove from you your heart of stone and give you a heart of flesh.

Ephesians 5:1 Follow God's example, therefore, as dearly loved children 2 and walk in the way of love, just as Christ loved us and gave himself up for us as a fragrant offering and sacrifice to God.

149	Obtain from a Nazarene place of worship some 'hosts' as used in their perverse and sordid rituals. If you are seeking Initiation into an	black mass communion hosts

established ceremonial group/Temple, this will probably be your task of fidelity to that group/Temple, with the hosts being used in the celebration of The Black Mass.

1 Corinthians 6:10 nor thieves nor the greedy nor drunkards nor slanderers nor swindlers will inherit the kingdom of God.

John 10:9 I am the gate; whoever enters through me will be saved. They will come in and go out, and find pasture. 10 The thief comes only to steal and kill and destroy; I have come that they may have life, and have it to the full.

Exodus 20:15 "You shall not steal."

Proverbs 10:2 Ill-gotten treasures have no lasting value, but righteousness delivers from death.

150 If however you are undertaking a Self-Initiation ... then immediately following that rite of Self-Initiation you should trample on or otherwise defile these 'hosts' (e.g. by urinating on them) saying as you do so the following: "By this deed I pledge myself to counter Nazarene filth, and give myself, body, blood and soul, to Satan, Prince of Darkness." You should then burn the hosts or what remains of them by placing them in a vessel containing flammable liquid and setting this alight, laughing as the burning seals your gesture and your oath.   Jesus temples sacrilege

1 Corinthians 3:16 Don't you know that you yourselves are God's temple and that God's Spirit dwells in your midst? 17 If anyone destroys God's temple, God will destroy that person; for God's temple is sacred, and you together are that temple.

Matthew 24:15 "So when you see standing in the holy place 'the abomination that causes desolation,' spoken of through the prophet Daniel—let the reader understand—

Matthew 21:13 "It is written," he said to them, "'My house will be called a house of prayer,' but you are making it 'a den of robbers.' 14 The blind and the lame came to him at the temple, and he healed them.

Exodus 20:7 "You shall not misuse the name of the Lord your God, for the Lord will not hold anyone guiltless who misuses his name.

2 Chronicles 24:7 Now the sons of that wicked woman Athaliah had broken into the temple of God and had used even its sacred objects for the Baals.

151 Train several members, and yourself, in the undertaking of the tests relevant to choosing an opfer - a human sacrifice. Select some suitable victims, using Satanic guidelines for so selecting a victim, and undertake the relevant tests on each chosen victim. The victim or victims having been so chosen by failing such tests, perform The Death Ritual with the intent of eliminating by magickal means the chosen victim(s).   murder

1 John 3:11 For this is the message you heard from the beginning: We should love one another. 12 Do not be like Cain, who belonged to the evil one and murdered his brother. And why did he murder him? Because his own actions were evil and his brother's were righteous.

Revelation 21:8 But the cowardly, the unbelieving, the vile, the murderers, the sexually immoral, those who practice magic arts, the idolaters and all liars—they will be consigned to the fiery lake of burning sulfur. This is the second death."

Matthew 5:21 "You have heard that it was said to the people long ago, 'You shall not murder, and anyone who murders will be subject to judgment.'

Leviticus 24:17 "'Anyone who takes the life of a human being is to be put to death.

152 Thereafter, and having completed all the necessary preparations, select a further victim using Aeonics or sinister strategy as a guide, and undertake a culling by disposing of the victim either during a suitable rite (e.g. The Ceremony of Recalling) or via practical means (e.g. assassination).   murder

Matthew 5:21 "You have heard that it was said to the people long ago, 'You shall not murder, and anyone who murders will be subject to judgment.'

Romans 13:9 The commandments, "You shall not commit adultery," "You shall not murder," "You shall not steal," "You shall not covet," and whatever other command there may be, are summed up in this one command: "Love your neighbor as yourself."

Matthew 26:52 "Put your sword back in its place," Jesus said to him, "for all who draw the sword will die by the sword.

Leviticus 24:17 "'Anyone who takes the life of a human being is to be put to death.

Exodus 21:12 "Anyone who strikes a person with a fatal blow is to be put to death.

153 Furthermore, the victims can be chosen either by you, or suggested by a member of your Temple, if those members are following the Satanic path in a committed way.   victims

Ecclesiastes 8:14 There is something else meaningless that occurs on earth: the righteous who get what the wicked deserve, and the wicked who get what the righteous deserve. This too, I say, is meaningless.

Psalms 37:9 For those who are evil will be destroyed, but those who hope in the Lord will inherit the land.

Genesis 9:6 "Whoever sheds human blood, by humans shall their blood be shed; for in the image of God has God made mankind.

Star-Gates

154 A black cloud spread about the ground, and moved slowly through the land, as a nameless god brought him these insights - and the Dark Gods manifest themselves throughout the rest of this world in the form of bloody war.   dark gods

Matthew 5:9 Blessed are the peacemakers, for they will be called children of God.

Matthew 26:52 "Put your sword back in its place," Jesus said to him, "for all who draw the sword will die by the sword.

John 1:5 The light shines in the darkness, and the darkness has not overcome it.

6.Guide To Black Magick

155 External Magick...Ceremonial magick can be done for basically two reasons: to create/draw down and then direct magickal energy for a specific aim (e.g. cursing), or to represent through words and symbolism the myths/knowledge of a particular tradition or cultus.   magick

Matthew 5:21 "You have heard that it was said to the people long ago, 'You shall not murder, and anyone who murders will be subject to judgment.' 22 But I tell you that anyone who is angry with a brother or sister will be subject to judgment. Again, anyone who says to a brother or sister, 'Raca,' is answerable to the court. And anyone who says, 'You fool!' will be in danger of the fire of hell.

James 3:9 With the tongue we praise our Lord and Father, and with it we curse human beings, who have been made in God's likeness. 10 Out of the same mouth come praise and cursing. My brothers and sisters, this should not be.

156 Internal Magick...This is when magickal techniques (e.g. Grade Rituals) are used to alter the consciousness of an individual. The rites of internal magick 'open the gates' between the causal and the acausal, and change the perception from 'ego' consciousness to the 'self' and what is beyond. In the Jungian sense, internal magick produces 'individuation', and leads to Adepthood.   sorcery
Jung

1 Peter 4:7 The end of all things is near. Therefore be alert and of sober mind so that you may pray.

Ephesians 5:11 Have nothing to do with the fruitless deeds of darkness, but rather expose them. 12 It is shameful even to mention what the disobedient do in secret.

1 Thessalonians 5:6 So then, let us not be like others, who are asleep, but let us be awake and sober. 7 For those who sleep, sleep at night, and those who get drunk, get drunk at night. 8 But since we belong to the day, let us be sober, putting on faith and love as a breastplate, and the hope of salvation as a helmet.

Romans 8:5 Those who live according to the flesh have their minds set on what the flesh desires; but those who live in accordance with the Spirit have their minds set on what the Spirit desires. 6 The mind governed by the flesh is death, but the mind governed by the Spirit is life and peace. 7 The mind governed by the flesh is hostile to God; it does not submit to God's law, nor can it do so. 8 Those who are in the realm of the flesh cannot please God.

157	Aeonic Magick...On one level, aeonic magick is the alteration/ distortion of such forces; on another, it is the 'creation' of new energies and their dispersion over the Earth to change conscious evolution. In one sense, this is the 'blackest' magick of all.	black magic

Romans 12:2 Do not conform to the pattern of this world, but be transformed by the renewing of your mind. Then you will be able to test and approve what God's will is—his good, pleasing and perfect will.

Philippians 4:6 Do not be anxious about anything, but in every situation, by prayer and petition, with thanksgiving, present your requests to God.

Philippians 4:8 Finally, brothers and sisters, whatever is true, whatever is noble, whatever is right, whatever is pure, whatever is lovely, whatever is admirable—if anything is excellent or praiseworthy—think about such things.

Psalm 139:23 Search me, God, and know my heart; test me and know my anxious thoughts.

158	However, this said, the full moon is rightly associated with ' lunacy' and 'demonic' possession - as any one who has worked nights at Mental Hospitals will testify. This power can also be harnessed during a ritual.	moon

Deuteronomy 4:19 And when you look up to the sky and see the sun, the moon and the

stars—all the heavenly array—do not be enticed into bowing down to them and worshiping things the Lord your God has apportioned to all the nations under heaven.

157 Celebratory rites in traditional Satanism are of two kinds - 1) those that express the energies of Satanism - e.g. the Black Mass, Ceremony of Recalling - and whose performance thus distorts the currents of the Nazarenes and the Old Aeon; and 2) those which create new energies appropriate to the Satanic age of fire to come - e.g. invokations to the 'Dark Gods'. — energy

Colossians 1:29 To this end I strenuously contend with all the energy Christ so powerfully works in me.

John 3:8 The wind blows wherever it pleases. You hear its sound, but you cannot tell where it comes from or where it is going. So it is with everyone born of the Spirit."

Isaiah 40:29 He gives strength to the weary and increases the power of the weak.

Ephesians 1:19 and his incomparably great power for us who believe. That power is the same as the mighty strength

158 The Black Mass is still celebrated simply because the Nazarenes (and their allies) are still powerful and still polluting us with their filth. — nazarenes

2 Timothy 3:12 In fact, everyone who wants to live a godly life in Christ Jesus will be persecuted, 13 while evildoers and impostors will go from bad to worse, deceiving and being deceived. 14 But as for you, continue in what you have learned and have become convinced of, because you know those from whom you learned it, 15 and how from infancy you have known the Holy Scriptures, which are able to make you wise for salvation through faith in Christ Jesus.

Matthew 16:24 Then Jesus said to his disciples, "Whoever wants to be my disciple must deny themselves and take up their cross and follow me.

John 15:19 If you belonged to the world, it

would love you as its own. As it is, you do not belong to the world, but I have chosen you out of the world. That is why the world hates you. 20 Remember what I told you: 'A servant is not greater than his master.' If they persecuted me, they will persecute you also. If they obeyed my teaching, they will obey yours also.

Matthew 5:10 Blessed are those who are persecuted because of righteousness, for theirs is the kingdom of heaven. 11 "Blessed are you when people insult you, persecute you and falsely say all kinds of evil against you because of me. 12 Rejoice and be glad, because great is your reward in heaven, for in the same way they persecuted the prophets who were before you.

Revelation 2:10 Do not be afraid of what you are about to suffer. I tell you, the devil will put some of you in prison to test you, and you will suffer persecution for ten days. Be faithful, even to the point of death, and I will give you life as your victor's crown. 11 Whoever has ears, let them hear what the Spirit says to the churches. The one who is victorious will not be hurt at all by the second death.

Matthew 10:16 "I am sending you out like sheep among wolves. Therefore be as shrewd as snakes and as innocent as doves. 17 Be on your guard; you will be handed over to the local councils and be flogged in the synagogues. 18 On my account you will be brought before governors and kings as witnesses to them and to the Gentiles.

159 The mysteries of the Nine Angles form an important aspect of genuine Black Magick. On the physical level, the nine represent energy vibrations - for according to tradition, a crystal shaped like a tetrahedron responds to voice vibration of the correct pitch and intensity. In simple terms, the crystal amplifies the power of thought and produces magickal change. Quartz gives the best results, although spinel may be used. The tetrahedron shape has to be created from the natural material by a skilled operator.

crystals

Revelation 4:6 Also in front of the throne there was what looked like a sea of glass, clear as crystal. In the center, around the throne, were four living creatures, and they were covered with eyes, in front and in back.

Acts 8:9 Now for some time a man named Simon had practiced sorcery in the city and amazed all the people of Samaria. He boasted that he was someone great, 10 and all the people, both high and low, gave him their attention and exclaimed, "This man is rightly called the Great Power of God." 11 They followed him because he had amazed them for a long time with his sorcery. 12 But when they believed Philip as he proclaimed the good news of the kingdom of God and the name of Jesus Christ, they were baptized, both men and women. 13 Simon himself believed and was baptized. And he followed Philip everywhere, astonished by the great signs and miracles he saw.

160 The Star Game has two sets of twenty- seven pieces - one set white, the other black, representing the two aspects of cosmic Change (or the causal and acausal). These pieces are spread over the seven boards. The Nine Angles also symbolize the seven plus two gates (or spheres) that join our causal universe with the acausal (or 'magickal') universe.

universe

Hebrews 11:3 By faith we understand that the universe was formed at God's command, so that what is seen was not made out of what was visible.

Genesis 1:14 And God said, "Let there be lights in the vault of the sky to separate the day from the night, and let them serve as signs to mark sacred times, and days and years,

Colossians 1:15 The Son is the image of the invisible God, the firstborn over all creation. 16 For in him all things were created: things in heaven and on earth, visible and invisible, whether thrones or powers or rulers or authorities; all things have been created through him and for him. 17 He is before all things, and in him all things hold together.

161 The other important form of Black Magick is to do with self-survival after death. This can be done in two ways, depending on the aim of the operator. The first is transference of the essence of selfhood, near the moment of physical death, into another physical body, ensuring thus the continuation of existence on the physical level.

demonic possession

Luke 4:33 In the synagogue there was a man possessed by a demon, an impure spirit. He cried out at the top of his voice, 34 "Go away! What do you want with us, Jesus of Nazareth? Have you come to destroy us? I know who you are—the Holy One of God!" 35 "Be quiet!" Jesus said sternly. "Come out of him!" Then the demon threw the man down before them all and came out without injuring him. 36 All the people were amazed and said to each other, "What words these are! With authority and power he gives orders to impure spirits and they come out!"

Matthew 8:28 When he arrived at the other side in the region of the Gadarenes, two demon-possessed men coming from the tombs met him. They were so violent that no one could pass that way. 29 "What do you want with us, Son of God?" they shouted. "Have you come here to torture us before the appointed time?" 30 Some distance from them a large herd of pigs was feeding. 31 The demons begged Jesus, "If you drive us out, send us into the herd of pigs." 32 He said to them, "Go!" So they came out and went into the pigs, and the whole herd rushed down the steep bank into the lake and died in the water. 33 Those tending the pigs ran off, went into the town and reported all this, including what had happened to the demon-possessed men. 34 Then the whole town went out to meet Jesus. And when they saw him, they pleaded with him to leave their region.

Acts 16:16 Once when we were going to the place of prayer, we were met by a female slave who had a spirit by which she predicted the future. She earned a great deal of money for her owners by fortune-telling. 17 She followed Paul and the rest of us, shouting, "These men are servants of the Most High God, who are telling you the way to be saved." 18 She kept this up for many days. Finally Paul became so annoyed that he turned around and said to the spirit, "In the name of Jesus Christ I command you to come out of her!" At that moment the spirit left her.

Matthew 12:43 "When an impure spirit comes out of a person, it goes through arid places seeking rest and does not find it. 44 Then it says, 'I will return to the house I left.' When it arrives, it finds the house unoccupied, swept clean and put in order. 45 Then it goes and takes with it seven other spirits more wicked than itself, and they go in and live there. And the final condition of that person is worse than the first. That is how it will be with this wicked generation."

Revelation 20:10 And the devil, who deceived them, was thrown into the lake of burning sulfur, where the beast and the false prophet had been thrown. They will be tormented day and night for ever and ever.

162   To see 'Satan' as simply a self symbol - as two recent 'satanic' groups do - is, firstly, to be self-deluded about the nature of cosmic forces, and second, to make (or attempt to make) Black Magick tame and safe. To deal with greater forces is to court danger - psychologically and physically. Traditional Satanists see this danger as a means: the strong survive and the weak perish; this simply being a reflection of genuine Satanist philosophy rather than the tame view spewed forth by the imitation and toy 'satanists' who abound today.   Satan is real

1 John 3:8 The one who does what is sinful is of the devil, because the devil has been sinning from the beginning. The reason the Son of God appeared was to destroy the devil's work.

84

Ephesians 6:11 Put on the full armor of God, so that you can take your stand against the devil's schemes. 12 For our struggle is not against flesh and blood, but against the rulers, against the authorities, against the powers of this dark world and against the spiritual forces of evil in the heavenly realms. 13 Therefore put on the full armor of God, so that when the day of evil comes, you may be able to stand your ground, and after you have done everything, to stand. 14 Stand firm then, with the belt of truth buckled around your waist, with the breastplate of righteousness in place, 15 and with your feet fitted with the readiness that comes from the gospel of peace. 16 In addition to all this, take up the shield of faith, with which you can extinguish all the flaming arrows of the evil one.

2 Corinthians 2:5 If anyone has caused grief, he has not so much grieved me as he has grieved all of you to some extent—not to put it too severely. 6 The punishment inflicted on him by the majority is sufficient. 7 Now instead, you ought to forgive and comfort him, so that he will not be overwhelmed by excessive sorrow. 8 I urge you, therefore, to reaffirm your love for him. 9 Another reason I wrote you was to see if you would stand the test and be obedient in everything. 10 Anyone you forgive, I also forgive. And what I have forgiven—if there was anything to forgive—I have forgiven in the sight of Christ for your sake, 11 in order that Satan might not outwit us. For we are not unaware of his schemes.

163   In a sense which few people will understand,   chaos
Satan is the essence of the acausal: the cosmic force of Chaos whose intrusion into our causal dimensions disrupts the entropy that linear time produces. Our species requires and has required symbols to enable apprehension and evolution - and this is true also of the Initiate (and to a lessor extent of the Adept) who belong to that lower order.

John 16:33 "I have told you these things, so

that in me you may have peace. In this world you will have trouble. But take heart! I have overcome the world."

2 Thessalonians 3:16 Now may the Lord of peace himself give you peace at all times and in every way. The Lord be with all of you.

John 14:27 Peace I leave with you; my peace I give you. I do not give to you as the world gives. Do not let your hearts be troubled and do not be afraid.

1 Corinthians 14:40 But everything should be done in a fitting and orderly way.

Isaiah 32:17 The fruit of that righteousness will be peace; its effect will be quietness and confidence forever. 18 My people will live in peaceful dwelling places, in secure homes, in undisturbed places of rest.

164 The Abyss destroys - or creates a new species, a new 'mind' capable of functioning on levels not normally accessible to those of the lower order. And the most potent symbol of certain cosmic forces has been, and still is, Satan.   new creation

2 Corinthians 5:17 Therefore, if anyone is in Christ, the new creation has come: The old has gone, the new is here! 18 All this is from God, who reconciled us to himself through Christ and gave us the ministry of reconciliation: 19 that God was reconciling the world to himself in Christ, not counting people's sins against them. And he has committed to us the message of reconciliation. 20 We are therefore Christ's ambassadors, as though God were making his appeal through us. We implore you on Christ's behalf: Be reconciled to God. 21 God made him who had no sin to be sin for us, so that in him we might become the righteousness of God.

Galatians 2:20 I have been crucified with Christ and I no longer live, but Christ lives in me. The life I now live in the body, I live by faith in the Son of God, who loved me and gave himself for me.

Ephesians 4:22 You were taught, with regard to your former way of life, to put off your old

self, which is being corrupted by its deceitful desires; 23 to be made new in the attitude of your minds; 24 and to put on the new self, created to be like God in true righteousness and holiness.

7- Darkness Is My Friend: The True Meaning Of The Sinister Way

165 Contrary to a current and growing misconception, the Sinister Way (and Sinister Magick) involves practical acts of darkness, of heresy, of chaos - involving such things as human sacrifice.

1 Corinthians 13:6 Love does not delight in evil but rejoices with the truth.

1 Thessalonians 5:22 reject every kind of evil.

2 Timothy 2:22 Flee the evil desires of youth and pursue righteousness, faith, love and peace, along with those who call on the Lord out of a pure heart.

Isaiah 32:6 For fools speak folly, their hearts are bent on evil: They practice ungodliness and spread error concerning the Lord; the hungry they leave empty and from the thirsty they withhold water.

166 The Sinister Way does not simply involve the history study of folk-traditions, of myths, of magick, of esoteric subjects, as it does not just involve individuals or groups experiencing (or claiming they have experienced) a certain "atmosphere" in certain "surroundings" which they or others believe or assume to be "sinister". Furthermore, the Sinister Way means the wholehearted acceptance, by the Sinister Initiate and Adept, of that particular way of living which has for centuries been called "Satanic".

Romans 10:9 If you declare with your mouth, "Jesus is Lord," and believe in your heart that God raised him from the dead, you will be saved. 10 For it is with your heart that you believe and are justified, and it is with your mouth that you profess your faith and are saved.

Romans 12:1 Therefore, I urge you, brothers

and sisters, in view of God's mercy, to offer your bodies as a living sacrifice, holy and pleasing to God—this is your true and proper worship. 2 Do not conform to the pattern of this world, but be transformed by the renewing of your mind. Then you will be able to test and approve what God's will is—his good, pleasing and perfect will.

Colossians 3:5 Put to death, therefore, whatever belongs to your earthly nature: sexual immorality, impurity, lust, evil desires and greed, which is idolatry. 6 Because of these, the wrath of God is coming. 7 You used to walk in these ways, in the life you once lived. 8 But now you must also rid yourselves of all such things as these: anger, rage, malice, slander, and filthy language from your lips. 9 Do not lie to each other, since you have taken off your old self with its practices 10 and have put on the new self, which is being renewed in knowledge in the image of its Creator.

167   The Sinister Way is still intrinsically Satanic because the Satanic archetype/mythos/image - the very Being, or life, which has been named Satan - still exists, still lives, and is still a becoming.   Satan

Revelation 12:12 Therefore rejoice, you heavens and you who dwell in them! But woe to the earth and the sea, because the devil has gone down to you! He is filled with fury, because he knows that his time is short."

Matthew 4:1 Then Jesus was led by the Spirit into the wilderness to be tempted by the devil. 2 After fasting forty days and forty nights, he was hungry. 3 The tempter came to him and said, "If you are the Son of God, tell these stones to become bread." 4 Jesus answered, "It is written: 'Man shall not live on bread alone, but on every word that comes from the mouth of God.

Isaiah 14:12 How you have fallen from heaven, morning star, son of the dawn! You have been cast down to the earth, you who once

laid low the nations!

168   This Being is the ethos of Heresy for this present civilization of ours - the presencing of the Dark, the Sinister, and thus a practical manifestation, in the world, of the workings of the sinister dialectic: a means to bring change, imbue life, and initiate further evolution.   *sinister dialectic*

Matthew 12:34 You brood of vipers, how can you who are evil say anything good? For the mouth speaks what the heart is full of. 35 A good man brings good things out of the good stored up in him, and an evil man brings evil things out of the evil stored up in him.

James 3:6 The tongue also is a fire, a world of evil among the parts of the body. It corrupts the whole body, sets the whole course of one's life on fire, and is itself set on fire by hell. 7 All kinds of animals, birds, reptiles and sea creatures are being tamed and have been tamed by mankind, 8 but no human being can tame the tongue. It is a restless evil, full of deadly poison.

James 1:13 When tempted, no one should say, "God is tempting me." For God cannot be tempted by evil, nor does he tempt anyone; 14 but each person is tempted when they are dragged away by their own evil desire and enticed.

Psalms 141:4 Do not let my heart be drawn to what is evil so that I take part in wicked deeds along with those who are evildoers; do not let me eat their delicacies.

Ephesians 6:12 For our struggle is not against flesh and blood, but against the rulers, against the authorities, against the powers of this dark world and against the spiritual forces of evil in the heavenly realms. 13 Therefore put on the full armor of God, so that when the day of evil comes, you may be able to stand your ground, and after you have done everything, to stand. 14 Stand firm then, with the belt of truth buckled around your waist, with the breastplate of righteousness in place, 15 and with your feet fitted with the readiness that comes from the gospel of peace. 16 In addition to all this, take up the shield of faith, with which you can extinguish all the flaming arrows of the evil one.

Proverbs 14:16 The wise fear the LORD and shun evil, but a fool is hotheaded and yet feels secure. 17 A quick-tempered person does foolish things, and the one who devises evil schemes is hated. 18 The simple inherit folly, but the prudent are crowned with knowledge. 19 Evildoers will bow down in the presence of the good, and the wicked at the gates of the righteous. 20 The poor are shunned even by their neighbors, but the rich have many friends. 21 It is a sin to despise one's neighbor, but blessed is the one who is kind to the needy. 22 Do not those who plot evil go astray? But those who plan what is good find love and faithfulness.

169 The reality of the present (and the next fifty to an hundred years or so) is that the majority need to be changed; they need to become human - and thus develop the potential latent within most. — talent

Romans 12:6 We have different gifts, according to the grace given to each of us. If your gift is prophesying, then prophesy in accordance with your faith; 7 if it is serving, then serve; if it is teaching, then teach; 8 if it is to encourage, then give encouragement; if it is giving, then give generously; if it is to lead, do it diligently; if it is to show mercy, do it cheerfully.

1 Peter 4:10 Each of you should use whatever gift you have received to serve others, as faithful stewards of God's grace in its various forms. 11 If anyone speaks, they should do so as one who speaks the very words of God. If anyone serves, they should do so with the strength God provides, so that in all things God may be praised through Jesus Christ. To him be the glory and the power for ever and ever. Amen.

1 Corinthians 12:7 Now to each one the

manifestation of the Spirit is given for the common good. 8 To one there is given through the Spirit a message of wisdom, to another a message of knowledge by means of the same Spirit, 9 to another faith by the same Spirit, to another gifts of healing by that one Spirit, 10 to another miraculous powers, to another prophecy, to another distinguishing between spirits, to another speaking in different kinds of tongues, and to still another the interpretation of tongues. 11 All these are the work of one and the same Spirit, and he distributes them to each one, just as he determines.

Colossians 3:23 Whatever you do, work at it with all your heart, as working for the Lord, not for human masters, 24 since you know that you will receive an inheritance from the Lord as a reward. It is the Lord Christ you are serving.

Ephesians 4:11 So Christ himself gave the apostles, the prophets, the evangelists, the pastors and teachers, 12 to equip his people for works of service, so that the body of Christ may be built up 13 until we all reach unity in the faith and in the knowledge of the Son of God and become mature, attaining to the whole measure of the fullness of Christ.

170   Only by such a change - in more that a few Initiates or Adepts - can the next civilization arise. It will not just "happen" - it has to be created, constructed, and controlled by Sinister Adepts who know what they are doing. The change that is necessary means that there must be a culling, or many cullings, which remove the worthless and those detrimental to further evolution.   culling

1 John 3:16 By this we know love, that he laid down his life for us, and we ought to lay down our lives for the brothers. 17 But if anyone has the world's goods and sees his brother in need, yet closes his heart against him, how does God's love abide in him? 18 Little children, let us not love in word or talk but in deed and in truth.

Luke 14:13 But when you give a feast, invite

the poor, the crippled, the lame, the blind, 14 and you will be blessed, because they cannot repay you. For you will be repaid at the resurrection of the just."

Luke 3:11 And he answered them, "Whoever has two tunics is to share with him who has none, and whoever has food is to do likewise."

Proverbs 14:21 It is a sin to despise one's neighbor, but blessed is the one who is kind to the needy.

Psalm 12:5 "Because the poor are plundered and the needy groan, I will now arise," says the LORD. "I will protect them from those who malign them."

Psalm 82:3 Defend the weak and the fatherless; uphold the cause of the poor and the oppressed.

Psalm 82:3 Defend the weak and the fatherless; uphold the cause of the poor and the oppressed. 4 Rescue the weak and the needy; deliver them from the hand of the wicked.

Proverbs 31:8 Speak up for those who cannot speak for themselves, for the rights of all who are destitute. 9 Speak up and judge fairly; defend the rights of the poor and needy.

Isaiah 25:4 You have been a refuge for the poor, a refuge for the needy in their distress, a shelter from the storm and a shade from the heat. For the breath of the ruthless is like a storm driving against a wall

171 This requires Sinister Initiates and Sinister Adepts "to presence the dark". Furthermore, the causal structures the majority rely on, such as societies, need to be changed, via the creative/sinister dialectic, and thus by such dark presencing.   society

Matthew 20:26 Not so with you. Instead, whoever wants to become great among you must be your servant, 27 and whoever wants to be first must be your slave— 28 just as the Son of Man did not come to be served, but to serve, and to give his life as a ransom for many."

1 Corinthians 14:33 For God is not a God of

disorder but of peace—as in all the congregations of the Lord's people.

Matthew 24:44 So you also must be ready, because the Son of Man will come at an hour when you do not expect him. 45 "Who then is the faithful and wise servant, whom the master has put in charge of the servants in his household to give them their food at the proper time? 46 It will be good for that servant whose master finds him doing so when he returns. 47 Truly I tell you, he will put him in charge of all his possessions. 48 But suppose that servant is wicked and says to himself, 'My master is staying away a long time,' 49 and he then begins to beat his fellow servants and to eat and drink with drunkards. 50 The master of that servant will come on a day when he does not expect him and at an hour he is not aware of. 51 He will cut him to pieces and assign him a place with the hypocrites, where there will be weeping and gnashing of teeth.

2 Chronicles 31:2 Hezekiah assigned the priests and Levites to divisions—each of them according to their duties as priests or Levites— to offer burnt offerings and fellowship offerings, to minister, to give thanks and to sing praises at the gates of the Lord's dwelling.

Exodus 18:21 But select capable men from all the people—men who fear God, trustworthy men who hate dishonest gain—and appoint them as officials over thousands, hundreds, fifties and tens.

172   In Initiate (and exoteric) terms, this new apprehension is an understanding of Satan as one of the Dark Gods (or even as the Father of the Dark Gods) and a further understanding of the Dark Gods themselves as chaotic, primal, sinister entities which provoke, create, cause change and evolution, and without which evolution is impossible.

    1 John 1:5 This is the message we have heard from him and declare to you: God is light; in him there is no darkness at all.

gods

Titus 3:4 But when the kindness and love of God our Savior appeared, 5 he saved us, not because of righteous things we had done, but because of his mercy. He saved us through the washing of rebirth and renewal by the Holy Spirit, 6 whom he poured out on us generously through Jesus Christ our Savior, 7 so that, having been justified by his grace, we might become heirs having the hope of eternal life.

1 John 4:7 Dear friends, let us love one another, for love comes from God. Everyone who loves has been born of God and knows God. 8 Whoever does not love does not know God, because God is love. 9 This is how God showed his love among us: He sent his one and only Son into the world that we might live through him. 10 This is love: not that we loved God, but that he loved us and sent his Son as an atoning sacrifice for our sins.

Deuteronomy 7:9 Know therefore that the Lord your God is God; he is the faithful God, keeping his covenant of love to a thousand generations of those who love him and keep his commandments.

Isaiah 40:28 Do you not know? Have you not heard? The LORD is the everlasting God, the Creator of the ends of the earth. He will not grow tired or weary, and his understanding no one can fathom. 29 He gives strength to the weary and increases the power of the weak.

173 In esoteric (and Adept) terms, this new apprehension is an understanding of the Dark Gods as causal manifestations, a presencing, of acausal energy - and a further understanding of how such acausal energy is the very life, the very Being, of both us as human beings, and of the cosmos itself.

life energy

1 Corinthians 6:19 Do you not know that your bodies are temples of the Holy Spirit, who is in you, whom you have received from God? You are not your own;

John 14:26 But the Advocate, the Holy Spirit, whom the Father will send in my name, will teach you all things and will remind you of everything I have said to you.

Galatians 5:22 But the fruit of the Spirit is love, joy, peace, forbearance, kindness, goodness, faithfulness, 23 gentleness and self-control. Against such things there is no law.

Isaiah 11:2 The Spirit of the LORD will rest on him— the Spirit of wisdom and of understanding, the Spirit of counsel and of might, the Spirit of the knowledge and fear of the LORD—

Deuteronomy 6:4 Hear, O Israel: The Lord our God, the Lord is one. 5 Love the Lord your God with all your heart and with all your soul and with all your strength.

Psalm 23:1 The LORD is my shepherd, I lack nothing. 2 He makes me lie down in green pastures, he leads me beside quiet waters, 3 he refreshes my soul. He guides me along the right paths for his name's sake.

174 The new Aeon means a new, and higher, Galactic civilization - several centuries after the energies of the new Aeon first become manifest and are presenced, via new nexions. The decline and ending of the current Aeon means the establishment of a new and expanding physical Empire: a New Order which is the last and most glorious manifestation of the genuine spirit, or ethos, of the old Aeon. Sinister esoteric groups must understand such things as these, and then act upon that understanding, esoterically and exoterically.   new aeon / the future

2 Corinthians 4:4 The god of this age has blinded the minds of unbelievers, so that they cannot see the light of the gospel that displays the glory of Christ, who is the image of God.

Matthew 24:6 You will hear of wars and rumors of wars, but see to it that you are not alarmed. Such things must happen, but the end is still to come.

Matthew 24:36 "But about that day or hour no one knows, not even the angels in heaven, nor the Son, but only the Father.

2 Corinthians 11:13 For such people are false apostles, deceitful workers, masquerading as apostles of Christ. 14 And no wonder, for Satan himself masquerades as an angel of light. 15 It is not surprising, then, if his servants also masquerade as servants of righteousness. Their end will be what their actions deserve.

Revelation 12:9 The great dragon was hurled down—that ancient serpent called the devil, or Satan, who leads the whole world astray. He was hurled to the earth, and his angels with him.

2 Peter 3:3 Above all, you must understand that in the last days scoffers will come, scoffing and following their own evil desires. 4 They will say, "Where is this 'coming' he promised? Ever since our ancestors died, everything goes on as it has since the beginning of creation."

8. An Introduction To Traditional Satanism

175 Essentially, the difference between the ONA and other groups which profess to belong to the 'Left Hand Path' or which claim to be Satanic is that the ONA seeks to realistically guide its members along the difficult and dangerous path of self-development, the goal of which is the creation of an entirely new individual. This path is fundamentally a quest for self-excellence and wisdom.

wisdom
excellence

James 1:5 If any of you lacks wisdom, you should ask God, who gives generously to all without finding fault, and it will be given to you.

James 3:13 Who is wise and understanding among you? Let them show it by their good life, by deeds done in the humility that comes from wisdom.

Ephesians 5:15 Be very careful, then, how you live—not as unwise but as wise, 16 making the most of every opportunity, because the days are evil. 17 Therefore do not be foolish, but understand what the Lord's will is.

Colossians 4:5 Be wise in the way you act toward outsiders; make the most of every opportunity. 6 Let your conversation be always full of grace, seasoned with salt, so that you may know how to answer everyone.

Proverbs 1:7 The fear of the LORD is the beginning of knowledge, but fools despise wisdom and instruction.

Proverbs 2:6 For the Lord gives wisdom; from his mouth come knowledge and understanding.

Proverbs 11:2 When pride comes, then comes disgrace, but with humility comes wisdom.

Ecclesiastes 2:26 To the person who pleases him, God gives wisdom, knowledge and happiness, but to the sinner he gives the task of gathering and storing up wealth to hand it over to the one who pleases God. This too is meaningless, a chasing after the wind.

176   There are no 'ceremonies', no magickal 'rites',   wisdom
not even any teachings which can provide the individual with genuine wisdom: real wisdom is only and always attained by the personal effort of the individual over many years. It is the result of a synthesis - a development of the dark side and an integration of that aspect of our being thus creating a complete, more evolved individual.

James 3:17 But the wisdom that comes from heaven is first of all pure; then peace-loving, considerate, submissive, full of mercy and good fruit, impartial and sincere.

Colossians 2:2 My goal is that they may be encouraged in heart and united in love, so that they may have the full riches of complete understanding, in order that they may know the mystery of God, namely, Christ, 3 in whom are hidden all the treasures of wisdom and knowledge.

James 1:5 If any of you lacks wisdom, you should ask God, who gives generously to all without finding fault, and it will be given to you.

1 Corinthians 1:30 It is because of him that you are in Christ Jesus, who has become for us wisdom from God—that is, our righteousness, holiness and redemption.

Proverbs 16:16 How much better to get wisdom than gold, to get insight rather than silver!

Proverbs 29:11 Fools give full vent to their rage, but the wise bring calm in the end.

Proverbs 15:12 Mockers resent correction, so they avoid the wise.

177 For us, Satanism is a quest involving real personal danger where the individual Initiate undertakes genuine challenges which take them to and beyond their limits: physical, 'mental' and psychic. — challenges

2 Timothy 2:15 Do your best to present yourself to God as one approved, a worker who does not need to be ashamed and who correctly handles the word of truth.

Galatians 5:1 It is for freedom that Christ has set us free. Stand firm, then, and do not let yourselves be burdened again by a yoke of slavery.

2 Timothy 1:7 For the Spirit God gave us does not make us timid, but gives us power, love and self-discipline.

1 Timothy 4:11 Command and teach these things. 12 Don't let anyone look down on you because you are young, but set an example for the believers in speech, in conduct, in love, in faith and in purity. 13 Until I come, devote yourself to the public reading of Scripture, to preaching and to teaching. 14 Do not neglect your gift, which was given you through prophecy when the body of elders laid their hands on you.

1 Peter 2:1 Therefore, rid yourselves of all malice and all deceit, hypocrisy, envy, and slander of every kind. 2 Like newborn babies, crave pure spiritual milk, so that by it you may grow up in your salvation, 3 now that you have tasted that the Lord is good. The Living Stone and a Chosen People 4 As you come to him, the living Stone—rejected by humans but chosen by God and precious to him— 5 you also, like living stones, are being built into a spiritual house to be a holy priesthood, offering spiritual sacrifices acceptable to God through Jesus Christ.

178	This quest, in its beginnings, involves the individual in exploring their 'hidden' or 'dark' side	dark side

Matthew 15:19 For out of the heart come evil thoughts—murder, adultery, sexual immorality, theft, false testimony, slander.

Mark 7:21 For it is from within, out of a person's heart, that evil thoughts come—sexual immorality, theft, murder, 22 adultery, greed, malice, deceit, lewdness, envy, slander, arrogance and folly. 23 All these evils come from inside and defile a person."

Proverbs 19:3 A person's own folly leads to their ruin, yet their heart rages against the Lord.

Jeremiah 17:9 The heart is deceitful above all things and beyond cure. Who can understand it? 10 "I the LORD search the heart and examine the mind, to reward each person according to their conduct, according to what their deeds deserve." 11 Like a partridge that hatches eggs it did not lay are those who gain riches by unjust means. When their lives are half gone, their riches will desert them, and in the end they will prove to be fools. 12 A glorious throne, exalted from the beginning, is the place of our sanctuary.

179	In Nietzschean terms, there is a practical living of a "master-morality". The person created via these experiences is the type to inspire a certain terror/awe in the supine majority, weaned as that majority have been by the softness of the Nazarene ethic.	morality following Jesus

Romans 13:8 Let no debt remain outstanding, except the continuing debt to love one another, for whoever loves others has fulfilled the law. 9 The commandments, "You shall not commit adultery," "You shall not murder," "You shall not steal," "You shall not covet," and whatever other command there may be, are summed up in

this one command: "Love your neighbor as yourself." 10 Love does no harm to a neighbor. Therefore love is the fulfillment of the law.

John 15:18 "If the world hates you, keep in mind that it hated me first. 19 If you belonged to the world, it would love you as its own. As it is, you do not belong to the world, but I have chosen you out of the world. That is why the world hates you.

Luke 9:23 Then he said to them all: "Whoever wants to be my disciple must deny themselves and take up their cross daily and follow me. 24 For whoever wants to save their life will lose it, but whoever loses their life for me will save it.

Luke 9:57 As they were walking along the road, a man said to him, "I will follow you wherever you go." 58 Jesus replied, "Foxes have dens and birds have nests, but the Son of Man has no place to lay his head." 59 He said to another man, "Follow me."But he replied, "Lord, first let me go and bury my father." 60 Jesus said to him, "Let the dead bury their own dead, but you go and proclaim the kingdom of God." 61 Still another said, "I will follow you, Lord; but first let me go back and say goodbye to my family." 62 Jesus replied, "No one who puts a hand to the plow and looks back is fit for service in the kingdom of God."

180 Thus, each stage of this way has associated with it certain tasks, certain experiences, which the individual must undertake by themselves in their own time. It is these and these alone which bring self-insight, mastery, understanding and skill - both 'occult' and personal. All the ONA does, at each stage and for each member, is offer advice - based on experience. That is, the ONA guides its members - it offers a practical system whereby real wisdom may be attained.

wisdom

James 3:13 Who is wise and understanding among you? Let them show it by their good life, by deeds done in the humility that comes from wisdom.

Colossians 4:5 Be wise in the way you act

toward outsiders; make the most of every opportunity. 6 Let your conversation be always full of grace, seasoned with salt, so that you may know how to answer everyone.

Proverbs 2:6 For the LORD gives wisdom; from his mouth come knowledge and understanding.

Ecclesiastes 2:26 To the person who pleases him, God gives wisdom, knowledge and happiness, but to the sinner he gives the task of gathering and storing up wealth to hand it over to the one who pleases God. This too is meaningless, a chasing after the wind.

181 For us, Satanism is all about the creation of proud, strong, characterful, insightful individuals - individuals who have gone beyond the majority and who thus represent a higher type.   highest type

2 Corinthians 9:10 Now he who supplies seed to the sower and bread for food will also supply and increase your store of seed and will enlarge the harvest of your righteousness.

Hebrews 5:12 In fact, though by this time you ought to be teachers, you need someone to teach you the elementary truths of God's word all over again. You need milk, not solid food! 13 Anyone who lives on milk, being still an infant, is not acquainted with the teaching about righteousness. 14 But solid food is for the mature, who by constant use have trained themselves to distinguish good from evil.

1 Peter 2:2 Like newborn babies, crave pure spiritual milk, so that by it you may grow up in your salvation, 3 now that you have tasted that the Lord is good.

Hebrews 6:1 Therefore let us move beyond the elementary teachings about Christ and be taken forward to maturity, not laying again the foundation of repentance from acts that lead to death, and of faith in God, 2 instruction about cleansing rites, the laying on of hands, the resurrection of the dead, and eternal judgment. 3 And God permitting, we will do so. 4 It is impossible for those who have once been enlightened, who have tasted the heavenly gift, who have shared in the Holy Spirit, 5 who have tasted the goodness of the word of God and the powers of the coming age 6 and who have fallen away, to be brought back to repentance. To their loss they are crucifying the Son of God all over again and subjecting him to public disgrace.

182 They seek to create a real elite - almost a new race of beings. Of course, this is not easy - it is really dangerous. Quite often, new Initiates fail because of the difficulty or because they lack the essential desire to succeed. But that is how evolution works - the strong overcome challenges and evolve; the others stay where they are, descend, or are destroyed. Thus, Satanism is elitist - it does not compromise.

⟶ elite
compromise

James 2:1 My brothers and sisters, believers in our glorious Lord Jesus Christ must not show favoritism. 2 Suppose a man comes into your meeting wearing a gold ring and fine clothes, and a poor man in filthy old clothes also comes in. 3 If you show special attention to the man wearing fine clothes and say, "Here's a good seat for you," but say to the poor man, "You stand there" or "Sit on the floor by my feet,"

1 Corinthians 1:26 Brothers and sisters, think of what you were when you were called. Not many of you were wise by human standards; not many were influential; not many were of noble birth. 27 But God chose the foolish things of the world to shame the wise; God chose the weak things of the world to shame the strong. 28 God chose the lowly things of this world and the despised things—and the things that are not—to nullify the things that are,

James 1:27 Religion that God our Father accepts as pure and faultless is this: to look after orphans and widows in their distress and to keep oneself from being polluted by the world.

James 4:6 But he gives us more grace. That is

why Scripture says: "God opposes the proud but shows favor to the humble." 7 Submit yourselves, then, to God. Resist the devil, and he will flee from you.

Matthew 6:24 "No one can serve two masters. Either you will hate the one and love the other, or you will be devoted to the one and despise the other. You cannot serve both God and money. 25 "Therefore I tell you, do not worry about your life, what you will eat or drink; or about your body, what you will wear. Is not life more than food, and the body more than clothes? 26 Look at the birds of the air; they do not sow or reap or store away in barns, and yet your heavenly Father feeds them. Are you not much more valuable than they?

183   This task requires the candidate for Adeptship to live alone, in an isolated area, for three months (usually from Spring Equinox to Summer Solstice) - to talk with no one, to live frugally, with no modern conveniences, no wireless, no modern 'distractions', in a shelter they have built [in recent years, the rules have been relaxed and a tent is allowed]. The aim of this is for them to experience themselves and Nature without any distractions - to really get to know themselves and the natural energies which exist, as those energies are   isolation

1 Corinthians 12:13 For we were all baptized by one Spirit so as to form one body—whether Jews or Gentiles, slave or free—and we were all given the one Spirit to drink. 14 Even so the body is not made up of one part but of many. 15 Now if the foot should say, "Because I am not a hand, I do not belong to the body," it would not for that reason stop being part of the body. 16 And if the ear should say, "Because I am not an eye, I do not belong to the body," it would not for that reason stop being part of the body. 17 If the whole body were an eye, where would the sense of hearing be? If the whole body were an ear, where would the sense of smell be? 18 But in fact God has placed the parts in the body, every one of them, just as he wanted them to be. 19 If they were all one part, where would the body be? 20 As it is, there are many parts, but one body.

Isaiah 41:10 So do not fear, for I am with you; do not be dismayed, for I am your God. I will strengthen you and help you; I will uphold you with my righteous right hand.

Genesis 2:18 The Lord God said, "It is not good for the man to be alone. I will make a helper suitable for him."

184 Hitherto, most of their experience/learning has been directly personal, relating to their personal development - now, aeonic perspective is gained, it becomes a part of them. That is, they develop still further, again via direct experience - this time, of the acausal itself. From this, further personal development takes place - they become complete, highly developed individuals who possess skills and an understanding few possess. *(uniqueness, understanding)*

James 1:5 If any of you lacks wisdom, you should ask God, who gives generously to all without finding fault, and it will be given to you.

Romans 12:2 Do not conform to the pattern of this world, but be transformed by the renewing of your mind. Then you will be able to test and approve what God's will is—his good, pleasing and perfect will.

Proverbs 2:6 For the LORD gives wisdom; from his mouth come knowledge and understanding.

Psalm 139:13 For you created my inmost being; you knit me together in my mother's womb. 14 I praise you because I am fearfully and wonderfully made; your works are wonderful, I know that full well.

Jeremiah 1:5 "Before I formed you in the womb I knew you, before you were born I set you apart; I appointed you as a prophet to the nations."

185 But to reach this stage - the fifth - takes at least ten years (more usual is fifteen to twenty). And *(spiritual development)*

there is another stage beyond this. Thus, it will be seen that our way is difficult and takes a long time.

Acts 2:38 Peter replied, "Repent and be baptized, every one of you, in the name of Jesus Christ for the forgiveness of your sins. And you will receive the gift of the Holy Spirit.

2 Peter 3:9 The Lord is not slow in keeping his promise, as some understand slowness. Instead he is patient with you, not wanting anyone to perish, but everyone to come to repentance. 10 But the day of the Lord will come like a thief. The heavens will disappear with a roar; the elements will be destroyed by fire, and the earth and everything done in it will be laid bare. 11 Since everything will be destroyed in this way, what kind of people ought you to be? You ought to live holy and godly lives 12 as you look forward to the day of God and speed its coming. That day will bring about the destruction of the heavens by fire, and the elements will melt in the heat.

2 Peter 3:8 But do not forget this one thing, dear friends: With the Lord a day is like a thousand years, and a thousand years are like a day. 9 The Lord is not slow in keeping his promise, as some understand slowness. Instead he is patient with you, not wanting anyone to perish, but everyone to come to repentance.

186 Satanism does not condone such things as 'human sacrifice'. We, on the contrary, are dark and really sinister - and propound culling. That is, we uphold human culling as beneficial, for both the individual who does the culling (it being a character-building experience) and for our species in general, since culling by its nature removes the worthless and thus improves the stock. Naturally, there are proper ways to choose who is to be culled - each victim is chosen because they have shown themselves to be suitable. They are never chosen at random, as they are never 'innocent'.   culling victims

Matthew 7:1 "Do not judge, or you too will be

judged. 2 For in the same way you judge others, you will be judged, and with the measure you use, it will be measured to you. 3 "Why do you look at the speck of sawdust in your brother's eye and pay no attention to the plank in your own eye? 4 How can you say to your brother, 'Let me take the speck out of your eye,' when all the time there is a plank in your own eye? 5 You hypocrite, first take the plank out of your own eye, and then you will see clearly to remove the speck from your brother's eye.

2 Corinthians 13:11 Finally, brothers and sisters, rejoice! Strive for full restoration, encourage one another, be of one mind, live in peace. And the God of love and peace will be with you.

Colossians 3:12 Therefore, as God's chosen people, holy and dearly loved, clothe yourselves with compassion, kindness, humility, gentleness and patience. 13 Bear with each other and forgive one another if any of you has a grievance against someone. Forgive as the Lord forgave you.

Psalms 11:5 The LORD examines the righteous, but the wicked, those who love violence, he hates with a passion.

Psalms 72:14 He will rescue them from oppression and violence, for precious is their blood in his sight.

Jeremiah 22:3 This is what the Lord says: Do what is just and right. Rescue from the hand of the oppressor the one who has been robbed. Do no wrong or violence to the foreigner, the fatherless or the widow, and do not shed innocent blood in this place.

Isaiah 35:3 Strengthen the feeble hands, steady the knees that give way;

4 say to those with fearful hearts, "Be strong, do not fear; your God will come, he will come with vengeance; with divine retribution he will come to save you."

187 We describe this system as Satanic, as Sinister because it is. It is a complete rejection of the   anti-christian

philosophy/religion of the Nazarene. The philosophy/religion of the Nazarene is anti-life and anti- evolutionary, as Nietzsche, for example, understood. For us, Satan is both an archetype or symbol of our defiance, and something real - the re-presentation of what we describe as 'the acausal'.

1 John 2:22 Who is the liar? It is whoever denies that Jesus is the Christ. Such a person is the antichrist—denying the Father and the Son.

John 12:48 There is a judge for the one who rejects me and does not accept my words; the very words I have spoken will condemn them at the last day.

Matthew 10:33 But whoever disowns me before others, I will disown before my Father in heaven.

Revelation 20:10 And the devil, who deceived them, was thrown into the lake of burning sulfur, where the beast and the false prophet had been thrown. They will be tormented day and night for ever and ever.

1 John 5:11 And this is the testimony: God has given us eternal life, and this life is in his Son. 12 Whoever has the Son has life; whoever does not have the Son of God does not have life.

188 Second, such groups and their members do not really understand the Sinister. They have had no real experience of the primal, numinous, supra-personal power of the dark forces - of how that power can destroy individuals. In effect, they have never really 'tapped into' the acausal itself - to what is really sinister. They have never really confronted Satan. They have never really striven to be like Satan - to become one with Him   acausal

Galatians 6:7 Do not be deceived: God cannot be mocked. A man reaps what he sows. 8 Whoever sows to please their flesh, from the flesh will reap destruction; whoever sows to please the Spirit, from the Spirit will reap eternal life.

Romans 6:23 For the wages of sin is death,

but the gift of God is eternal life in Christ Jesus our Lord.

Romans 2:6 God "will repay each person according to what they have done." 7 To those who by persistence in doing good seek glory, honor and immortality, he will give eternal life. 8 But for those who are self-seeking and who reject the truth and follow evil, there will be wrath and anger. 9 There will be trouble and distress for every human being who does evil: first for the Jew, then for the Gentile; 10 but glory, honor and peace for everyone who does good: first for the Jew, then for the Gentile.

Proverbs 1:31 they will eat the fruit of their ways and be filled with the fruit of their schemes. 32 For the waywardness of the simple will kill them, and the complacency of fools will destroy them;

Jeremiah 17:10 "I the LORD search the heart and examine the mind, to reward each person according to their conduct, according to what their deeds deserve." 11 Like a partridge that hatches eggs it did not lay are those who gain riches by unjust means. When their lives are half gone, their riches will desert them, and in the end they will prove to be fools.

189 There is thus a real, a genuine, transcending beyond 'good' and 'evil'; beyond 'light' and 'dark'.   neither good nor evil

1 John 5:19 We know that we are children of God, and that the whole world is under the control of the evil one.

1 Thessalonians 5:21 21 but test them all; hold on to what is good, 22 reject every kind of evil.

Psalm 14:1 The fool says in his heart, "There is no God." They are corrupt, their deeds are vile; there is no one who does good.

Ephesians 6:12 For our struggle is not against flesh and blood, but against the rulers, against the authorities, against the powers of this dark world and against the spiritual forces of evil in the heavenly realms.

2 Chronicles 29:6 Our parents were unfaithful; they did evil in the eyes of the Lord our God and forsook him. They turned their faces away from the Lord's dwelling place and turned their backs on him.

1 Samuel 15:23 For rebellion is like the sin of divination, and arrogance like the evil of idolatry. Because you have rejected the word of the LORD, he has rejected you as king."

190   A genuine Satanist can be like a beast of prey -   rebellion
in real life. They can be and sometimes are, in real life, assassins, warriors, outlaws.

Hebrews 3:15 As has just been said: "Today, if you hear his voice, do not harden your hearts as you did in the rebellion."

Romans 13:1 Let everyone be subject to the governing authorities, for there is no authority except that which God has established. The authorities that exist have been established by God. 2 Consequently, whoever rebels against the authority is rebelling against what God has instituted, and those who do so will bring judgment on themselves.

2 Timothy 4:3 For the time will come when people will not put up with sound doctrine. Instead, to suit their own desires, they will gather around them a great number of teachers to say what their itching ears want to hear. 4 They will turn their ears away from the truth and turn aside to myths.

Isaiah 1:19 If you are willing and obedient, you will eat the good things of the land; 20 but if you resist and rebel, you will be devoured by the sword." For the mouth of the LORD has spoken.

1 Samuel 15:23 For rebellion is like the sin of divination, and arrogance like the evil of idolatry. Because you have rejected the word of the LORD, he has rejected you as king."

Proverbs 17:11 Evildoers foster rebellion against God; the messenger of death will be sent against them.

Isaiah 14:12 How you have fallen from

heaven, morning star, son of the dawn! You have been cast down to the earth, you who once laid low the nations! 13 You said in your heart, "I will ascend to the heavens; I will raise my throne above the stars of God; I will sit enthroned on the mount of assembly, on the utmost heights of Mount Zaphon. 14 I will ascend above the tops of the clouds; I will make myself like the Most High." 15 But you are brought down to the realm of the dead, to the depths of the pit.

191 The Satanist is sinister and dark, in real life - and then they move on, to new experiences, to even higher levels of understanding until eventually they acquire real wisdom, or are destroyed.   wisdom

James 3:13 Who is wise and understanding among you? Let them show it by their good life, by deeds done in the humility that comes from wisdom.

Colossians 4:5 Be wise in the way you act toward outsiders; make the most of every opportunity. 6 Let your conversation be always full of grace, seasoned with salt, so that you may know how to answer everyone.

Proverbs 2:6 For the LORD gives wisdom; from his mouth come knowledge and understanding.

Proverbs 11:2 When pride comes, then comes disgrace, but with humility comes wisdom.

192 Whatever, they will have really lived, 'on the edge'; they will really have achieved something with their lives.   achievement

1 John 5:4 for everyone born of God overcomes the world. This is the victory that has overcome the world, even our faith.

Ephesians 1:11 In him we were also chosen, having been predestined according to the plan of him who works out everything in conformity with the purpose of his will, 12 in order that we, who were the first to put our hope in Christ, might be for the praise of his glory.

Colossians 3:23 Whatever you do, work at it

with all your heart, as working for the Lord, not for human masters, 24 since you know that you will receive an inheritance from the Lord as a reward. It is the Lord Christ you are serving.

193   They will in some way by their living have 'presenced' the dark forces on earth. If they survive - their rewards are their achievements and the wisdom that awaits. If they do not survive, at least they will have done something with their lives.   rewards

Romans 2:6 God "will repay each person according to what they have done."

1 Corinthians 2:9 However, as it is written: "What no eye has seen, what no ear has heard, and what no human mind has conceived" — *the things God has prepared for those who love him*—

Proverbs 22:4 Humility is the fear of the LORD; its wages are riches and honor and life.

Deuteronomy 5:33 Walk in obedience to all that the LORD your God has commanded you, so that you may live and prosper and prolong your days in the land that you will possess.

9- The Tradition Of The Sinister Way

194   The essence of genuine Satanism can be simply stated: it is a way to inner development, the goal of which is a new individual.   individualism

1 Peter 4:10 Each of you should use whatever gift you have received to serve others, as faithful stewards of God's grace in its various forms.

Philippians 2:3 Do nothing out of selfish ambition or vain conceit. Rather, in humility value others above yourselves, 4 not looking to your own interests but each of you to the interests of the others.

Romans 12:3 For by the grace given me I say to every one of you: Do not think of yourself more highly than you ought, but rather think of yourself with sober judgment, in accordance with the faith God has distributed to each of you. 4 For just as each of us has one body with many members, and these members do not all have the same function, 5 so in Christ we, though many, form one body, and each member belongs to all the others.

1 Corinthians 12:4 There are different kinds of gifts, but the same Spirit distributes them. 5 There are different kinds of service, but the same Lord. 6 There are different kinds of working, but in all of them and in everyone it is the same God at work.

195 A Satanist is an individual explorer - following in the footsteps of others (and perhaps using their guide books) but always seeking further horizons, daring to defy convention (in ideas as well as in morals and attitude) yet part of an evolutionary succession enabling what is experienced to be understood and become beneficial.   evolution defiance

Romans 13:2 Consequently, whoever rebels against the authority is rebelling against what God has instituted, and those who do so will bring judgment on themselves.

Galatians 6:7 Do not be deceived: God cannot be mocked. A man reaps what he sows. 8 Whoever sows to please their flesh, from the flesh will reap destruction; whoever sows to please the Spirit, from the Spirit will reap eternal life.

Numbers 15:30 "'But anyone who sins defiantly, whether native-born or foreigner, blasphemes the Lord and must be cut off from the people of Israel.

10- The Meaning Of Sinister Initiation

196 Along the Seven-Fold Sinister Way these Initiation rites (for in one sense all the rituals involved during the various stages of the Sinister Way are initiation rites in themselves) are primarily concerned with presenting the Darkness or acausal component of the psyche in the conscious world, or mind, of the Initiate.   mental darkness

John 8:12 When Jesus spoke again to the people, he said, "I am the light of the world. Whoever follows me will never walk in darkness, but will have the light of life."

1 Peter 2:9 But you are a chosen people, a royal priesthood, a holy nation, God's special possession, that you may declare the praises of him who called you out of darkness into his wonderful light.

Colossians 1:13 For he has rescued us from the dominion of darkness and brought us into the kingdom of the Son he loves, 14 in whom we have redemption, the forgiveness of sins.

Isaiah 29:15 Woe to those who go to great depths to hide their plans from the LORD, who do their work in darkness and think, "Who sees us? Who will know?"

197 In regard to this latter aspect, by undertaking such actions these actions themselves will or may (dependant upon Individual Destiny) aid to the manifestation or creation of a Sinister Temple.

sinister temple

Ephesians 2:19 Consequently, you are no longer foreigners and strangers, but fellow citizens with God's people and also members of his household, 20 built on the foundation of the apostles and prophets, with Christ Jesus himself as the chief cornerstone. 21 In him the whole building is joined together and rises to become a holy temple in the Lord. 22 And in him you too are being built together to become a dwelling in which God lives by his Spirit.

Acts 2:42 They devoted themselves to the apostles' teaching and to fellowship, to the breaking of bread and to prayer. 43 Everyone was filled with awe at the many wonders and signs performed by the apostles. 44 All the believers were together and had everything in common. 45 They sold property and possessions to give to anyone who had need. 46 Every day they continued to meet together in the temple courts. They broke bread in their homes and ate together with glad and sincere hearts, 47 praising God and enjoying the favor of all the people. And the Lord added to their number daily those who were being saved.

Psalm 150:1 Praise the LORD. Praise God in

his sanctuary; praise him in his mighty heavens. 2 Praise him for his acts of power; praise him for his surpassing greatness. 3 Praise him with the sounding of the trumpet, praise him with the harp and lyre, 4 praise him with timbrel and dancing, praise him with the strings and pipe, 5 praise him with the clash of cymbals, praise him with resounding cymbals. 6 Let everything that has breath praise the LORD. Praise the LORD.

198 Further to previous Order guide-lines, a new method of Initiate development advises that the Initiate begins with the Dark Pathways themselves (instead of the Sinister Sphereworkings). The aim is to invoke one Dark God per week, meditating each night leading up to the ritual for no less than fifteen minutes on the respective sigil whilst slowly repeating the name of the Dark God or the Word of Power.   dark gods prayer

Matthew 6:9 "This, then, is how you should pray: " 'Our Father in heaven, hallowed be your name, 10 your kingdom come, your will be done, on earth as it is in heaven. 11 Give us today our daily bread. 12 And forgive us our debts, as we also have forgiven our debtors. 13 And lead us not into temptation, but deliver us from the evil one.'

Romans 8:26 In the same way, the Spirit helps us in our weakness. We do not know what we ought to pray for, but the Spirit himself intercedes for us through wordless groans. 27 And he who searches our hearts knows the mind of the Spirit, because the Spirit intercedes for God's people in accordance with the will of God.

1 Chronicles 16:8 Give praise to the LORD, proclaim his name; make known among the nations what he has done. 9 Sing to him, sing praise to him; tell of all his wonderful acts. 10 Glory in his holy name; let the hearts of those who seek the LORD rejoice. 11 Look to the LORD and his strength; seek his face always.

199 The aim is to invoke one Dark God per week,   possession

meditating each night leading up to the ritual for no less than fifteen minutes on the respective sigil whilst slowly repeating the name of the Dark God or the Word of Power.

Acts 16:16 Once when we were going to the place of prayer, we were met by a female slave who had a spirit by which she predicted the future. She earned a great deal of money for her owners by fortune-telling. 17 She followed Paul and the rest of us, shouting, "These men are servants of the Most High God, who are telling you the way to be saved." 18 She kept this up for many days. Finally Paul became so annoyed that he turned around and said to the spirit, "In the name of Jesus Christ I command you to come out of her!" At that moment the spirit left her.

Luke 11:24 "When an impure spirit comes out of a person, it goes through arid places seeking rest and does not find it. Then it says, 'I will return to the house I left.' 25 When it arrives, it finds the house swept clean and put in order.

Leviticus 19:31 "'Do not turn to mediums or seek out spiritists, for you will be defiled by them. I am the Lord your God.

200   The wearing of such an item of jewelry further   jewelry
stimulates the Initiates awareness that he or she is a member of a Tradition, one that is far more important and potent than the frankly rather pathetic past-times that most people take as an interest or hobby. This ring or necklace becomes for the Initiate a 'Mark of Satan', a symbol of the Initiates quest and a constant reminder of the Sinister in the Initiates life, that is the Initiate is constantly aware that he or she is wearing an outward symbol - that others can see - of his or her Sinister Quest.

1 Peter 3:3 Your beauty should not come from outward adornment, such as elaborate hairstyles and the wearing of gold jewelry or fine clothes. 4 Rather, it should be that of your inner self, the unfading beauty of a gentle and quiet spirit, which is of great worth in God's sight.

Galatians 3:26 So in Christ Jesus you are all children of God through faith, 27 for all of you who were baptized into Christ have clothed yourselves with Christ.

Exodus 20:4 "You shall not make for yourself an image in the form of anything in heaven above or on the earth beneath or in the waters below. 5 You shall not bow down to them or worship them; for I, the Lord your God, am a jealous God, punishing the children for the sin of the parents to the third and fourth generation of those who hate me, 6 but showing love to a thousand generations of those who love

Isaiah 3:18 In that day the Lord will snatch away their finery: the bangles and headbands and crescent necklaces, 19 the earrings and bracelets and veils, 20 the headdresses and anklets and sashes, the perfume bottles and charms,

201 Yet even now I do not know what lies ahead   gods
Now is my time to seek the glory of my Gods
That I may one day walk with Satan In His
world, With His Bride And that I may also
Become Something far greater than the moral I
am leaving behind, The mortal that must die
That a God may be born.

2 John 1:7 I say this because many deceivers, who do not acknowledge Jesus Christ as coming in the flesh, have gone out into the world. Any such person is the deceiver and the antichrist.

John 12:48 There is a judge for the one who rejects me and does not accept my words; the very words I have spoken will condemn them at the last day. 49 For I did not speak on my own, but the Father who sent me commanded me to say all that I have spoken. 50 I know that his command leads to eternal life. So whatever I say is just what the Father has told me to say."

Luke 10:16 "Whoever listens to you listens to me; whoever rejects you rejects me; but whoever rejects me rejects him who sent me."

17 The seventy-two returned with joy and said, "Lord, even the demons submit to us in your name." 18 He replied, "I saw Satan fall like lightning from heaven. 19 I have given you authority to trample on snakes and scorpions and to overcome all the power of the enemy; nothing will harm you.

11- The Seven-Fold Way : Training And Grades

202 Such tests and encounters are not games but merely devices which enable the candidate to begin to understand their own motives and expectations and as such are an important preparation to Initiation. It is to be understood that it is not the order, which tests the candidate - but the candidates themselves. Initiation is the beginning of the breaking of the illusion of roles, and to be successful this breaking must be done by the individual, from within.

tests

James 1:2 Consider it pure joy, my brothers and sisters, whenever you face trials of many kinds, 3 because you know that the testing of your faith produces perseverance. 4 Let perseverance finish its work so that you may be mature and complete, not lacking anything.

1 Peter 1:7 These have come so that the proven genuineness of your faith—of greater worth than gold, which perishes even though refined by fire—may result in praise, glory and honor when Jesus Christ is revealed.

1 John 4:1 Dear friends, do not believe every spirit, but test the spirits to see whether they are from God, because many false prophets have gone out into the world. 2 This is how you can recognize the Spirit of God: Every spirit that acknowledges that Jesus Christ has come in the flesh is from God, 3 but every spirit that does not acknowledge Jesus is not from God. This is the spirit of the antichrist, which you have heard is coming and even now is already in the world. 4 You, dear children, are from God and have overcome them, because the one who is in you is greater than the one who is in the world.

2 Peter 2:8 (for that righteous man, living

among them day after day, was tormented in his righteous soul by the lawless deeds he saw and heard)— 9 if this is so, then the Lord knows how to rescue the godly from trials and to hold the unrighteous for punishment on the day of judgment.

Job 23:10 But he knows the way that I take; when he has tested me, I will come forth as gold.

Psalm 66:10 For you, God, tested us; you refined us like silver.

203 Besides this breaking of self-delusion, Initiation is an awakening of the occult faculties - that is, the experience by the candidate of the reality of magickal forces.   self-delusion

1 Corinthians 3:18 Do not deceive yourselves. If any of you think you are wise by the standards of this age, you should become "fools" so that you may become wise. 19 For the wisdom of this world is foolishness in God's sight. As it is written: "He catches the wise in their craftiness"; 20 and again, "The Lord knows that the thoughts of the wise are futile."

1 John 1:8 If we claim to be without sin, we deceive ourselves and the truth is not in us. 9 If we confess our sins, he is faithful and just and will forgive us our sins and purify us from all unrighteousness. 10 If we claim we have not sinned, we make him out to be a liar and his word is not in us.

2 Thessalonians 2:3 Don't let anyone deceive you in any way, for that day will not come until the rebellion occurs and the man of lawlessness is revealed, the man doomed to destruction. 4 He will oppose and will exalt himself over everything that is called God or is worshiped, so that he sets himself up in God's temple, proclaiming himself to be God. 5 Don't you remember that when I was with you I used to tell you these things?

204 The most usual magickal task involved the novice assuming the 'role' of a dark sorcerer/sorceress for example, dressing in   dissent
rebellion

black and cultivating a satanic appearance - and in this guise attending various Occult functions and generally trying to provoke argument and dissent.

Matthew 5:37 All you need to say is simply 'Yes' or 'No'; anything beyond this comes from the evil one. 38 "You have heard that it was said, 'Eye for eye, and tooth for tooth.' 39 But I tell you, do not resist an evil person. If anyone slaps you on the right cheek, turn to them the other cheek also.

Titus 3:10 Warn a divisive person once, and then warn them a second time. After that, have nothing to do with them.

Romans 16:17 I urge you, brothers and sisters, to watch out for those who cause divisions and put obstacles in your way that are contrary to the teaching you have learned. Keep away from them. 18 For such people are not serving our Lord Christ, but their own appetites. By smooth talk and flattery they deceive the minds of naive people. 19 Everyone has heard about your obedience, so I rejoice because of you; but I want you to be wise about what is good, and innocent about what is evil. 20 The God of peace will soon crush Satan under your feet. The grace of our Lord Jesus be with you.

Proverbs 6:16 There are six things the LORD hates, seven that are detestable to him: 17 haughty eyes, a lying tongue, hands that shed innocent blood, 18 a heart that devises wicked schemes, feet that are quick to rush into evil, 19 a false witness who pours out lies and a person who stirs up conflict in the community.

205 The novice in this is advised to cultivate an attitude of arrogance and pride and must be prepared to defend forcefully their Satanic views.   arrogance

Romans 11:20 Granted. But they were broken off because of unbelief, and you stand by faith. Do not be arrogant, but tremble. 21 For if God did not spare the natural branches, he will not

spare you either. 22 Consider therefore the kindness and sternness of God: sternness to those who fell, but kindness to you, provided that you continue in his kindness. Otherwise, you also will be cut off.

James 4:16 As it is, you boast in your arrogant schemes. All such boasting is evil. 17 If anyone, then, knows the good they ought to do and doesn't do it, it is sin for them.

1 Corinthians 4:18 Some of you have become arrogant, as if I were not coming to you. 19 But I will come to you very soon, if the Lord is willing, and then I will find out not only how these arrogant people are talking, but what power they have. 20 For the kingdom of God is not a matter of talk but of power.

Proverbs 16:5 The LORD detests all the proud of heart. Be sure of this: They will not go unpunished.

1 Samuel 2:3 "Do not keep talking so proudly or let your mouth speak such arrogance, for the LORD is a God who knows, and by him deeds are weighed.

Isaiah 13:11 I will punish the world for its evil, the wicked for their sins. I will put an end to the arrogance of the haughty and will humble the pride of the ruthless.

206 This stage generally takes from six months to two years and is concluded when the novice finds changes of perspective arising as a consequence of the self-understanding brought through following the goals and tasks.   self-awareness

2 Timothy 1:7 For the Spirit God gave us does not make us timid, but gives us power, love and self-discipline.

2 Corinthians 13:5 Examine yourselves to see whether you are in the faith; test yourselves. Do you not realize that Christ Jesus is in you—unless, of course, you fail the test?

Matthew 11:28 "Come to me, all you who are weary and burdened, and I will give you rest. 29 Take my yoke upon you and learn from me, for I am gentle and humble in heart, and you will

find rest for your souls. 30 For my yoke is easy and my burden is light."

Matthew 16:24 Then Jesus said to his disciples, "Whoever wants to be my disciple must deny themselves and take up their cross and follow me. 25 For whoever wants to save their life will lose it, but whoever loses their life for me will find it.

207 Thus it will be seen that the seven-fold way is not easy. It is a way of life, which any individual may follow. Those who only follow its early stages gain something of benefit - those who go further may achieve the goal that awaits us all: the next stage of human evolution. — evolution

Ephesians 2:10 For we are God's handiwork, created in Christ Jesus to do good works, which God prepared in advance for us to do.

1 Cor 15:39 Not all flesh is the same: People have one kind of flesh, animals have another, birds another and fish another. 40 There are also heavenly bodies and there are earthly bodies; but the splendor of the heavenly bodies is one kind, and the splendor of the earthly bodies is another. 41 The sun has one kind of splendor, the moon another and the stars another; and star differs from star in splendor.

209 The seven-fold way possesses the potential to create (given good guidance) in ten years what it has taken seven civilizations, five Aeons or nearly ten thousand years to achieve. Every individual is free to choose between this path to the divine and a continuation of the sleep that keeps the potentiality of life at bay. All magick is a glimpse of this path - it is up to the individual to walk along it. — pathway

Mark 1:3 "a voice of one calling in the wilderness, 'Prepare the way for the Lord, make straight paths for him.' "

2 Timothy 3:16 All Scripture is God-breathed and is useful for teaching, rebuking, correcting and training in righteousness, 17 so that the servant of God may be thoroughly equipped for every good work.

Proverbs 3: 5 Trust in the LORD with all your heart and lean not on your own understanding; 6 in all your ways submit to him, and he will make your paths straight.

Proverbs 1:7 The fear of the Lord is the beginning of knowledge, but fools despise wisdom and instruction.

Jeremiah 29:11 For I know the plans I have for you," declares the Lord, "plans to prosper you and not to harm you, plans to give you hope and a future. 12 Then you will call on me and come and pray to me, and I will listen to you. 13 You will seek me and find me when you seek me with all your heart. 14 I will be found by you," declares the Lord, "and will bring you back from captivity. I will gather you from all the nations and places where I have banished you," declares the Lord, "and will bring you back to the place from which I carried you into exile."

13- Dark Pathworking: Satanas

210 The Dark Gods embody the spirit of life, and give it the Acausal Charge implicit in any conscious being. Once the Dark Gods intruded upon our Causal world, and caused the terror, unrest, and destructiveness which forced the evolution of our species by way of increasing our consciousness.   spirit of life

John 6:63 The Spirit gives life; the flesh counts for nothing. The words I have spoken to you—they are full of the Spirit and life. 64 Yet there are some of you who do not believe." For Jesus had known from the beginning which of them did not believe and who would betray him.

John 6:27 Do not work for food that spoils, but for food that endures to eternal life, which the Son of Man will give you. For on him God the Father has placed his seal of approval."

Luke 4:4 Jesus answered, "It is written: 'Man shall not live on bread alone.'

Romans 12:2 Do not conform to the pattern of this world, but be transformed by the renewing of your mind. Then you will be able to test and approve what God's will is—his good, pleasing

and perfect will. 3 For by the grace given me I say to every one of you: Do not think of yourself more highly than you ought, but rather think of yourself with sober judgment, in accordance with the faith God has distributed to each of you. 4 For just as each of us has one body with many members, and these members do not all have the same function, 5 so in Christ we, though many, form one body, and each member belongs to all the others.

1 Peter 2:2 Like newborn babies, crave pure spiritual milk, so that by it you may grow up in your salvation, 3 now that you have tasted that the Lord is good. 4 As you come to him, the living Stone—rejected by humans but chosen by God and precious to him— 5 you also, like living stones, are being built into a spiritual house to be a holy priesthood, offering spiritual sacrifices acceptable to God through Jesus Christ.

Isaiah 55:1 "Come, all you who are thirsty, come to the waters; and you who have no money, come, buy and eat! Come, buy wine and milk without money and without cost. 2 Why spend money on what is not bread, and your labor on what does not satisfy? Listen, listen to me, and eat what is good, and you will delight in the richest of fare.

211   My body weakened, and exhaustion gripped firmly as I struggled to retain the strength to stand and complete the rite. I was not being drained, as some might take it. But rather I was experiencing a realm in which my consciousness was hitherto unaware. It was an intrusion which I unknowingly desired to be harsh. And the harsher the better, so long as I retained the ability to move on. The exhaustion I experienced during the dance had not lasted, as it was merely a result of frenzy. But with Satanas, quickly came a deeper felt exhaustion, not only one of the body, but one of the spirit.   demonic possession

1 Peter 5:8 Be alert and of sober mind. Your enemy the devil prowls around like a roaring

lion looking for someone to devour.

1 John 4:1 Dear friends, do not believe every spirit, but test the spirits to see whether they are from God, because many false prophets have gone out into the world. 2 This is how you can recognize the Spirit of God: Every spirit that acknowledges that Jesus Christ has come in the flesh is from God, 3 but every spirit that does not acknowledge Jesus is not from God. This is the spirit of the antichrist, which you have heard is coming and even now is already in the world.

2 Corinthians 11:13 For such people are false apostles, deceitful workers, masquerading as apostles of Christ. 14 And no wonder, for Satan himself masquerades as an angel of light. 15 It is not surprising, then, if his servants also masquerade as servants of righteousness. Their end will be what their actions deserve.

15. Magickal Mastery - A Novice's Guide

212	This aim must then become your desire - and a ritual is a means whereby this desire may be achieved. It is essential, of course, for this desire to be strong, and the techniques of magick are simply a means whereby this desire can be strengthened and directed.	desires

Romans 13:13 Let us behave decently, as in the daytime, not in carousing and drunkenness, not in sexual immorality and debauchery, not in dissension and jealousy. 14 Rather, clothe yourselves with the Lord Jesus Christ, and do not think about how to gratify the desires of the flesh.

Psalm 37:4 Take delight in the LORD, and he will give you the desires of your heart. 5 Commit your way to the LORD; trust in him and he will do this:

213	It is no good just saying the words, doing a bit of chanting or waving implements about: you must be emotional. You must literally drive yourself almost to the point of possession, of divine/diabolic madness but always with your desire (i.e. the aim of the ritual) firmly before	demonic possession emotionalism

you, stopping just short of total abandonment.

1 Corinthians 14:33 For God is not a God of disorder but of peace—as in all the congregations of the Lord's people.

1 Thessalonians 4:11 and to make it your ambition to lead a quiet life: You should mind your own business and work with your hands, just as we told you, 12 so that your daily life may win the respect of outsiders and so that you will not be dependent on anybody.

16. Magick With Tears

214 Quite simply Satanism is not an escape from, but the partaking in life. The challenge of living life as a self contained entity, creating a lifestyle that intuitively follows the path of individual Destiny (by this process Destiny becomes, gradually, consciously apparent) is just too disturbing for the majority of the human race to accept.

partakers
extraversion
vs introject

1 Peter 4:13 But rejoice inasmuch as you participate in the sufferings of Christ, so that you may be overjoyed when his glory is revealed.

2 Peter 1:4 Through these he has given us his very great and precious promises, so that through them you may participate in the divine nature, having escaped the corruption in the world caused by evil desires.

Luke 5:12 While Jesus was in one of the towns, a man came along who was covered with leprosy. When he saw Jesus, he fell with his face to the ground and begged him, "Lord, if you are willing, you can make me clean." 13 Jesus reached out his hand and touched the man. "I am willing," he said. "Be clean!" And immediately the leprosy left him. 14 Then Jesus ordered him, "Don't tell anyone, but go, show yourself to the priest and offer the sacrifices that Moses commanded for your cleansing, as a testimony to them." 15 Yet the news about him spread all the more, so that crowds of people came to hear him and to be healed of their sicknesses. 16 But Jesus often withdrew to lonely places and prayed.

1 Corinthians 13:13 If I speak in the tongues of men or of angels, but do not have love, I am only a resounding gong or a clanging cymbal. 2 If I have the gift of prophecy and can fathom all mysteries and all knowledge, and if I have a faith that can move mountains, but do not have love, I am nothing. 3 If I give all I possess to the poor and give over my body to hardship that I may boast, but do not have love, I gain nothing. 4 Love is patient, love is kind. It does not envy, it does not boast, it is not proud. 5 It does not dishonor others, it is not self-seeking, it is not easily angered, it keeps no record of wrongs. 6 Love does not delight in evil but rejoices with the truth. 7 It always protects, always trusts, always hopes, always perseveres.

215   To achieve the highest success possible should always be totally desirable, but the individual should arrive at their own concept of success and not that of the general consensus.   true success

Matthew 16:26 What good will it be for someone to gain the whole world, yet forfeit their soul? Or what can anyone give in exchange for their soul? 27 For the Son of Man is going to come in his Father's glory with his angels, and then he will reward each person according to what they have done.

Luke 16:10 "Whoever can be trusted with very little can also be trusted with much, and whoever is dishonest with very little will also be dishonest with much. 11 So if you have not been trustworthy in handling worldly wealth, who will trust you with true riches?

Romans 12:2 Do not conform to the pattern of this world, but be transformed by the renewing of your mind. Then you will be able to test and approve what God's will is—his good, pleasing and perfect will.

Jeremiah 17:7 "But blessed is the one who trusts in the Lord, whose confidence is in him.

Proverbs 16:3 Commit to the LORD whatever you do, and he will establish your plans.

Proverbs 3:1 My son, do not forget my teaching, but keep my commands in your heart, 2 for they will prolong your life many years and bring you peace and prosperity. 3 Let love and faithfulness never leave you; bind them around your neck, write them on the tablet of your heart. 4 Then you will win favor and a good name in the sight of God and man.

17. Sinister Shadow Magick

216 Satanism is dark, and Satanists revel in evil. As a word, evil is regarded as deriving for the Gothic (via Old English) "ubils" implying "beyond" and "going beyond due limits". Later, the word - like so many others - was re-interpreted "morally", in the abstract terms of Nazarene fundamentalism and "evil" became a general term, applied to one's opponents and those excesses which timed and psychically ailing Nazarenes feared. — evil defined

Ephesians 6:12 For our struggle is not against flesh and blood, but against the rulers, against the authorities, against the powers of this dark world and against the spiritual forces of evil in the heavenly realms. 13 Therefore put on the full armor of God, so that when the day of evil comes, you may be able to stand your ground, and after you have done everything, to stand.

Luke 11:13 If you then, though you are evil, know how to give good gifts to your children, how much more will your Father in heaven give the Holy Spirit to those who ask him!"

John 3:20 Everyone who does evil hates the light, and will not come into the light for fear that their deeds will be exposed. 21 But whoever lives by the truth comes into the light, so that it may be seen plainly that what they have done has been done in the sight of God.

1 Peter 2:15 For it is God's will that by doing good you should silence the ignorant talk of foolish people. 16 Live as free people, but do not use your freedom as a cover-up for evil; live as God's slaves.

James 3:16 For where you have envy and selfish ambition, there you find disorder and every evil practice.

Proverbs 8:13 To fear the LORD is to hate evil; I hate pride and arrogance, evil behavior and perverse speech.

Zechariah 7:9 "This is what the Lord Almighty said: 'Administer true justice; show mercy and compassion to one another. 10 Do not oppress the widow or the fatherless, the foreigner or the poor. Do not plot evil against each other.'

217 The Satanic novice will aspire - to what is beyond, in all things. This means personal experience, testing Destiny and achieving difficult goals in personal life. It means real danger in the real world, not cheap manufactured "thrills" of self-induced stupor and loss of control - but rather, life and liberty threatening situations. These may be and often are amoral, illegal and evil - all laws are "fundamentally an accumulation of tireless attempts to stop creative individuals making life into instants of poetry".

illegal activity

Romans 13:1 Let everyone be subject to the governing authorities, for there is no authority except that which God has established. The authorities that exist have been established by God. 2 Consequently, whoever rebels against the authority is rebelling against what God has instituted, and those who do so will bring judgment on themselves. 3 For rulers hold no terror for those who do right, but for those who do wrong. Do you want to be free from fear of the one in authority? Then do what is right and you will be commended. 4 For the one in authority is God's servant for your good. But if you do wrong, be afraid, for rulers do not bear the sword for no reason. They are God's servants, agents of wrath to bring punishment on the wrongdoer. 5 Therefore, it is necessary to submit to the authorities, not only because of possible punishment but also as a matter of conscience. 6 This is also why you pay taxes, for the authorities are God's servants, who give their full time to governing. 7 Give to everyone what you owe them: If you owe taxes, pay taxes; if revenue, then revenue; if respect, then respect; if honor, then honor.

218 However, the acts of a Satanist are not random nor motiveless and neither do they arise from a weakness of character nor uncontrolled desire. Instead, they arise from fulfilling Satanic wyrd - or, viewed another way, from presencing the energies of "darkness"/Satan on the Earth with sinister intent.   strength of character

John 15:5 "I am the vine; you are the branches. If you remain in me and I in you, you will bear much fruit; apart from me you can do nothing.

Romans 5:3 Not only so, but we also glory in our sufferings, because we know that suffering produces perseverance; 4 perseverance, character; and character, hope. 5 And hope does not put us to shame, because God's love has been poured out into our hearts through the Holy Spirit, who has been given to us.

Romans 1:20 For since the creation of the world God's invisible qualities—his eternal power and divine nature—have been clearly seen, being understood from what has been made, so that people are without excuse. 21 For although they knew God, they neither glorified him as God nor gave thanks to him, but their thinking became futile and their foolish hearts were darkened.

Ezekiel 36:26 I will give you a new heart and put a new spirit in you; I will remove from you your heart of stone and give you a heart of flesh. 27 And I will put my Spirit in you and move you to follow my decrees and be careful to keep my laws.

219 For this, practical experience and some guidance is needed. Let us assume the novice is advised or chooses to use a political form to achieve this experience - and thus becomes   politics

involved with radical "right wing" politics because such people already possess an element or two of Satanic spirit, the "other sides" in this form and at this moment in the history of this aeon representing the Nazarene disease in another guise.

John 18:36 Jesus said, "My kingdom is not of this world. If it were, my servants would fight to prevent my arrest by the Jewish leaders. But now my kingdom is from another place." 37 "You are a king, then!" said Pilate. Jesus answered, "You say that I am a king. In fact, the reason I was born and came into the world is to testify to the truth. Everyone on the side of truth listens to me."

Philippians 3:20 But our citizenship is in heaven. And we eagerly await a Savior from there, the Lord Jesus Christ, 21 who, by the power that enables him to bring everything under his control, will transform our lowly bodies so that they will be like his glorious body.

Proverbs 28:15 Like a roaring lion or a charging bear is a wicked ruler over a helpless people.

Ecclesiastes 4:13 Better a poor but wise youth than an old but foolish king who no longer knows how to heed a warning.

220   For example, a political form may be chosen and used. After some time, violence, riots somewhere, the spread of a new idea... The rising of a type of State in essence inspired with sinister energies and thus contributing to aeonic evolution... Perhaps a war, to propitiate the darker forces... Thus, it will be understood that Satanists act in a directed way, whether they are novices or Adepts.   incitement of war

Matthew 5:38 "You have heard that it was said, 'Eye for eye, and tooth for tooth.' 39 But I tell you, do not resist an evil person. If anyone slaps you on the right cheek, turn to them the other cheek also.

Matthew 26:52 "Put your sword back in its

place," Jesus said to him, "for all who draw the sword will die by the sword. 53 Do you think I cannot call on my Father, and he will at once put at my disposal more than twelve legions of angels? 54 But how then would the Scriptures be fulfilled that say it must happen in this way?"

James 4:1 What causes fights and quarrels among you? Don't they come from your desires that battle within you? 2 You desire but do not have, so you kill. You covet but you cannot get what you want, so you quarrel and fight. You do not have because you do not ask God. 3 When you ask, you do not receive, because you ask with wrong motives, that you may spend what you get on your pleasures.

Isaiah 60:18 No longer will violence be heard in your land, nor ruin or destruction within your borders, but you will call your walls Salvation and your gates Praise.

Psalms 11:5 The LORD examines the righteous, but the wicked, those who love violence, he hates with a passion.

19. The Aims Of The ONA

221 To implement sinister strategy - i.e. to presence the acausal (or 'the dark forces') via nexions and so change evolution. One immediate aim is to presence acausal energies in a particular way so creating a new aeon and then a new, higher, civilization from the energies unleashed.

Acts 2:40 With many other words he warned them; and he pleaded with them, "Save yourselves from this corrupt generation." 41 Those who accepted his message were baptized, and about three thousand were added to their number that day.

Hebrews 12:14 Make every effort to live in peace with everyone and to be holy; without holiness no one will see the Lord.

Matthew 5:13 "You are the salt of the earth. But if the salt loses its saltiness, how can it be made salty again? It is no longer good for anything, except to be thrown out and trampled underfoot. 14 "You are the light of the world. A town built on a hill cannot be hidden.

Isaiah 1:4 Woe to the sinful nation, a people whose guilt is great, a brood of evildoers, children given to corruption! They have forsaken the LORD; they have spurned the Holy One of Israel and turned their backs on him.

222 Expressed simply, the aim of the ONA is to create a new species – to significantly change our evolution as a species. This will take time - many centuries, in fact. The Seven-Fold Way is a practical means whereby an individual, now, can develop and so become a part of this new species.   evolution

Genesis 1:26 Then God said, "Let us make mankind in our image, in our likeness, so that they may rule over the fish in the sea and the birds in the sky, over the livestock and all the wild animals, and over all the creatures that move along the ground." 27 So God created mankind in his own image, in the image of God he created them; male and female he created them.

1 John 3:1 See what great love the Father has lavished on us, that we should be called children of God! And that is what we are! The reason the world does not know us is that it did not know him. 2 Dear friends, now we are children of God, and what we will be has not yet been made known. But we know that when Christ appears, we shall be like him, for we shall see him as he is.

20. Ritual Magick: Dure And Sedue Ceremonial

223 Magick enables us to capture again and again those moments which not only shape our lives but which can extend the possibilities of our existence: those moments when we know with an exhileration and an insight that transcends words, when we become more than a single isolated individual burdened with a causal existence.   insights

Matthew 7:22 Many will say to me on that day, 'Lord, Lord, did we not prophesy in your

name and in your name drive out demons and in your name perform many miracles?' 23 Then I will tell them plainly, 'I never knew you. Away from me, you evildoers!' 24 "Therefore everyone who hears these words of mine and puts them into practice is like a wise man who built his house on the rock.

1 Corinthians 2:9 However, as it is written: "What no eye has seen, what no ear has heard, and what no human mind has conceived" — the things God has prepared for those who love him—10 these are the things God has revealed to us by his Spirit. The Spirit searches all things, even the deep things of God.

Proverbs 2:3 indeed, if you call out for insight and cry aloud for understanding, 4 and if you look for it as for silver and search for it as for hidden treasure, 5 then you will understand the fear of the LORD and find the knowledge of God. 6 For the LORD gives wisdom; from his mouth come knowledge and understanding. 7 He holds success in store for the upright, he is a shield to those whose walk is blameless, 8 for he guards the course of the just and protects the way of his faithful ones.

Proverbs 1:2 for gaining wisdom and instruction; for understanding words of insight; 3 for receiving instruction in prudent behavior, doing what is right and just and fair; 4 for giving prudence to those who are simple, knowledge and discretion to the young—5 let the wise listen and add to their learning, and let the discerning get guidance—6 for understanding proverbs and parables, the sayings and riddles of the wise. 7 The fear of the LORD is the beginning of knowledge, but fools despise wisdom and instruction.

21. Adeptship - Its Real Meaning And Purpose

224 Adeptship results from a transformation - a transmutation of the individual. This begins at Initiation, whether that be ceremonial or hermetic [i.e. as part of a group or alone]. It is an internal alchemical process of change, and

adeptship
discipleship

occurs on all levels - the psychic, the magickal, the intellectual, the psychological and the physical. It is the birth of a new individual who has skills, knowledge, understanding and judgment not possessed by the majority.

Acts 1:8 But you will receive power when the Holy Spirit comes on you; and you will be my witnesses in Jerusalem, and in all Judea and Samaria, and to the ends of the earth."

John 15:16 You did not choose me, but I chose you and appointed you so that you might go and bear fruit—fruit that will last—and so that whatever you ask in my name the Father will give you. 17 This is my command: Love each other.

Hebrews 3:12 See to it, brothers and sisters, that none of you has a sinful, unbelieving heart that turns away from the living God. 13 But encourage one another daily, as long as it is called "Today," so that none of you may be hardened by sin's deceitfulness. 14 We have come to share in Christ, if indeed we hold our original conviction firmly to the very end.

Ephesians 5:1 Follow God's example, therefore, as dearly loved children 2 and walk in the way of love, just as Christ loved us and gave himself up for us as a fragrant offering and sacrifice to God.

23. The Left Handed Path - An Analysis

225 In contradistinction, the LHP in its methods is non-structured. In the genuine LHP there is nothing that is not permitted - nothing that is forbidden or restricted. That is, the LHP means the individual takes sole responsibility for their actions and their quest. This makes the LHP both difficult and dangerous - its methods can be used as an excuse for anti-social behaviour as they can be used to aid the fetishes and weaknesses of some individuals as well as lead some into forbidden and illegal acts.

right hand path
left hand path

Romans 7:11 For sin, seizing the opportunity afforded by the commandment, deceived me, and through the commandment put me to death.

12 So then, the law is holy, and the commandment is holy, righteous and good.

Matthew 5:17 "Do not think that I have come to abolish the Law or the Prophets; I have not come to abolish them but to fulfill them. 18 For truly I tell you, until heaven and earth disappear, not the smallest letter, not the least stroke of a pen, will by any means disappear from the Law until everything is accomplished. 19 Therefore anyone who sets aside one of the least of these commands and teaches others accordingly will be called least in the kingdom of heaven, but whoever practices and teaches these commands will be called great in the kingdom of heaven. 20 For I tell you that unless your righteousness surpasses that of the Pharisees and the teachers of the law, you will certainly not enter the kingdom of heaven.

Romans 3:19 Now we know that whatever the law says, it says to those who are under the law, so that every mouth may be silenced and the whole world held accountable to God. 20 Therefore no one will be declared righteous in God's sight by the works of the law; rather, through the law we become conscious of our sin. 21 But now apart from the law the righteousness of God has been made known, to which the Law and the Prophets testify. 22 This righteousness is given through faith in Jesus Christ to all who believe. There is no difference between Jew and Gentile,

Psalm 19:7 The law of the LORD is perfect, refreshing the soul. The statutes of the LORD are trustworthy, making wise the simple. 8 The precepts of the LORD are right, giving joy to the heart. The commands of the LORD are radiant, giving light to the eyes.

Psalm 119:1 Blessed are those whose ways are blameless, who walk according to the law of the LORD.

Deuteronomy 30:15 See, I set before you today life and prosperity, death and destruction. 16 For I command you today to love the Lord your God, to walk in obedience to him, and to keep his commands, decrees and laws; then you will live and increase, and the Lord your God will bless you in the land you are entering to possess.

226 Further, the goal or aim of the LHP is individual specific - it is the raising of that individual to 'godhead'; the fulfillment of individual potential and thus a discovery and fulfillment of their unique Destiny. That is, it breeds a unique character, a unique individual. destiny

Ephesians 2:8 For it is by grace you have been saved, through faith—and this is not from yourselves, it is the gift of God— 9 not by works, so that no one can boast.

Romans 12:2 Do not conform to the pattern of this world, but be transformed by the renewing of your mind. Then you will be able to test and approve what God's will is—his good, pleasing and perfect will.

Revelation 20:12 And I saw the dead, great and small, standing before the throne, and books were opened. Another book was opened, which is the book of life. The dead were judged according to what they had done as recorded in the books.

John 16:33 "I have told you these things, so that in me you may have peace. In this world you will have trouble. But take heart! I have overcome the world."

Jeremiah 17:10 "I the LORD search the heart and examine the mind, to reward each person according to their conduct, according to what their deeds deserve."

227 Essentially, the LHP Initiate is a free spirit, already possessed of a certain willful character, while the RHP Initiate is in thrall to other people's ideas and ways of doing things. free will

Galatians 5:13 You, my brothers and sisters, were called to be free. But do not use your freedom to indulge the flesh; rather, serve one another humbly in love.

Romans 10:9 If you declare with your mouth,

"Jesus is Lord," and believe in your heart that God raised him from the dead, you will be saved. 10 For it is with your heart that you believe and are justified, and it is with your mouth that you profess your faith and are saved.

Proverbs 16:9 In their hearts humans plan their course, but the Lord establishes their steps.

Isaiah 55:6 Seek the LORD while he may be found; call on him while he is near. 7 Let the wicked forsake their ways and the unrighteous their thoughts. Let them turn to the LORD, and he will have mercy on them, and to our God, for he will freely pardon.

228   In summary, the RHP is soft. The LHP is hard. The RHP is like a comfortable game - and one which can be played, left for a while, then taken up again. The LHP is a struggle which takes years. The RHP prescribes behaviour and limits personal responsibility. The LHP means self-responsibility and self-effort. The RHP requires the individual to conform in certain way. The LHP is non-restrictive. RHP organizations and 'teachers' require the Initiate to conform and accept the authority of that organization/ 'teacher'. LHP organizations and Masters/ Mistresses only offer advice and guidance, based on their own experience.   Left hand path   Right hand path

Matthew 16:24 Then Jesus said to his disciples, "Whoever wants to be my disciple must deny themselves and take up their cross and follow me. 25 For whoever wants to save their life will lose it, but whoever loses their life for me will find it.

2 Corinthians 3:17 Now the Lord is the Spirit, and where the Spirit of the Lord is, there is freedom. 18 And we all, who with unveiled faces contemplate the Lord's glory, are being transformed into his image with ever-increasing glory, which comes from the Lord, who is the Spirit.

James 1:25 But whoever looks intently into

the perfect law that gives freedom, and continues in it—not forgetting what they have heard, but doing it—they will be blessed in what they do.

Luke 4:18 "The Spirit of the Lord is on me, because he has anointed me to proclaim good news to the poor. He has sent me to proclaim freedom for the prisoners and recovery of sight for the blind, to set the oppressed free,

19 to proclaim the year of the Lord's favor."

Romans 8:1 Therefore, there is now no condemnation for those who are in Christ Jesus, 2 because through Christ Jesus the law of the Spirit who gives life has set you free from the law of sin and death. 3 For what the law was powerless to do because it was weakened by the flesh, God did by sending his own Son in the likeness of sinful flesh to be a sin offering. And so he condemned sin in the flesh, 4 in order that the righteous requirement of the law might be fully met in us, who do not live according to the flesh but according to the Spirit.

Isaiah 61:1 The Spirit of the Sovereign LORD is on me, because the LORD has anointed me to proclaim good news to the poor. He has sent me to bind up the brokenhearted, to proclaim freedom for the captives and release from darkness for the prisoners, 2 to proclaim the year of the LORD's favor and the day of vengeance of our God, to comfort all who mourn, 3 and provide for those who grieve in Zion— to bestow on them a crown of beauty instead of ashes, the oil of joy instead of mourning, and a garment of praise instead of a spirit of despair. They will be called oaks of righteousness, a planting of the LORD for the display of his splendor.

Psalm 119:45 I will walk about in freedom, for I have sought out your precepts.

229	The Satanist effectively learns to play at being god.	atheism blasphemy

2 Timothy 4:3 For the time will come when people will not put up with sound doctrine.

Instead, to suit their own desires, they will gather around them a great number of teachers to say what their itching ears want to hear. 4 They will turn their ears away from the truth and turn aside to myths.

Romans 12:3 For by the grace given me I say to every one of you: Do not think of yourself more highly than you ought, but rather think of yourself with sober judgment, in accordance with the faith God has distributed to each of you. 4 For just as each of us has one body with many members, and these members do not all have the same function, 5 so in Christ we, though many, form one body, and each member belongs to all the others.

Ephesians 2:10 For we are God's handiwork, created in Christ Jesus to do good works, which God prepared in advance for us to do.

Romans 12:6 We have different gifts, according to the grace given to each of us. If your gift is prophesying, then prophesy in accordance with your faith; 7 if it is serving, then serve; if it is teaching, then teach; 8 if it is to encourage, then give encouragement; if it is giving, then give generously; if it is to lead, do it diligently; if it is to show mercy, do it cheerfully.

230   Satan is the Prince of Darkness - Master of all that is hidden or secret, both within ourselves and external to ourselves. He is the ruler of this world - the force behind its evolutionary change; the 'fire' of life. He is Lord of Life - of all the sensual delights and pleasures. He is also 'evil' or 'dark' or 'sinister' - merciless, ruthless, Master of Death. He can and does promote suffering, misery, death. But all these things are impersonal - they are natural consequences of life, of change and evolution.   Satan

Revelation 20:10 And the devil, who deceived them, was thrown into the lake of burning sulfur, where the beast and the false prophet had been thrown. They will be tormented day and night for ever and ever.

2 Corinthians 4:4 The god of this age has blinded the minds of unbelievers, so that they cannot see the light of the gospel that displays the glory of Christ, who is the image of God.

2 Corinthians 11:14 And no wonder, for Satan himself masquerades as an angel of light.

John 12:31 Now is the time for judgment on this world; now the prince of this world will be driven out. 32 And I, when I am lifted up from the earth, will draw all people to myself." 33 He said this to show the kind of death he was going to die.

Job 1:6 One day the angels came to present themselves before the Lord, and Satan also came with them. 7 The Lord said to Satan, "Where have you come from?" Satan answered the Lord, "From roaming throughout the earth, going back and forth on it."

Matthew 16:23 Jesus turned and said to Peter, "Get behind me, Satan! You are a stumbling block to me; you do not have in mind the concerns of God, but merely human concerns."

231 Rather, the satanic approach is to glory in Satanic deeds and chants and such like because they are Satanic - because by so doing them there is an exultation, an affirmation and a being like Satan: not because something is 'expected' or done out of fear of the consequences. It is by living life, by deeds, that a Satanist becomes like Satan and so evolves to partake of a new and higher existence. Such deeds are those to bring insight, self-discovery, to achieve, esoteric knowledge, experience of the 'forbidden', of the pleasures of living - and they are also those which change others and the world and which thus can and do bring suffering, misery, death: which are, in short, evil.

knowledge
pleasure

Luke 8:14 The seed that fell among thorns stands for those who hear, but as they go on their way they are choked by life's worries, riches and pleasures, and they do not mature.

1 Corinthians 13:2 If I have the gift of prophecy and can fathom all mysteries and all knowledge, and if I have a faith that can move mountains, but do not have love, I am nothing.

2 Peter 1:3 His divine power has given us everything we need for a godly life through our knowledge of him who called us by his own glory and goodness.

Romans 1:25 They exchanged the truth about God for a lie, and worshiped and served created things rather than the Creator—who is forever praised. Amen.

James 5:5 You have lived on earth in luxury and self-indulgence. You have fattened yourselves in the day of slaughter. 6 You have condemned and murdered the innocent one, who was not opposing you.

1 Corinthians 10:13 No temptation has overtaken you except what is common to mankind. And God is faithful; he will not let you be tempted beyond what you can bear. But when you are tempted, he will also provide a way out so that you can endure it.

Colossians 3:5 Put to death, therefore, whatever belongs to your earthly nature: sexual immorality, impurity, lust, evil desires and greed, which is idolatry. 6 Because of these, the wrath of God is coming. 7 You used to walk in these ways, in the life you once lived.

232 Evil, correctly defined, is part of the cosmic dialectic - it is force, which is a-moral: i.e. it is beyond the bounds of 'morals'. Morals derive from a limited (human - or, rather, pseudo-human) perspective, and a morality is a projection by individual consciousness onto reality. Nothing that is 'moral' or immoral exists. All morals are therefore artifice - they are abstractions.   morals

2 Peter 1:5 For this very reason, make every effort to add to your faith goodness; and to goodness, knowledge; 6 and to knowledge, self-control; and to self-control, perseverance; and to perseverance, godliness; 7 and to godliness, mutual affection; and to mutual affection, love. 8 For if you possess these qualities in increasing measure, they will keep you from being ineffective and unproductive in your knowledge of our Lord Jesus Christ.

1 Corinthians 15:33 Do not be misled: "Bad company corrupts good character." 34 Come back to your senses as you ought, and stop sinning; for there are some who are ignorant of God—I say this to your shame.

3 John 1:11 Dear friend, do not imitate what is evil but what is good. Anyone who does what is good is from God. Anyone who does what is evil has not seen God.

Proverbs 1:7 The fear of the LORD is the beginning of knowledge, but fools despise wisdom and instruction.

26. The Practical Esoteric Aims Of Satanism

233 The practical aims arise from Satanic strategy which has its foundation in Aeonics [qv. the various Aeonics and Cliology]. These aims are essentially tactics to achieve the long-term strategic goal. This goal is the creation of a new species - and this means (a) a new Aeon; (b) a new aeonic civilization. For this to be achieved, present structures, forms, ideas and so on, have to be changed. Aeonics shows that the present Aeonic civilization, the Western, has been distorted in its ethos and its structures. One of the most potent forms of the distortion has been the Nazarene religion.

creation

Revelation 4:11 "You are worthy, our Lord and God, to receive glory and honor and power, for you created all things, and by your will they were created and have their being."

Colossians 1:16 For in him all things were created: things in heaven and on earth, visible and invisible, whether thrones or powers or rulers or authorities; all things have been created through him and for him.

John 1:1 In the beginning was the Word, and the Word was with God, and the Word was God. 2 He was with God in the beginning. 3

Through him all things were made; without him nothing was made that has been made.

Genesis 1:1 In the beginning God created the heavens and the earth. 2 Now the earth was formless and empty, darkness was over the surface of the deep, and the Spirit of God was hovering over the waters.

Jeremiah 32:17 "Ah, Sovereign Lord, you have made the heavens and the earth by your great power and outstretched arm. Nothing is too hard for you.

Psalm 139:13 For you created my inmost being; you knit me together in my mother's womb. 14 I praise you because I am fearfully and wonderfully made; your works are wonderful, I know that full well.

234 There has been a 'silent revolution' in all Western societies and they all now conform to unhealthy Nazarene induced forms - the power structures of these societies now actively seek to eradicate all heretical pro-Promethean ideas/groups/individuals, and use the full force of the 'Law', as well as covert tactics, against those who hold out against the relentless onslaught to enslave the peoples of the West to what are essentially 'Magian' created ideas. Thus the campaigns, in Schools and throughout society, against "racism". To implement this Magian revolution, a myth was created - 'the Holocaust'. — holocaust

John 4:22 You Samaritans worship what you do not know; we worship what we do know, for salvation is from the Jews.

Genesis 12:2 "I will make you into a great nation, and I will bless you; I will make your name great, and you will be a blessing. 3 I will bless those who bless you, and whoever curses you I will curse; and all peoples on earth will be blessed through you."

235 On the practical level, it is considered necessary, in order to achieve strategic goals, to support the creation of a Western Imperium - that is, to support those forces trying to — racism

undermine in a practical way the current Nazarene/Magian status quo. This means upholding heretical views such as racial inequality, and denying 'the Holocaust' - as well as aiding/supporting National-Socialist/"racist" causes. The tactical aim here is the creation of a pro-Aryan, National-Socialist type State which has a noble, conquering spirit or ethos, and thus which re-presents Satanic values in action in the real world.

Galatians 3:28 There is neither Jew nor Gentile, neither slave nor free, nor is there male and female, for you are all one in Christ Jesus.

Acts 10:34 Then Peter began to speak: "I now realize how true it is that God does not show favoritism 35 but accepts from every nation the one who fears him and does what is right.

James 2:8 If you really keep the royal law found in Scripture, "Love your neighbor as yourself," you are doing right. 9 But if you show favoritism, you sin and are convicted by the law as lawbreakers.

Deuteronomy 10:17 For the Lord your God is God of gods and Lord of lords, the great God, mighty and awesome, who shows no partiality and accepts no bribes. 18 He defends the cause of the fatherless and the widow, and loves the foreigner residing among you, giving them food and clothing. 19 And you are to love those who are foreigners, for you yourselves were foreigners in Egypt. 20 Fear the Lord your God and serve him. Hold fast to him and take your oaths in his name. 21 He is the one you praise; he is your God, who performed for you those great and awesome wonders you saw with your own eyes. 22 Your ancestors who went down into Egypt were seventy in all, and now the Lord your God has made you as numerous as the stars in the sky.

236	This means disrupting societies supporting armed insurrection, spreading heretical ideas, aiding those groups/ forms which weaken societies from within (in the moral sense - e.g.	chaos illegal activity

drug dealing) and thus engendering a healthy, noble resurgence. A primary aim is to cause chaos, on the streets, economically, and socially - to thus provide opportunities for a revolutionary pro- Aryan group to take or seize power.

1 Corinthians 14:33 For God is not a God of disorder but of peace—as in all the congregations of the Lord's people.

Romans 13:1 Let everyone be subject to the governing authorities, for there is no authority except that which God has established. The authorities that exist have been established by God. 2 Consequently, whoever rebels against the authority is rebelling against what God has instituted, and those who do so will bring judgment on themselves. 3 For rulers hold no terror for those who do right, but for those who do wrong. Do you want to be free from fear of the one in authority? Then do what is right and you will be commended. 4 For the one in authority is God's servant for your good. But if you do wrong, be afraid, for rulers do not bear the sword for no reason. They are God's servants, agents of wrath to bring punishment on the wrongdoer.

Genesis 9:5 And for your lifeblood I will surely demand an accounting. I will demand an accounting from every animal. And from each human being, too, I will demand an accounting for the life of another human being. 6 "Whoever sheds human blood, by humans shall their blood be shed; for in the image of God has God made mankind.

Proverbs 6:16 There are six things the LORD hates, seven that are detestable to him: 17 haughty eyes, a lying tongue, hands that shed innocent blood, 18 a heart that devises wicked schemes, feet that are quick to rush into evil, 19 a false witness who pours out lies and a person who stirs up conflict in the community.

| 237 | A magickal and practical aim is to destroy the power structure of America, for that country | America Israel |

effectively is acting to maintain a global control in accord with Magian dictates and thus impose the Magian world-view. The real power of the Magian heart-land resides in America and in the control excercised in the minds of Europeans by the idea of 'multi-racialism' and the myth of the holocaust. If the present power structure of America was destroyed, the practical power-base, both financial and military, of the Magian heart-land (ie. Israel) would collapse - what has prevented the destruction of this heart-land by the Arabs is the military superiority given to it by America.

John 4:22 You Samaritans worship what you do not know; we worship what we do know, for salvation is from the Jews.

Romans 9:4 the people of Israel. Theirs is the adoption to sonship; theirs the divine glory, the covenants, the receiving of the law, the temple worship and the promises. 5 Theirs are the patriarchs, and from them is traced the human ancestry of the Messiah, who is God over all, forever praised! Amen.

Genesis 12:1 The LORD had said to Abram, "Go from your country, your people and your father's household to the land I will show you. 2 "I will make you into a great nation, and I will bless you; I will make your name great, and you will be a blessing. 3 I will bless those who bless you, and whoever curses you I will curse; and all peoples on earth will be blessed through you."

Amos 9:14 and I will bring my people Israel back from exile. "They will rebuild the ruined cities and live in them. They will plant vineyards and drink their wine; they will make gardens and eat their fruit. 15 I will plant Israel in their own land, never again to be uprooted from the land I have given them," says the LORD your God.

Ezekiel 11:17 "Therefore say: 'This is what the Sovereign Lord says: I will gather you from the nations and bring you back from the countries where you have been scattered, and I will give you back the land of Israel again.'

238 The present Aeon is the Western - and this Aeon dates from c.500 eh to c.2000eh in terms of the energies being predominant. The aeonic civilization follows some centuries later: for the West, arising c. 900 eh and ending c. 2400eh. The energies of the next Aeon follow or arise some centuries after the last Aeonic ones: in practice, this means at the end of the civilization of the last Aeonc; when the Imperium is collapsing. Thus, the new Aeonic manifestations will arise c.2400eh.
    prophesy

2 Peter 2:1 But there were also false prophets among the people, just as there will be false teachers among you. They will secretly introduce destructive heresies, even denying the sovereign Lord who bought them—bringing swift destruction on themselves.

1 Corinthians 14:1 Follow the way of love and eagerly desire gifts of the Spirit, especially prophecy. 2 For anyone who speaks in a tongue does not speak to people but to God. Indeed, no one understands them; they utter mysteries by the Spirit. 3 But the one who prophesies speaks to people for their strengthening, encouraging and comfort. 4 Anyone who speaks in a tongue edifies themselves, but the one who prophesies edifies the church. 5 I would like every one of you to speak in tongues, but I would rather have you prophesy. The one who prophesies is greater than the one who speaks in tongues, unless someone interprets, so that the church may be edified.

239 This insight means that a genuine Initiate understands a transient form such as 'National-Socialism' as a practical expression of some of the principles of Satanism and as, in the long-term, contributing to evolutionary change via its inherent dynamism and acceptance of the forces of Nature. Such an Initiate understands that, at this moment in aeonic history, such a form is necessary: ie. this form (or something very
    nazism

similar) and only this form presences the sinister in the way that sinister must be presenced to achieve the strategic goal of Satanism over centuries.

Matthew 22:37 Jesus replied: "'Love the Lord your God with all your heart and with all your soul and with all your mind.' 38 This is the first and greatest commandment. 39 And the second is like it: 'Love your neighbor as yourself.'

Isaiah 5:20 Woe to those who call evil good and good evil, who put darkness for light and light for darkness, who put bitter for sweet and sweet for bitter.

Psalm 94:4 They pour out arrogant words; all the evildoers are full of boasting. 5 They crush your people, LORD; they oppress your inheritance. 6 They slay the widow and the foreigner; they murder the fatherless. 7 They say, "The LORD does not see; the God of Jacob takes no notice." 8 Take notice, you senseless ones among the people; you fools, when will you become wise?

240   The tactics are geared to this. Thus, an encouragement of Islam in certain Arab states may be a tactic used - because Islam acts to discourage the 'American' materialism which would otherwise flourish, and thus offsets 'American' (read covert Zionist) influence. This in itself poses problems for America and thus the Magian.   Islam

Acts 4:9 If we are being called to account today for an act of kindness shown to a man who was lame and are being asked how he was healed, 10 then know this, you and all the people of Israel: It is by the name of Jesus Christ of Nazareth, whom you crucified but whom God raised from the dead, that this man stands before you healed. 11 Jesus is " 'the stone you builders rejected, which has become the cornerstone.' 12 Salvation is found in no one else, for there is no other name under heaven given to mankind by which we must be saved."

Romans 6:23 For the wages of sin is death, but the gift of God is eternal life in Christ Jesus our Lord.

John 14:6 Jesus answered, "I am the way and the truth and the life. No one comes to the Father except through me. 7 If you really know me, you will know my Father as well. From now on, you do know him and have seen him."

John 3:3 Jesus replied, "Very truly I tell you, no one can see the kingdom of God unless they are born again." 4 "How can someone be born when they are old?" Nicodemus asked. "Surely they cannot enter a second time into their mother's womb to be born!" 5 Jesus answered, "Very truly I tell you, no one can enter the kingdom of God unless they are born of water and the Spirit. 6 Flesh gives birth to flesh, but the Spirit gives birth to spirit.

John 3:16 For God so loved the world that he gave his one and only Son, that whoever believes in him shall not perish but have eternal life. 17 For God did not send his Son into the world to condemn the world, but to save the world through him. 18 Whoever believes in him is not condemned, but whoever does not believe stands condemned already because they have not believed in the name of God's one and only Son.

27. Satanism, Blasphemy And The Black Mass

In one important respect, Satanism may be regarded by new Initiates as a catharsis - a means whereby individuals may divest themselves of those limiting roles that often are the creation of the ethos or ethics of the society in which those individuals find themselves. — catharsis

Mark 5:34 He said to her, "Daughter, your faith has healed you. Go in peace and be freed from your suffering."

Matthew 10:1 Jesus called his twelve disciples to him and gave them authority to drive out impure spirits and to heal every disease and sickness.

Jeremiah 33:6 "'Nevertheless, I will bring

health and healing to it; I will heal my people and will let them enjoy abundant peace and security.
Isaiah 53:4 Surely he took up our pain and bore our suffering, yet we considered him punished by God, stricken by him, and afflicted. 5 But he was pierced for our transgressions, he was crushed for our iniquities; the punishment that brought us peace was on him, and by his wounds we are healed.

242 For the Satanic novice [the first two stages of the seven-fold Satanic path] Satanism represents the dark aspect of the individual psyche - and by identifying with this, the individual is enabled, by the transformation that results, to begin the 'Great Work' whose attainment is the goal of the Adept. This 'Great Work' is simply the creation of a new individual - and this new type, by virtue of the path followed, often inspires in others a certain terror.

    new individual

Ephesians 4:22 You were taught, with regard to your former way of life, to put off your old self, which is being corrupted by its deceitful desires; 23 to be made new in the attitude of your minds; 24 and to put on the new self, created to be like God in true righteousness and holiness
2 Corinthians 5:17 Therefore, if anyone is in Christ, the new creation has come: The old has gone, the new is here!
Romans 6:4 We were therefore buried with him through baptism into death in order that, just as Christ was raised from the dead through the glory of the Father, we too may live a new life. 5 For if we have been united with him in a death like his, we will certainly also be united with him in a resurrection like his. 6 For we know that our old self was crucified with him so that the body ruled by sin might be done away with, [a] that we should no longer be slaves to sin— 7 because anyone who has died has been set free from sin. 8 Now if we died with Christ, we believe that we will also live with him. 9 For

we know that since Christ was raised from the dead, he cannot die again; death no longer has mastery over him. 10 The death he died, he died to sin once for all; but the life he lives, he lives to God.

243   That is, those who fail in their quest along this path [and Gilles de Rais is an example] often do so because they fundamentally accept the dichotomy of 'evil' and 'good' and identify with what they perceive or believe to be, 'evil' - this perception and understanding almost always deriving from what the 'opposition' have declared to be 'evil'. The reality is that this dichotomy does not exist in the cosmos - the convention of what is 'evil' has been imposed, by the projection of mostly Nazarene dogmatists, upon reality.   dichotomy good vs evil

Matthew 7:15 "Watch out for false prophets. They come to you in sheep's clothing, but inwardly they are ferocious wolves. 16 By their fruit you will recognize them. Do people pick grapes from thornbushes, or figs from thistles? 17 Likewise, every good tree bears good fruit, but a bad tree bears bad fruit. 18 A good tree cannot bear bad fruit, and a bad tree cannot bear good fruit.

James 1:13 When tempted, no one should say, "God is tempting me." For God cannot be tempted by evil, nor does he tempt anyone; 14 but each person is tempted when they are dragged away by their own evil desire and enticed. 15 Then, after desire has conceived, it gives birth to sin; and sin, when it is full-grown, gives birth to death.

John 8:44 You belong to your father, the devil, and you want to carry out your father's desires. He was a murderer from the beginning, not holding to the truth, for there is no truth in him. When he lies, he speaks his native language, for he is a liar and the father of lies.

Isaiah 5:20 Woe to those who call evil good and good evil, who put darkness for light and light for darkness, who put bitter for sweet and

sweet for bitter.

Isaiah 45:7 I form the light and create darkness, I bring prosperity and create disaster; I, the LORD, do all these things.

244   One of the Satanic masses in use today is based on an evokation of Adolf Hitler - and not as something artificial, still less as a psychological 'game'. Rather, there is a genuine identification with the positive, life-enhancing, aspects of National-Socialism. [To most readers, this will be shocking - a blasphemy; which is exactly the point.] As with the traditional Black Mass, it is the stress placed on the positive, vital qualities of opposition that are important - because these contradict in their very essence all that is assumed about what or whom the mass is concerned with. Thus, in this particular Satanic Mass, Adolf Hitler is not represented as he is today portrayed by his opponents - as some sort of 'evil' monster - but as exactly the opposite, as a noble saviour.   Hitler

Romans 1:16 For I am not ashamed of the gospel, because it is the power of God that brings salvation to everyone who believes: first to the Jew, then to the Gentile.

Genesis 12:1 The LORD had said to Abram, "Go from your country, your people and your father's household to the land I will show you. 2 "I will make you into a great nation, and I will bless you; I will make your name great, and you will be a blessing. 3 I will bless those who bless you, and whoever curses you I will curse; and all peoples on earth will be blessed through you."

Romans 9:5 Theirs are the patriarchs, and from them is traced the human ancestry of the Messiah, who is God over all, forever praised! Amen.

Matthew 10:5 These twelve Jesus sent out with the following instructions: "Do not go among the Gentiles or enter any town of the Samaritans. 6 Go rather to the lost sheep of Israel.

Romans 11:28 As far as the gospel is concerned, they are enemies for your sake; but as far as election is concerned, they are loved on account of the patriarchs, 29 for God's gifts and his call are irrevocable. 30 Just as you who were at one time disobedient to God have now received mercy as a result of their disobedience, 31 so they too have now become disobedient in order that they too may now receive mercy as a result of God's mercy to you. 32 For God has bound everyone over to disobedience so that he may have mercy on them all.

245 In a very important sense, Satanism uncovers what the ethos of a particular society or societies have covered up through images, dogma, ethics, words and ideas - and it returns the individual to the primal chaos out of which opposites were formed. This uncovering gives the individual control, a conscious understanding and an awareness of their unique Destiny.   destiny

Matthew 16:24 Then Jesus said to his disciples, "Whoever wants to be my disciple must deny themselves and take up their cross and follow me. 25 For whoever wants to save their life will lose it, but whoever loses their life for me will find it.

Ephesians 2:10 For we are God's handiwork, created in Christ Jesus to do good works, which God prepared in advance for us to do.

Romans 8:28 And we know that in all things God works for the good of those who love him, who have been called according to his purpose. 29 For those God foreknew he also predestined to be conformed to the image of his Son, that he might be the firstborn among many brothers and sisters.

John 16:33 "I have told you these things, so that in me you may have peace. In this world you will have trouble. But take heart! I have overcome the world."

Psalm 139:2 You know when I sit and when I rise; you perceive my thoughts from afar. 3 You

discern my going out and my lying down; you are familiar with all my ways. 4 Before a word is on my tongue you, LORD, know it completely.

Isaiah 55:11 so is my word that goes out from my mouth: It will not return to me empty, but will accomplish what I desire and achieve the purpose for which I sent it.

Jeremiah 29:11 For I know the plans I have for you," declares the Lord, "plans to prosper you and not to harm you, plans to give you hope and a future. 12 Then you will call on me and come and pray to me, and I will listen to you. 13 You will seek me and find me when you seek me with all your heart. 14 I will be found by you," declares the Lord, "and will bring you back from captivity. I will gather you from all the nations and places where I have banished you," declares the Lord, "and will bring you back to the place from which I carried you into exile."

29- Satanism And Satanic Influence

246 First, let us consider what Satanism is not. It is not an acceptance of conventional morality or ways of living; it is not a belief, or a faith, which causes a rejection of the reality (and harshness) of life; it is not a refuge for the failures, the cowards and the weak. Satanism is about pride, an acceptance of individual worth.   pride

Romans 11:18 do not consider yourself to be superior to those other branches. If you do, consider this: You do not support the root, but the root supports you. 19 You will say then, "Branches were broken off so that I could be grafted in." 20 Granted. But they were broken off because of unbelief, and you stand by faith. Do not be arrogant, but tremble.

James 4:6 But he gives us more grace. That is why Scripture says: "God opposes the proud but shows favor to the humble."

1 John 2:16 For everything in the world—the lust of the flesh, the lust of the eyes, and the pride of life—comes not from the Father but from the world.

Deuteronomy 8:2 Remember how the Lord

your God led you all the way in the wilderness these forty years, to humble and test you in order to know what was in your heart, whether or not you would keep his commands. 3 He humbled you, causing you to hunger and then feeding you with manna, which neither you nor your ancestors had known, to teach you that man does not live on bread alone but on every word that comes from the mouth of the Lord.

Proverbs 11:2 When pride comes, then comes disgrace, but with humility comes wisdom.

Psalm 75:4 To the arrogant I say, 'Boast no more,' and to the wicked, 'Do not lift up your horns.

Jeremiah 9:23 This is what the LORD says: "Let not the wise boast of their wisdom or the strong boast of their strength or the rich boast of their riches, 24 but let the one who boasts boast about this: that they have the understanding to know me, that I am the LORD, who exercises kindness, justice and righteousness on earth, for in these I delight," declares the LORD.

247 The chief contributions of the ONA, toward an tarot understanding of Satanism in particular, and the Occult in general, may be briefly described ... The creation of a Sinister Tarot whose images are Sinister, and thus imbued with Satanic energy.

Matthew 7:15 "Watch out for false prophets. They come to you in sheep's clothing, but inwardly they are ferocious wolves. 16 By their fruit you will recognize them. Do people pick grapes from thornbushes, or figs from thistles? 17 Likewise, every good tree bears good fruit, but a bad tree bears bad fruit. 18 A good tree cannot bear bad fruit, and a bad tree cannot bear good fruit. 19 Every tree that does not bear good fruit is cut down and thrown into the fire. 20 Thus, by their fruit you will recognize them.

Deuteronomy 18:9 When you enter the land the Lord your God is giving you, do not learn to imitate the detestable ways of the nations there. 10 Let no one be found among you who sacrifices their son or daughter in the fire, who practices divination or sorcery, interprets omens, engages in witchcraft, 11 or casts spells, or who is a medium or spiritist or who consults the dead. 12 Anyone who does these things is detestable to the Lord; because of these same detestable practices the Lord your God will drive out those nations before you.

248   The chief contributions of the ONA, toward an understanding of Satanism in particular, and the Occult in general, may be briefly described ... Bringing an awareness of the Dark Gods - of the Sinister energies/forces which exist and which have been symbolized by 'Satan'/the Devil...
      occult energies

Colossians 1:9 For this reason, since the day we heard about you, we have not stopped praying for you. We continually ask God to fill you with the knowledge of his will through all the wisdom and understanding that the Spirit gives, 10 so that you may live a life worthy of the Lord and please him in every way: bearing fruit in every good work, growing in the knowledge of God, 11 being strengthened with all power according to his glorious might so that you may have great endurance and patience, 12 and giving joyful thanks to the Father, who has qualified you[b] to share in the inheritance of his holy people in the kingdom of light.

Ephesians 6:10 Finally, be strong in the Lord and in his mighty power. 11 Put on the full armor of God, so that you can take your stand against the devil's schemes. 12 For our struggle is not against flesh and blood, but against the rulers, against the authorities, against the powers of this dark world and against the spiritual forces of evil in the heavenly realms. 13 Therefore put on the full armor of God, so that when the day of evil comes, you may be able to stand your ground, and after you have done everything, to stand. 14 Stand firm then, with the belt of truth buckled around your waist, with the breastplate of righteousness in place, 15 and with your feet fitted with the readiness that comes from the gospel of peace. 16 In addition to all this, take up the shield of faith, with which you can extinguish all the flaming arrows of the evil one. 17 Take the helmet of salvation and the sword of the Spirit, which is the word of God.

Isaiah 40:28 Do you not know? Have you not heard? The LORD is the everlasting God, the Creator of the ends of the earth. He will not grow tired or weary, and his understanding no one can fathom. 29 He gives strength to the weary and increases the power of the weak. 30 Even youths grow tired and weary, and young men stumble and fall; 31 but those who hope in the LORD will renew their strength. They will soar on wings like eagles; they will run and not grow weary, they will walk and not be faint.

249 The chief contributions of the ONA, toward an understanding of Satanism in particular, and the Occult in general, may be briefly described ... An emphasis of the personal qualities - the character - of a Satanist, enshrined in the concepts of Excellence, Honour and the motto "die, rather than submit to anyone or anything".   excellence submission

James 4:7 Submit yourselves, then, to God. Resist the devil, and he will flee from you. 8 Come near to God and he will come near to you. Wash your hands, you sinners, and purify your hearts, you double-minded. 9 Grieve, mourn and wail. Change your laughter to mourning and your joy to gloom. 10 Humble yourselves before the Lord, and he will lift you up.

1 Peter 5:6 Humble yourselves, therefore, under God's mighty hand, that he may lift you up in due time. 7 Cast all your anxiety on him because he cares for you. 8 Be alert and of sober mind. Your enemy the devil prowls around like a roaring lion looking for someone to devour. 9 Resist him, standing firm in the faith, because you know that the family of believers throughout the world is undergoing the same kind of sufferings. 10 And the God of all grace, who called you to his eternal glory in Christ, after you have suffered a little while, will himself restore you and make you strong, firm and steadfast.

Romans 12:1 Therefore, I urge you, brothers and sisters, in view of God's mercy, to offer your bodies as a living sacrifice, holy and pleasing to God—this is your true and proper worship. 2 Do not conform to the pattern of this world, but be transformed by the renewing of your mind. Then you will be able to test and approve what God's will is—his good, pleasing and perfect will.

Ephesians 5:21 Submit to one another out of reverence for Christ.

Proverbs 3:5 Trust in the LORD with all your heart and lean not on your own understanding; 6 in all your ways submit to him, and he will make your paths straight.

30. Makrokosmos

250	Satanic reasoning, and the judgment of a 'thing', derive from direct personal experience. Thus, for the Satanist, there can be no real understanding of something until that something is lived. Before then, understanding is merely academic, relying as it does on the validity of sources other than one's own experience.	knowledge

James 1:5 If any of you lacks wisdom, you should ask God, who gives generously to all without finding fault, and it will be given to you.

Isaiah 11:2 The Spirit of the LORD will rest on him— the Spirit of wisdom and of understanding, the Spirit of counsel and of might, the Spirit of the knowledge and fear of the LORD—

Proverbs 18:15 The heart of the discerning acquires knowledge, for the ears of the wise seek it out.

251	The development of Satanic reasoning is part of the purpose of the Insight Role (qv.). This	insight role

alchemical method is very hard, as it requires the Satanist to believe in their role - and convince other non-Satanists of their sincerity via practical acts [it is no use just editing a (for example) National-Socialist journal - or writing learned articles for existing journals]. The role usually brings an alienation of occult comrades; family; other friends - sometimes the loss of personal freedom. It severely tests, and thus develops - or destroys - character.

2 Timothy 3:12 In fact, everyone who wants to live a godly life in Christ Jesus will be persecuted, 13 while evildoers and impostors will go from bad to worse, deceiving and being deceived. 14 But as for you, continue in what you have learned and have become convinced of, because you know those from whom you learned it, 15 and how from infancy you have known the Holy Scriptures, which are able to make you wise for salvation through faith in Christ Jesus.

1 Peter 2:16 Live as free people, but do not use your freedom as a cover-up for evil; live as God's slaves. 17 Show proper respect to everyone, love the family of believers, fear God, honor the emperor. 18 Slaves, in reverent fear of God submit yourselves to your masters, not only to those who are good and considerate, but also to those who are harsh. 19 For it is commendable if someone bears up under the pain of unjust suffering because they are conscious of God. 20 But how is it to your credit if you receive a beating for doing wrong and endure it? But if you suffer for doing good and you endure it, this is commendable before God.

Matthew 23:27 "Woe to you, teachers of the law and Pharisees, you hypocrites! You are like whitewashed tombs, which look beautiful on the outside but on the inside are full of the bones of the dead and everything unclean. 28 In the same way, on the outside you appear to people as righteous but on the inside you are full of hypocrisy and wickedness.

252   An Insight Role thus creates a real understanding of Aeonics - an understanding beyond the self, and thus the cultivation of the faculty of Reason, and the glimmerings of genuine Wisdom. As stated, without this (arduous) experience, there is a staying where one is - despite whatever level of intellectual esoteric apprehension gained - centered around a mostly self-indulgent life-style. Essentially, without experiencing this bifurcation, the psyche will not be changed, thus preventing it from travelling towards those realms that separate the Initiate from the Adept.   *reasoning*

1 Peter 3:15 But in your hearts revere Christ as Lord. Always be prepared to give an answer to everyone who asks you to give the reason for the hope that you have. But do this with gentleness and respect, 16 keeping a clear conscience, so that those who speak maliciously against your good behavior in Christ may be ashamed of their slander. 17 For it is better, if it is God's will, to suffer for doing good than for doing evil.

Matthew 16:8 Aware of their discussion, Jesus asked, "You of little faith, why are you talking among yourselves about having no bread? 9 Do you still not understand? Don't you remember the five loaves for the five thousand, and how many basketfuls you gathered? 10 Or the seven loaves for the four thousand, and how many basketfuls you gathered? 11 How is it you don't understand that I was not talking to you about bread? But be on your guard against the yeast of the Pharisees and Sadducees." 12 Then they understood that he was not telling them to guard against the yeast used in bread, but against the teaching of the Pharisees and Sadducees.

Mark 2:6 Now some teachers of the law were sitting there, thinking to themselves, 7 "Why does this fellow talk like that? He's blaspheming! Who can forgive sins but God alone?" 8 Immediately Jesus knew in his spirit that this was what they were thinking in their hearts, and he said to them, "Why are you thinking these things? 9 Which is easier: to say to this paralyzed man, 'Your sins are forgiven,' or to say, 'Get up, take your mat and walk'? 10 But I want you to know that the Son of Man has authority on earth to forgive sins." So he said to the man, 11 "I tell you, get up, take your mat and go home." 12 He got up, took his mat and walked out in full view of them all. This amazed everyone and they praised God, saying, "We have never seen anything like this!"

32- Manipulation II

253 One of the fundamental principles of Black Magick is elitism: the belief that the majority are essentially beneath Initiates in terms of understanding, intelligence and ability. This gives the foundation for manipulation - both on the personal and the magickal level. The Black Magick novice is generally scornful of others - until and unless worth has been proved or shown.   elitism

Romans 2:8 But for those who are self-seeking and who reject the truth and follow evil, there will be wrath and anger. 9 There will be trouble and distress for every human being who does evil: first for the Jew, then for the Gentile; 10 but glory, honor and peace for everyone who does good: first for the Jew, then for the Gentile. 11 For God does not show favoritism.

Galatians 3:28 There is neither Jew nor Gentile, neither slave nor free, nor is there male and female, for you are all one in Christ Jesus.

John 13:16 Very truly I tell you, no servant is greater than his master, nor is a messenger greater than the one who sent him.

Leviticus 19:33 "'When a foreigner resides among you in your land, do not mistreat them. 34 The foreigner residing among you must be treated as your native-born. Love them as yourself, for you were foreigners in Egypt. I am the Lord your God.

Proverbs 22:2 Rich and poor have this in common: The Lord is the Maker of them all.

254 For a true Black Magickian is essentially a strong individualist who finds his or her own company preferable to that of others - unless those others can be useful in some way. That is, there is no dependence of any kind, particularly not emotional. on any other individual or individuals. This, of course, is what the novice strives to achieve. It cannot be achieved quickly - or even by "will" alone. Rather, it is a cumulative process - an alchemical change, a re-orientation of personality, and such changes take time.

individualism

Philippians 2:3 Do nothing out of selfish ambition or vain conceit. Rather, in humility value others above yourselves, 4 not looking to your own interests but each of you to the interests of the others.

Romans 12:3 For by the grace given me I say to every one of you: Do not think of yourself more highly than you ought, but rather think of yourself with sober judgment, in accordance with the faith God has distributed to each of you. 4 For just as each of us has one body with many members, and these members do not all have the same function, 5 so in Christ we, though many, form one body, and each member belongs to all the others.

1 Corinthians 12:27 Now you are the body of Christ, and each one of you is a part of it.

Romans 12:4 For just as each of us has one body with many members, and these members do not all have the same function, 5 so in Christ we, though many, form one body, and each member belongs to all the others. 6 We have different gifts, according to the grace given to each of us. If your gift is prophesying, then prophesy in accordance with your faith; 7 if it is serving, then serve; if it is teaching, then teach; 8 if it is to encourage, then give encouragement; if it is giving, then give generously; if it is to lead, do it diligently; if it is to show mercy, do it cheerfully.

255 The arrogence of the Black Magickian is not an empty one: it is not a posturing. Instead, it arises from within: from the knowledge and insight the novice has gained into him/her self - by having achieved in both the personal and magickal sense. Thus the magickal and practical goals which are set for novices - they develop self-assurance, a pride and that arrogence which is truly Satanic.

arrogance

James 3:13 Who is wise and understanding among you? Let them show it by their good life, by deeds done in the humility that comes from wisdom. 14 But if you harbor bitter envy and selfish ambition in your hearts, do not boast about it or deny the truth. 15 Such "wisdom" does not come down from heaven but is earthly, unspiritual, demonic. 16 For where you have envy and selfish ambition, there you find disorder and every evil practice.

1 Peter 5:5 In the same way, you who are younger, submit yourselves to your elders. All of you, clothe yourselves with humility toward one another, because, "God opposes the proud but shows favor to the humble." 6 Humble yourselves, therefore, under God's mighty hand, that he may lift you up in due time.

1 Samuel 15:23 For rebellion is like the sin of divination, and arrogance like the evil of idolatry. Because you have rejected the word of the Lord, he has rejected you as king."

Psalm 73:6 Therefore pride is their necklace; they clothe themselves with violence. 7 From their callous hearts comes iniquity; their evil imaginations have no limits. 8 They scoff, and speak with malice; with arrogance they threaten oppression. 9 Their mouths lay claim to heaven, and their tongues take possession of the earth.

Isaiah 14:12 How you have fallen from heaven, morning star, son of the dawn! You have been cast down to the earth, you who once laid low the nations! 13 You said in your heart, "I will ascend to the heavens; I will raise my throne above the stars of God; I will sit enthroned on the mount of assembly, on the utmost heights of Mount Zaphon. 14 I will ascend above the tops of the clouds; I will make myself like the Most High." 15 But you are brought down to the realm of the dead, to the depths of the pit.

34- The Morality Of Satanism

256 The essence of satanic morality - insofar as the individual Satanist is concerned - can be simply expressed: a Satanist makes an assessment of others, judging them, and then decides whether those others, on an individual basis, are suitable victims. If they are suitable, as victims, then the Satanist acts accordingly - e.g. by manipulating them, using them and so on. The judgement is based on character - i.e. does the person who is being judged possess a weak character? Are they dross, worthless? If they are judged to be so, by the individual Satanist, then they are suitable subjects.

Satanic morality

Matthew 7:1 "Do not judge, or you too will be judged. 2 For in the same way you judge others, you will be judged, and with the measure you use, it will be measured to you. 3 "Why do you look at the speck of sawdust in your brother's eye and pay no attention to the plank in your own eye? 4 How can you say to your brother, 'Let me take the speck out of your eye,' when all the time there is a plank in your own eye? 5 You hypocrite, first take the plank out of your own eye, and then you will see clearly to remove the speck from your brother's eye.

Luke 6:37 "Do not judge, and you will not be judged. Do not condemn, and you will not be condemned. Forgive, and you will be forgiven. 38 Give, and it will be given to you. A good measure, pressed down, shaken together and running over, will be poured into your lap. For with the measure you use, it will be measured to you."

Luke 6:35 But love your enemies, do good to them, and lend to them without expecting to get anything back. Then your reward will be great, and you will be children of the Most High, because he is kind to the ungrateful and wicked. 36 Be merciful, just as your Father is merciful.

Proverbs 31:9 Speak up and judge fairly; defend the rights of the poor and needy.

35- Notes On Study And Practice In Modern Satanism

257   Satanic practice in the real world would arise from (a) forming and running a Satanic Temple; and (b) undertaking Insight Roles and other Satanic tasks. Aside from a specific Insight Role, which the novice would choose, they would undertake the various physical challenges required [qv. the MS 'Adeptship - Its Real Meaning and Significance', for example] and strive to increase their experience by living Satanically in a way which aided the sinister dialectic.   *self-insight*

Matthew 16:24 Then Jesus said to his disciples, "Whoever wants to be my disciple must deny themselves and take up their cross and follow me. 25 For whoever wants to save their life will lose it, but whoever loses their life for me will find it.

Galatians 2:20 I have been crucified with Christ and I no longer live, but Christ lives in me. The life I now live in the body, I live by faith in the Son of God, who loved me and gave himself for me.

John 8:34 Jesus replied, "Very truly I tell you, everyone who sins is a slave to sin. 35 Now a slave has no permanent place in the family, but a son belongs to it forever. 36 So if the Son sets you free, you will be free indeed. 37 I know that you are Abraham's descendants. Yet you are looking for a way to kill me, because you have no room for my word. 38 I am telling you what I have seen in the Father's presence, and you are doing what you have heard from your father."

258   One of the tasks might be to plan and undertake a culling.   *culling*

1 John 3:11 For this is the message you heard

from the beginning: We should love one another. 12 Do not be like Cain, who belonged to the evil one and murdered his brother. And why did he murder him? Because his own actions were evil and his brother's were righteous.

Romans 12:19 Do not take revenge, my dear friends, but leave room for God's wrath, for it is written: "It is mine to avenge; I will repay," says the Lord.

Ezekiel 33:8 When I say to the wicked, 'You wicked person, you will surely die,' and you do not speak out to dissuade them from their ways, that wicked person will die for their sin, and I will hold you accountable for their blood. 9 But if you do warn the wicked person to turn from their ways and they do not do so, they will die for their sin, though you yourself will be saved.

259 Another might be to aid Heretical forms by, for example, becoming involved with an extremist group which seeks the destruction of 'the System' and whose principles and aims are in accord with the Satanic ethos and whose actions aid the sinister dialectic.   rebellion authority

Romans 13:1 Let everyone be subject to the governing authorities, for there is no authority except that which God has established. The authorities that exist have been established by God. 2 Consequently, whoever rebels against the authority is rebelling against what God has instituted, and those who do so will bring judgment on themselves.

Matthew 22:19 Show me the coin used for paying the tax." They brought him a denarius, 20 and he asked them, "Whose image is this? And whose inscription?" 21 "Caesar's," they replied. Then he said to them, "So give back to Caesar what is Caesar's, and to God what is God's."

Ephesians 6:5 Slaves, obey your earthly masters with respect and fear, and with sincerity of heart, just as you would obey Christ.

1 Peter 2:13 Submit yourselves for the Lord's sake to every human authority: whether to the emperor, as the supreme authority, 14 or to governors, who are sent by him to punish those who do wrong and to commend those who do right. 15 For it is God's will that by doing good you should silence the ignorant talk of foolish people. 16 Live as free people, but do not use your freedom as a cover-up for evil; live as God's slaves. 17 Show proper respect to everyone, love the family of believers, fear God, honor the emperor.

260 Another might be to undermine present structures by fostering their decline - e.g. dealing in drugs.   drug dealing

1 Peter 5:8 Be alert and of sober mind. Your enemy the devil prowls around like a roaring lion looking for someone to devour.

1 Corinthians 5:11 But now I am writing to you that you must not associate with anyone who claims to be a brother or sister but is sexually immoral or greedy, an idolater or slanderer, a drunkard or swindler. Do not even eat with such people.

1 Corinthians 6:19 Do you not know that your bodies are temples of the Holy Spirit, who is in you, whom you have received from God? You are not your own; 20 you were bought at a price. Therefore honor God with your bodies.

36. The Satanic Way Of Living

261 The way of living that a Satanist undertakes is one which allows an exultation - an affirmation of individual existence. This way is an intentional one - that is, a conscious striving to achieve something, to excel, to experience and learn and discover. Furthermore, the Satanist makes his or her own rules as they progress. That is, they rely on their own judgement, their own instinct.   individualism

Romans 12:3 For by the grace given me I say to every one of you: Do not think of yourself more highly than you ought, but rather think of yourself with sober judgment, in accordance

with the faith God has distributed to each of you. 4 For just as each of us has one body with many members, and these members do not all have the same function, 5 so in Christ we, though many, form one body, and each member belongs to all the others.

1 Corinthians 12:8 To one there is given through the Spirit a message of wisdom, to another a message of knowledge by means of the same Spirit, 9 to another faith by the same Spirit, to another gifts of healing by that one Spirit, 10 to another miraculous powers, to another prophecy, to another distinguishing between spirits, to another speaking in different kinds of tongues, and to still another the interpretation of tongues. 11 All these are the work of one and the same Spirit, and he distributes them to each one, just as he determines.

1 Peter 4:10 Each of you should use whatever gift you have received to serve others, as faithful stewards of God's grace in its various forms.

Philippians 2:3 Do nothing out of selfish ambition or vain conceit. Rather, in humility value others above yourselves, 4 not looking to your own interests but each of you to the interests of the others. 5 In your relationships with one another, have the same mindset as Christ Jesus: 6 Who, being in very nature God, did not consider equality with God something to be used to his own advantage; 7 rather, he made himself nothing by taking the very nature of a servant, being made in human likeness.

37- Thernn - An Introduction To Natural Septenary Magick

262 "Magick" on the individual level is, quite simply, the attainment of conscious integration with natural forces - or with "Nature", and the Cosmos that is beyond. This integration implies a loss of the "self-image", and a gradual expansion of consciousness into the acausal realms. There is thus achieved a natural balance

acausal
spirit

within living, and the cultivation of a more noble, higher type of human being

Ephesians 6:12 For our struggle is not against flesh and blood, but against the rulers, against the authorities, against the powers of this dark world and against the spiritual forces of evil in the heavenly realms.

Matthew 6:19 "Do not store up for yourselves treasures on earth, where moths and vermin destroy, and where thieves break in and steal. 20 But store up for yourselves treasures in heaven, where moths and vermin do not destroy, and where thieves do not break in and steal. 21 For where your treasure is, there your heart will be also.

Galatians 5:16 So I say, walk by the Spirit, and you will not gratify the desires of the flesh. 17 For the flesh desires what is contrary to the Spirit, and the Spirit what is contrary to the flesh. They are in conflict with each other, so that you are not to do whatever you want. 18 But if you are led by the Spirit, you are not under the law. 19 The acts of the flesh are obvious: sexual immorality, impurity and debauchery; 20 idolatry and witchcraft; hatred, discord, jealousy, fits of rage, selfish ambition, dissensions, factions 21 and envy; drunkenness, orgies, and the like. I warn you, as I did before, that those who live like this will not inherit the kingdom of God.

263 Dark Gods: These are 'living' entities which exist in an acausal space-time. They may be likened to "antimatter" as against the "matter" which exists in our causal space-time - thus, their intrusion into the causal, disrupts. This disruption is primarily psychic because the psyche of an individual by its nature intrudes or is a part of the acausal. The entities can assume physical forms, but only briefly ~ and then only when a nexion is fully opened. And where the causal and acausal intersect on Earth.   *dark gods*
antimatter

Matthew 12:43 "When an impure spirit comes

out of a person, it goes through arid places seeking rest and does not find it. 44 Then it says, 'I will return to the house I left.' When it arrives, it finds the house unoccupied, swept clean and put in order. 45 Then it goes and takes with it seven other spirits more wicked than itself, and they go in and live there. And the final condition of that person is worse than the first. That is how it will be with this wicked generation."

2 Peter 2:4 For if God did not spare angels when they sinned, but sent them to hell, putting them in chains of darkness[b] to be held for judgment; 5 if he did not spare the ancient world when he brought the flood on its ungodly people, but protected Noah, a preacher of righteousness, and seven others; 6 if he condemned the cities of Sodom and Gomorrah by burning them to ashes, and made them an example of what is going to happen to the ungodly; 7 and if he rescued Lot, a righteous man, who was distressed by the depraved conduct of the lawless 8 (for that righteous man, living among them day after day, was tormented in his righteous soul by the lawless deeds he saw and heard)— 9 if this is so, then the Lord knows how to rescue the godly from trials and to hold the unrighteous for punishment on the day of judgment.

264   As far as Adepts of the sinister tradition are concerned, there are only two realistic options: the creation of Imperium [the fulfilment of Western wyrd via a practical form], or disruption of existing forms with the aim of undermining and destroying Nazarene/ Magian influence, leading to chaos from which a New Aeon will emerge, this Aeon being Satanic. The latter involves the 'pruning' of unnecessary elements on a large scale - the creation of an elite capable of making the Aeon a reality.   anti-Christian

2 Thessalonians 2:3 Don't let anyone deceive you in any way, for that day will not come until the rebellion occurs and the man of lawlessness

*is revealed, the man doomed to destruction. 4
He will oppose and will exalt himself over
everything that is called God or is worshiped,
so that he sets himself up in God's temple,
proclaiming himself to be God. 5 Don't you
remember that when I was with you I used to
tell you these things? 6 And now you know what
is holding him back, so that he may be revealed
at the proper time. 7 For the secret power of
lawlessness is already at work; but the one who
now holds it back will continue to do so till he is
taken out of the way. 8 And then the lawless one
will be revealed, whom the Lord Jesus will
overthrow with the breath of his mouth and
destroy by the splendor of his coming. 9 The
coming of the lawless one will be in accordance
with how Satan works. He will use all sorts of
displays of power through signs and wonders
that serve the lie, 10 and all the ways that
wickedness deceives those who are perishing.
They perish because they refused to love the
truth and so be saved. 11 For this reason God
sends them a powerful delusion so that they will
believe the lie 12 and so that all will be
condemned who have not believed the truth but
have delighted in wickedness.*

52 Adeptship - Its Real Meaning And Significance

265 An Adept is an individual who has undertaken an Occult quest and who has, as a result of that quest, the following abilities/attributes: a) a real understanding of esoteric, Occult matters, and a deep esoteric knowledge/insight; b) esoteric skills - chief of which is empathy: with both natural and 'Occult' forces/energies. An important aspect of this empathy [an intuitive understanding of things as those things are in their essence] is with living beings and that species mis-named Homo Sapiens Sapiens; c) a unique character - formed via experience; d) a unique 'philosophy of life' attained via self-discovery and self-experience ~ by finding answers unaided.

adept
empathy

Matthew 16:1 The Pharisees and Sadducees came to Jesus and tested him by asking him to show them a sign from heaven. 2 He replied, "When evening comes, you say, 'It will be fair weather, for the sky is red,' 3 and in the morning, 'Today it will be stormy, for the sky is red and overcast.' You know how to interpret the appearance of the sky, but you cannot interpret the signs of the times.

1 Peter 3:8 Finally, all of you, be like-minded, be sympathetic, love one another, be compassionate and humble.

Colossians 3:12 Therefore, as God's chosen people, holy and dearly loved, clothe yourselves with compassion, kindness, humility, gentleness and patience.

Proverbs 14:31 Whoever oppresses the poor shows contempt for their Maker, but whoever is kind to the needy honors God.

266   Adeptship results from a transformation - a transmutation of the individual. This begins at Initiation, whether that be ceremonial or hermetic [i.e. as part of a group or alone]. It is an internal alchemical process of change and occurs on all levels - the psychic, the magickal, the intellectual, the psychological and the physical. It is the birth of a new individual who has skills, knowledge, understanding and judgement not possessed by the majority.   *transmutation*

Ephesians 4:22 You were taught, with regard to your former way of life, to put off your old self, which is being corrupted by its deceitful desires; 23 to be made new in the attitude of your minds; 24 and to put on the new self, created to be like God in true righteousness and holiness.

2 Corinthians 5:17 Therefore, if anyone is in Christ, the new creation has come: The old has gone, the new is here!

1 John 5:4 for everyone born of God overcomes the world. This is the victory that has overcome the world, even our faith.

1 Peter 2:2 Like newborn babies, crave pure

spiritual milk, so that by it you may grow up in your salvation, 3 now that you have tasted that the Lord is good. 4 As you come to him, the living Stone—rejected by humans but chosen by God and precious to him— 5 you also, like living stones, are being built into a spiritual house to be a holy priesthood, offering spiritual sacrifices acceptable to God through Jesus Christ.

56 Way The Means. The End

267 The Aim of the Seven-Fold Way is Enlightenment. This is a wisdom, an understanding, and a new way of being. It is an apprehension of what IS, as against what Appears-To-Be, and it is also a practical living in the world in a manner which changes the world. Enlightenment is beyond the duality of Good and Evil - beyond the Light and the Dark. It is beyond the conventional words used to express understanding.

enlightenment

Hebrews 6:4 It is impossible for those who have once been enlightened, who have tasted the heavenly gift, who have shared in the Holy Spirit, 5 who have tasted the goodness of the word of God and the powers of the coming age 6 and who have fallen away, to be brought back to repentance. To their loss they are crucifying the Son of God all over again and subjecting him to public disgrace.

Ephesians 1:18 I pray that the eyes of your heart may be enlightened in order that you may know the hope to which he has called you, the riches of his glorious inheritance in his holy people, 19 and his incomparably great power for us who believe. That power is the same as the mighty strength 20 he exerted when he raised Christ from the dead and seated him at his right hand in the heavenly realms, 21 far above all rule and authority, power and dominion, and every name that is invoked, not only in the present age but also in the one to come.

2 Corinthians 4:6 For God, who said, "Let

light shine out of darkness," made his light shine in our hearts to give us the light of the knowledge of God's glory displayed in the face of Christ.

268 60. A Gift For The Prince (A Guide To Human Sacrifice)

A Satanist revels in life because by living life in a joyful, ecstatic way, the acausal that exists within us all by virtue of our being, is strengthened. For Satanists, not only the manner of living is important, but also the manner of death. We must live well and die at the right time, proud and defiant to the end - not waiting sickly and weak. The scum of the Earth wail and tremble as they face Death: we stand laughing and spit with contempt. Thus do we learn how to live.

death

John 11:25 Jesus said to her, "I am the resurrection and the life. The one who believes in me will live, even though they die; 26 and whoever lives by believing in me will never die. Do you believe this?" 27 "Yes, Lord," she replied, "I believe that you are the Messiah, the Son of God, who is to come into the world.

John 14:1 "Do not let your hearts be troubled. You believe in God; believe also in me. 2 My Father's house has many rooms; if that were not so, would I have told you that I am going there to prepare a place for you? 3 And if I go and prepare a place for you, I will come back and take you to be with me that you also may be where I am. 4 You know the way to the place where I am going."

2 Corinthians 4:14 because we know that the one who raised the Lord Jesus from the dead will also raise us with Jesus and present us with you to himself.

62 The Abyss

269 The Abyss is where the causal and the acausal meet: a nexus of temporal and spatial dimensions. Because of the nature of our consciousness, the Abyss lies latent within all of us - that is, our consciousness consists of both

soul

causal and acausal aspects. In this sense, we are all 'Gates'/ to the acausal dimensions, although this Gate - and the pathways leading to/from it - often lies undiscovered. Magickal training is essentially the discovery, exploration and use of these pathways.

Matthew 16:26 What good will it be for someone to gain the whole world, yet forfeit their soul? Or what can anyone give in exchange for their soul?

Matthew 10:28 Do not be afraid of those who kill the body but cannot kill the soul. Rather, be afraid of the One who can destroy both soul and body in hell.

Hebrews 4:12 For the word of God is alive and active. Sharper than any double-edged sword, it penetrates even to dividing soul and spirit, joints and marrow; it judges the thoughts and attitudes of the heart.

64. In Praise Of War

War is necessary - it ensures the health of a people and it encourages those warrior virtues which are essential to civilization. When a people, nation or race goes for decades without engaging in a war which involves all or most of the communities of that people, nation or race, then that people, nation or race tends toward decadence - with cowardly scum coming to the surface, the young becoming feckless and undisciplined, and society generally declining. War breeds and reveals character - in combat, there is no where to hide.

Matthew 5:9 Blessed are the peacemakers, for they will be called children of God. 10 Blessed are those who are persecuted because of righteousness, for theirs is the kingdom of heaven. 11 "Blessed are you when people insult you, persecute you and falsely say all kinds of evil against you because of me. 12 Rejoice and be glad, because great is your reward in heaven, for in the same way they persecuted the prophets who were before you.

Matthew 26:52 "Put your sword back in its

place," Jesus said to him, "for all who draw the sword will die by the sword.

Ephesians 6:11 Put on the full armor of God, so that you can take your stand against the devil's schemes.

Micah 7:8 Do not gloat over me, my enemy! Though I have fallen, I will rise. Though I sit in darkness, the LORD will be my light.

271   For too long, the pacifists, the cowards, the decadent and the pursuers of selfish, material goals, have been unchallenged. We who believe in war - who know its value and its purpose - have been silent for too long. We need to once again proudly and defiantly sing the praises of war!   pacifism

Matthew 5:39 But I tell you, do not resist an evil person. If anyone slaps you on the right cheek, turn to them the other cheek also. 40 And if anyone wants to sue you and take your shirt, hand over your coat as well. 41 If anyone forces you to go one mile, go with them two miles. 42 Give to the one who asks you, and do not turn away from the one who wants to borrow from you. 43 "You have heard that it was said, 'Love your neighbor and hate your enemy.' 44 But I tell you, love your enemies and pray for those who persecute you, 45 that you may be children of your Father in heaven. He causes his sun to rise on the evil and the good, and sends rain on the righteous and the unrighteous.

1 Peter 3:9 Do not repay evil with evil or insult with insult. On the contrary, repay evil with blessing, because to this you were called so that you may inherit a blessing.

John 14:27 Peace I leave with you; my peace I give you. I do not give to you as the world gives. Do not let your hearts be troubled and do not be afraid.

65 To Presence The Dark

272   If this means killing, wars, suffering, sacrifice, terror, disease. tragedy and disruption, then such things must be - for it is one of the duties of a Satanic Initiate to so presence the dark, and   presencing the dark

prepare the way for, or initiate, the change and evolution which always result from such things. Such things as these must be, and always will be, because the majority of people are or will remain, inert and sub-human unless changed.

1 John 5:19 We know that we are children of God, and that the whole world is under the control of the evil one.

Isaiah 32:6 For fools speak folly, their hearts are bent on evil: They practice ungodliness and spread error concerning the LORD; the hungry they leave empty and from the thirsty they withhold water.

66. Culling

273 As has been written - opfers are human culling in action. That is, Satanic sacrifice makes a contribution to improving the human stock: removing the worthless, the weak, the diseased (in terms of character). Naturally, this culling occurs on a somewhat larger scale by using magickal means to direct / influence / control events in real time (i.e. in the causal) and so produce historical change [war / strife / struggle / revolution and so on] than it does by choosing a specific opfer and executing an act of sacrifice.   culling

2 Corinthians 12:9 But he said to me, "My grace is sufficient for you, for my power is made perfect in weakness." Therefore I will boast all the more gladly about my weaknesses, so that Christ's power may rest on me.

Isaiah 40:29 He gives strength to the weary and increases the power of the weak.

Psalm 10:2 In his arrogance the wicked man hunts down the weak, who are caught in the schemes he devises.

71 Victims - A Sinister Expose

274 It should be understood that all acts undertaken by a Satanic novice to gain experience are perpetrated/done against those (the victims) whose character has been revealed to be or shown to be, by their deeds, defective. This character is judged from a Satanic perspective.   victimization

The actions of a Satanic novice in the real world, arise as a consequence of that novice following, at the time of a particular act, a particular stage of the Satanic way to Adeptship and beyond. Thus, each act has a purpose and an intent which are beyond the moment(s) of that act. The purpose is to achieve experience (and consequently that maturity of character which experience brings), and the intent is Satanic

Matthew 18:6 "If anyone causes one of these little ones—those who believe in me—to stumble, it would be better for them to have a large millstone hung around their neck and to be drowned in the depths of the sea.

1 Peter 5:8 Be alert and of sober mind. Your enemy the devil prowls around like a roaring lion looking for someone to devour. 9 Resist him, standing firm in the faith, because you know that the family of believers throughout the world is undergoing the same kind of sufferings.

1 John 2:16 For everything in the world—the lust of the flesh, the lust of the eyes, and the pride of life—comes not from the Father but from the world.

72 Revenge

275 Any healthy flourishing society not only allows revenge, but encourages it, and any society which does not is already a form of tyranny, however much clever, vapid, intellectual and political words may be used to try and obscure this reality. A healthy society is one that tends to respect the individual right to justice and thus revenge   vengeance

Romans 12:19 Do not take revenge, my dear friends, but leave room for God's wrath, for it is written: "It is mine to avenge; I will repay," says the Lord.

Hebrews 10:30 For we know him who said, "It is mine to avenge; I will repay," and again, "The Lord will judge his people."

Romans 12:19 Do not take revenge, my dear friends, but leave room for God's wrath, for it is

written: "It is mine to avenge; I will repay," says the Lord. 20 On the contrary: "If your enemy is hungry, feed him; if he is thirsty, give him something to drink. In doing this, you will heap burning coals on his head." 21 Do not be overcome by evil, but overcome evil with good.

82* The Creative Dialectic, Aeonic Strategy and National-Socialism

276 There are only two possibilities in respect of the immediate future: (1) The triumph of the Zionist, with the creation of world-wide repressive, multiracial and "politically correct" Police-States, which are Marxist in all but name, since the term "politically correct" has become a euphemism for "Marxism by stealth". (2) The triumph of National-Socialism, with the gradual spread of the ethnic and evolutionary ideals of National-Socialism leading to the creation of ethnic States. A new civilization would arise, created by a new race of higher beings forged from the anvil of struggle, with numinous goals striven for. Gradually, the civilization would spread outward, from the Earth, and on toward the stars, with star-systems discovered and planets colonized. The promise of our own race, and our own species, would be fulfilled.

Marxism
National socialism

Romans 13:1 Let everyone be subject to the governing authorities, for there is no authority except that which God has established. The authorities that exist have been established by God. 2 Consequently, whoever rebels against the authority is rebelling against what God has instituted, and those who do so will bring judgment on themselves. 3 For rulers hold no terror for those who do right, but for those who do wrong. Do you want to be free from fear of the one in authority? Then do what is right and you will be commended. 4 For the one in authority is God's servant for your good. But if you do wrong, be afraid, for rulers do not bear the sword for no reason. They are God's servants, agents of wrath to bring punishment on the wrongdoer. 5 Therefore, it is necessary to submit to the authorities, not only because of possible punishment but also as a matter of conscience. 6 This is also why you pay taxes, for the authorities are God's servants, who give their full time to governing. 7 Give to everyone what you owe them: If you owe taxes, pay taxes; if revenue, then revenue; if respect, then respect; if honor, then honor.

1 Thessalonians 5:14 And we urge you, brothers and sisters, warn those who are idle and disruptive, encourage the disheartened, help the weak, be patient with everyone.

Galatians 6:2 Carry each other's burdens, and in this way you will fulfill the law of Christ.

1 Peter 2:13 Submit yourselves for the Lord's sake to every human authority: whether to the emperor, as the supreme authority, 14 or to governors, who are sent by him to punish those who do wrong and to commend those who do right. 15 For it is God's will that by doing good you should silence the ignorant talk of foolish people. 16 Live as free people, but do not use your freedom as a cover-up for evil; live as God's slaves. 17 Show proper respect to everyone, love the family of believers, fear God, honor the emperor.

85 Aeonics And Manipulation II

277 That this is so seldom understood, today, is evident of how few really understand: of how precious wisdom still is. Further, the fact that the above statements re guarding National-Socialist Germany are heresy (in the literal sense) today, explicates the distortion that has occurred in the Faustian civilization far better than dozens of words. This ethos, exoterically, Satanic. That is, the true ethos of the West enshrines a Satanic view of the world - a pa g an joy in conquest, experience, living , in seeking and going beyond limits, physically and intellectually. The morbidity of the Nazarene has undermined all this distorted it. in essence, therefore, a Faustian Imperium would have been

evolution
Nazism

180

a type of Satanic State on Earth: a fulfilment of the first part of the sinister dialectic of history, and would have made possible the next part or stag e, that of a Galactic Empire. It would be during this later stage that another goal would have been achieved - a genuine evolution in consciousness

1 Corinthians 12:13 For we were all baptized by one Spirit so as to form one body—whether Jews or Gentiles, slave or free—and we were all given the one Spirit to drink.

Romans 9:3 For I could wish that I myself were cursed and cut off from Christ for the sake of my people, those of my own race, 4 the people of Israel. Theirs is the adoption to sonship; theirs the divine glory, the covenants, the receiving of the law, the temple worship and the promises. 5 Theirs are the patriarchs, and from them is traced the human ancestry of the Messiah, who is God over all, forever praised! Amen.

Romans 9:4 the people of Israel. Theirs is the adoption to sonship; theirs the divine glory, the covenants, the receiving of the law, the temple worship and the promises.

Ezekiel 36:24 " 'For I will take you out of the nations; I will gather you from all the countries and bring you back into your own land. 25 I will sprinkle clean water on you, and you will be clean; I will cleanse you from all your impurities and from all your idols. 26 I will give you a new heart and put a new spirit in you; I will remove from you your heart of stone and give you a heart of flesh. 27 And I will put my Spirit in you and move you to follow my decrees and be careful to keep my laws.

98. Aeonic Insight Roles

278　The following are suggested Aeonic Insight Roles, based on a knowledge of the sinister dialectic and the situation as exists at the time of writing (114yf). Some of these suggested Insight Roles are relatively easy; some are especially hard and dangerous, and thus suited

insight roles
aeonic

only to the most daring and sinister individuals. (1) Join or form a covert insurrectionary organization, dedicated to National Socialism, whose aim is to undermine by practical means the status quo and which uses the strategy and tactics outlined in The Strategy and Tactics of Revolution (Parts I and II) (2) Undertake the role of assassin, selecting as your opfers those who publicly support or aid, ZOG, the NWO, The System. (3) Convert to Islam and aid, through words, or deeds, or both, those undertaking Jihad against Zionism and the NWO. (4) Join or form an active anarchist organization or group dedicated to fighting the capitalist System. (5) Join or form a National Socialist group or organization, and aid that organization and especially aid and propagate "historical revisionism".

John 3:16 For God so loved the world that he gave his one and only Son, that whoever believes in him shall not perish but have eternal life.

John 5:24 "Very truly I tell you, whoever hears my word and believes him who sent me has eternal life and will not be judged but has crossed over from death to life.

Galatians 6:8 Whoever sows to please their flesh, from the flesh will reap destruction; whoever sows to please the Spirit, from the Spirit will reap eternal life.

1 John 5:20 We know also that the Son of God has come and has given us understanding, so that we may know him who is true. And we are in him who is true by being in his Son Jesus Christ. He is the true God and eternal life.

The Satanic Bible
Prelude

1 Called "The Black Pope" by many of his followers, Anton LaVey began the road to High Priesthood of the Church of Satan when he was

carnal nature

only 16 years old and an organ player in a carnival: "I knew then that the Christian Church thrives on hypocrisy, and that man's carnal nature will out!"

Romans 8:6 The mind governed by the flesh is death, but the mind governed by the Spirit is life and peace. 7 The mind governed by the flesh is hostile to God; it does not submit to God's law, nor can it do so. 8 Those who are in the realm of the flesh cannot please God.

1 Corinthians 2:14 The person without the Spirit does not accept the things that come from the Spirit of God but considers them foolishness, and cannot understand them because they are discerned only through the Spirit.

Galatians 5:16 So I say, walk by the Spirit, and you will not gratify the desires of the flesh.

1 Thessalonians 4:3 It is God's will that you should be sanctified: that you should avoid sexual immorality; 4 that each of you should learn to control your own body in a way that is holy and honorable, 5 not in passionate lust like the pagans, who do not know God; 6 and that in this matter no one should wrong or take advantage of a brother or sister. The Lord will punish all those who commit such sins, as we told you and warned you before. 7 For God did not call us to be impure, but to live a holy life.

The Nine Satanic Statements

2 Satan represents kindness to those who deserve it, instead of love wasted on ingrates!   charity

2 Corinthians 9:6 Remember this: Whoever sows sparingly will also reap sparingly, and whoever sows generously will also reap generously. 7 Each of you should give what you have decided in your heart to give, not reluctantly or under compulsion, for God loves a cheerful giver. 8 And God is able to bless you abundantly, so that in all things at all times, having all that you need, you will abound in every good work.

Proverbs 11:25 A generous person will

	prosper; whoever refreshes others will be refreshed.	
3	Satan represents vengeance, instead of turning the other cheek!	vengeance
	1 Peter 3:9 Do not repay evil with evil or insult with insult. On the contrary, repay evil with blessing, because to this you were called so that you may inherit a blessing.	
	1 Thessalonians 5:15 Make sure that nobody pays back wrong for wrong, but always strive to do what is good for each other and for everyone else.	
	Hebrews 10:30 For we know him who said, "It is mine to avenge; I will repay," and again, "The Lord will judge his people." 31 It is a dreadful thing to fall into the hands of the living God.	

The Book of Satan II

4	Behold the crucifix; what does it symbolize? Pallid incompetence hanging on a tree.	the cross
	1 Corinthians 1:18 For the message of the cross is foolishness to those who are perishing, but to us who are being saved it is the power of God.	
	Hebrews 12:1 Therefore, since we are surrounded by such a great cloud of witnesses, let us throw off everything that hinders and the sin that so easily entangles. And let us run with perseverance the race marked out for us, 2 fixing our eyes on Jesus, the pioneer and perfecter of faith. For the joy set before him he endured the cross, scorning its shame, and sat down at the right hand of the throne of God.	
	Philippians 2:6 Who, being in very nature God, did not consider equality with God something to be used to his own advantage; 7 rather, he made himself nothing by taking the very nature of a servant, being made in human likeness. 8 And being found in appearance as a man, he humbled himself by becoming obedient to death— even death on a cross!	
5	The chief duty of every new age is to upraise new men to determine its liberties, to lead it	materialism

towards material success - to rend the rusty padlocks and chains of dead custom that always prevent healthy expansion. Theories and ideas that may have meant life and hope and freedom for our ancestors may now mean destruction, slavery, and dishonor to us!

1 Timothy 6:7 For we brought nothing into the world, and we can take nothing out of it. 8 But if we have food and clothing, we will be content with that.

Ecclesiastes 5:10 Whoever loves money never has enough; whoever loves wealth is never satisfied with their income. This too is meaningless.

Mark 8:36 What good is it for someone to gain the whole world, yet forfeit their soul?

Proverbs 30:8 Keep falsehood and lies far from me; give me neither poverty nor riches, but give me only my daily bread.

Exodus 20:17 "You shall not covet your neighbor's house. You shall not covet your neighbor's wife, or his male or female servant, his ox or donkey, or anything that belongs to your neighbor."

The Book of Satan III

1. "Love one another" it has been said is the supreme law, but what power made it so? Upon what rational authority does the gospel of love rest? Why should I not hate mine enemies - if I "love" them does that not place me at their mercy? 2. Is it natural for enemies to do good unto each other - and WHAT IS GOOD? 3. Can the torn and bloody victim "love" the blood-splashed jaws that rend him limb from limb?

1 John 4:8 Whoever does not love does not know God, because God is love.

Matthew 5:43 "You have heard that it was said, 'Love your neighbor and hate your enemy.' 44 But I tell you, love your enemies and pray for those who persecute you, 45 that you may be children of your Father in heaven. He causes his sun to rise on the evil and the good, and sends rain on the righteous and the

love one another

unrighteous. 46 If you love those who love you, what reward will you get? Are not even the tax collectors doing that? 47 And if you greet only your own people, what are you doing more than others? Do not even pagans do that? 48 Be perfect, therefore, as your heavenly Father is perfect.

Leviticus 19:18 "'Do not seek revenge or bear a grudge against anyone among your people, but love your neighbor as yourself. I am the Lord.

7 Is not "lust and carnal desire" a more truthful term to describe "love" when applied to the continuance of the race? Is not the "love" of the fawning scriptures simply a euphemism for sexual activity, or was the "great teacher" a glorifier of eunuchs? eunuchs

Matthew 19:12 For there are eunuchs who were born that way, and there are eunuchs who have been made eunuchs by others—and there are those who choose to live like eunuchs for the sake of the kingdom of heaven. The one who can accept this should accept it."

1 Corinthians 7:1 Now for the matters you wrote about: "It is good for a man not to have sexual relations with a woman." 2 But since sexual immorality is occurring, each man should have sexual relations with his own wife, and each woman with her own husband.

Isaiah 56:3 Let no foreigner who is bound to the LORD say, "The LORD will surely exclude me from his people." And let no eunuch complain, "I am only a dry tree." 4 For this is what the LORD says: "To the eunuchs who keep my Sabbaths, who choose what pleases me and hold fast to my covenant—5 to them I will give within my temple and its walls a memorial and a name better than sons and daughters; I will give them an everlasting name that will endure forever.

8 Give blow for blow, scorn for scorn, doom for doom - with compound interest liberally added thereunto! Eye for eye, tooth for tooth, aye business enemies

fourfold, a hundred-fold! Make yourself a Terror to your adversary, and when he goeth his way, he will possess much additional wisdom to ruminate over. Thus shall you make yourself respected in all the walks of life, and your spirit - your immortal spirit - shall live, not in an intangible paradise, but in the brains and sinews of those whose respect you have gained.

1 Timothy 2:1 I urge, then, first of all, that petitions, prayers, intercession and thanksgiving be made for all people— 2 for kings and all those in authority, that we may live peaceful and quiet lives in all godliness and holiness.

Proverbs 25:21 If your enemy is hungry, give him food to eat; if he is thirsty, give him water to drink. 22 In doing this, you will heap burning coals on his head, and the LORD will reward you.

Proverbs 24:17 Do not gloat when your enemy falls; when they stumble, do not let your heart rejoice, 18 or the LORD will see and disapprove and turn his wrath away from them. 19 Do not fret because of evildoers or be envious of the wicked, 20 for the evildoer has no future hope, and the lamp of the wicked will be snuffed out.

9   6. Love your enemies and do good to them that hate and use you - is this not the despicable philosophy of the spaniel that rolls upon its back when kicked?   love your enemies

1 Peter 3:8 Finally, all of you, be like-minded, be sympathetic, love one another, be compassionate and humble.

Matthew 22:37 Jesus replied: "'Love the Lord your God with all your heart and with all your soul and with all your mind.' 38 This is the first and greatest commandment. 39 And the second is like it: 'Love your neighbor as yourself.' 40 All the Law and the Prophets hang on these two commandments."

Hebrews 13:1 Keep on loving one another as brothers and sisters. 2 Do not forget to show

hospitality to strangers, for by so doing some people have shown hospitality to angels without knowing it.

Romans 14:13 Therefore let us stop passing judgment on one another. Instead, make up your mind not to put any stumbling block or obstacle in the way of a brother or sister. 14 I am convinced, being fully persuaded in the Lord Jesus, that nothing is unclean in itself. But if anyone regards something as unclean, then for that person it is unclean. 15 If your brother or sister is distressed because of what you eat, you are no longer acting in love. Do not by your eating destroy someone for whom Christ died. 16 Therefore do not let what you know is good be spoken of as evil.

The Book of Satan IV

10 1. Life is the great indulgence - death, the great abstinence. Therefore, make the most of life – Here and Now! 2. There is no heaven of glory bright, and no hell where sinners roast. Here and now is our day of torment! Here and now is our day of joy! Here and now is our opportunity! Choose ye this day, this hour, for no redeemer liveth!

afterlife

Revelation 20:11 Then I saw a great white throne and him who was seated on it. The earth and the heavens fled from his presence, and there was no place for them. 12 And I saw the dead, great and small, standing before the throne, and books were opened. Another book was opened, which is the book of life. The dead were judged according to what they had done as recorded in the books. 13 The sea gave up the dead that were in it, and death and Hades gave up the dead that were in them, and each person was judged according to what they had done. 14 Then death and Hades were thrown into the lake of fire. The lake of fire is the second death. 15 Anyone whose name was not found written in the book of life was thrown into the lake of fire.

1 Corinthians 15:21 For since death came

through a man, the resurrection of the dead comes also through a man.

John 11:25 Jesus said to her, "I am the resurrection and the life. The one who believes in me will live, even though they die;

John 3:16 For God so loved the world that he gave his one and only Son, that whoever believes in him shall not perish but have eternal life. 17 For God did not send his Son into the world to condemn the world, but to save the world through him. 18 Whoever believes in him is not condemned, but whoever does not believe stands condemned already because they have not believed in the name of God's one and only Son.

John 8:51 Very truly I tell you, whoever obeys my word will never see death."

Isaiah 25:8 he will swallow up death forever. The Sovereign LORD will wipe away the tears from all faces; he will remove his people's disgrace from all the earth. The LORD has spoken.

The Book of Satan V

11 1. Blessed are the strong, for they shall possess the earth - Cursed are the weak, for they shall inherit the yoke! 2. Blessed are the powerful, for they shall be reverenced among men – Cursed are the feeble, for they shall be blotted out!

    weakness
    business

1 John 3:17 If anyone has material possessions and sees a brother or sister in need but has no pity on them, how can the love of God be in that person? 18 Dear children, let us not love with words or speech but with actions and in truth.

Luke 14:12 Then Jesus said to his host, "When you give a luncheon or dinner, do not invite your friends, your brothers or sisters, your relatives, or your rich neighbors; if you do, they may invite you back and so you will be repaid. 13 But when you give a banquet, invite the poor, the crippled, the lame, the blind, 14 and you will be blessed. Although they cannot repay you, you will be repaid at the resurrection of the righteous."

Psalm 82:3 Defend the weak and the fatherless; uphold the cause of the poor and the oppressed. 4 Rescue the weak and the needy; deliver them from the hand of the wicked.

Isaiah 1:17 Learn to do right; seek justice. Defend the oppressed. Take up the cause of the fatherless; plead the case of the widow.

Zechariah 7:10 Do not oppress the widow or the fatherless, the foreigner or the poor. Do not plot evil against each other.' 11 "But they refused to pay attention; stubbornly they turned their backs and covered their ears. 12 They made their hearts as hard as flint and would not listen to the law or to the words that the LORD Almighty had sent by his Spirit through the earlier prophets. So the LORD Almighty was very angry. 13 " 'When I called, they did not listen; so when they called, I would not listen,' says the LORD Almighty. 14 'I scattered them with a whirlwind among all the nations, where they were strangers. The land they left behind them was so desolate that no one traveled through it. This is how they made the pleasant land desolate.' "

Psalm 10:17 You, LORD, hear the desire of the afflicted; you encourage them, and you listen to their cry, 18 defending the fatherless and the oppressed, so that mere earthly mortals will never again strike terror.

12   3. Blessed are the bold, for they shall be masters of the world - Cursed are the righteously humble, for they shall be trodden under cloven hoofs! 4. Blessed are the victorious, for victory is the basis of right - Cursed are the vanquished, for they shall be vassals forever!   humility business

Ephesians 4:2 Be completely humble and gentle; be patient, bearing with one another in love. 3 Make every effort to keep the unity of the Spirit through the bond of peace. 4 There is one body and one Spirit, just as you were called to one hope when you were called; 5 one Lord, one faith, one baptism; 6 one God and Father of all, who is over all and through all and in all.

Romans 12:16 Live in harmony with one another. Do not be proud, but be willing to associate with people of low position. Do not be conceited.

2 Chronicles 7:13 "When I shut up the heavens so that there is no rain, or command locusts to devour the land or send a plague among my people, 14 if my people, who are called by my name, will humble themselves and pray and seek my face and turn from their wicked ways, then I will hear from heaven, and I will forgive their sin and will heal their land.

Luke 14:7 When he noticed how the guests picked the places of honor at the table, he told them this parable: 8 "When someone invites you to a wedding feast, do not take the place of honor, for a person more distinguished than you may have been invited. 9 If so, the host who invited both of you will come and say to you, 'Give this person your seat.' Then, humiliated, you will have to take the least important place. 10 But when you are invited, take the lowest place, so that when your host comes, he will say to you, 'Friend, move up to a better place.' Then you will be honored in the presence of all the other guests. 11 For all those who exalt themselves will be humbled, and those who humble themselves will be exalted."

James 4:6 But he gives us more grace. That is why Scripture says: "God opposes the proud but shows favor to the humble." 7 Submit yourselves, then, to God. Resist the devil, and he will flee from you. 8 Come near to God and he will come near to you. Wash your hands, you sinners, and purify your hearts, you double-minded. 9 Grieve, mourn and wail. Change your laughter to mourning and your joy to gloom. 10 Humble yourselves before the Lord, and he will lift you up.

Proverbs 11:2 When pride comes, then comes disgrace, but with humility comes wisdom.

The Enlightenment

13 Entertaining as they might be, most stories and plays about Devil worship must be recognized as the obsolete absurdities they are. It has been said "the truth will make men free". The truth alone has never set anyone free. It is only "doubt" which will bring mental emancipation. — freedom

Galatians 5:13 You, my brothers and sisters, were called to be free. But do not use your freedom to indulge the flesh; rather, serve one another humbly in love. 14 For the entire law is fulfilled in keeping this one command: "Love your neighbor as yourself."

2 Corinthians 3:17 Now the Lord is the Spirit, and where the Spirit of the Lord is, there is freedom.

1 Corinthians 6:12 "I have the right to do anything," you say—but not everything is beneficial. "I have the right to do anything"— but I will not be mastered by anything.

Ephesians 3:10 His intent was that now, through the church, the manifold wisdom of God should be made known to the rulers and authorities in the heavenly realms, 11 according to his eternal purpose that he accomplished in Christ Jesus our Lord. 12 In him and through faith in him we may approach God with freedom and confidence. 13 I ask you, therefore, not to be discouraged because of my sufferings for you, which are your glory.

Isaiah 61:1 The Spirit of the Sovereign LORD is on me, because the LORD has anointed me to proclaim good news to the poor. He has sent me to bind up the brokenhearted, to proclaim freedom for the captives and release from darkness for the prisoners,

14 The Satanist knows that praying does absolutely no good – in fact, it actually lessens the chance of success, for the devoutly religious too often sit back complacently and pray for a situation which, if they were to do something about it on their own, could be accomplished much quicker! The Satanist shuns terms such as — prayer

"hope" and "prayer" as they are indicative of apprehension. If we hope and pray for something to come about, we will not act in a positive way which will make it happen. The Satanist, realizing that anything he gets is of his own doing, takes command of the situation instead of praying to God for it to happen.

1 John 5:14 This is the confidence we have in approaching God: that if we ask anything according to his will, he hears us. 15 And if we know that he hears us—whatever we ask—we know that we have what we asked of him.

Matthew 6:9 "This, then, is how you should pray: " 'Our Father in heaven, hallowed be your name, 10 your kingdom come, your will be done, on earth as it is in heaven. 11 Give us today our daily bread. 12 And forgive us our debts, as we also have forgiven our debtors. 13 And lead us not into temptation, but deliver us from the evil one. '

Mark 11:24 Therefore I tell you, whatever you ask for in prayer, believe that you have received it, and it will be yours.

James 5:16 Therefore confess your sins to each other and pray for each other so that you may be healed. The prayer of a righteous person is powerful and effective.

Matthew 6:5 "And when you pray, do not be like the hypocrites, for they love to pray standing in the synagogues and on the street corners to be seen by others. Truly I tell you, they have received their reward in full. 6 But when you pray, go into your room, close the door and pray to your Father, who is unseen. Then your Father, who sees what is done in secret, will reward you. 7 And when you pray, do not keep on babbling like pagans, for they think they will be heard because of their many words. 8 Do not be like them, for your Father knows what you need before you ask him.

15 Just as the Satanist does not pray to God for forgiveness assistance, he does not pray for forgiveness for his wrong doings. In other religions, when one

commits a wrong he either prays to God for forgiveness, or confesses to an intermediary and asks him to pray to God for forgiveness for his sins. The Satanist knows that praying does no good, confessing to another human being, like himself, accomplishes even less - and is, furthermore, degrading.

Luke 6:37 "Do not judge, and you will not be judged. Do not condemn, and you will not be condemned. Forgive, and you will be forgiven. 38 Give, and it will be given to you. A good measure, pressed down, shaken together and running over, will be poured into your lap. For with the measure you use, it will be measured to you."

Ephesians 4:31 Get rid of all bitterness, rage and anger, brawling and slander, along with every form of malice. 32 Be kind and compassionate to one another, forgiving each other, just as in Christ God forgave you.

James 5:16 Therefore confess your sins to each other and pray for each other so that you may be healed. The prayer of a righteous person is powerful and effective. 17 Elijah was a human being, even as we are. He prayed earnestly that it would not rain, and it did not rain on the land for three and a half years. 18 Again he prayed, and the heavens gave rain, and the earth produced its crops. 19 My brothers and sisters, if one of you should wander from the truth and someone should bring that person back, 20 remember this: Whoever turns a sinner from the error of their way will save them from death and cover over a multitude of sins.

Matthew 18:21 Then Peter came to Jesus and asked, "Lord, how many times shall I forgive my brother or sister who sins against me? Up to seven times?" 22 Jesus answered, "I tell you, not seven times, but seventy-seven times.

Acts 2:38 Peter replied, "Repent and be baptized, every one of you, in the name of Jesus Christ for the forgiveness of your sins. And you will receive the gift of the Holy Spirit.

16 THE seven deadly sins of the Christian Church are: greed, pride, envy, anger, gluttony, lust, and sloth. Satanism advocates indulging in each of these "sins" as they all lead to physical, mental, or emotional gratification. — sins / gratification

John 16:24 Until now you have not asked for anything in my name. Ask and you will receive, and your joy will be complete.

Colossians 3:5 Put to death, therefore, whatever belongs to your earthly nature: sexual immorality, impurity, lust, evil desires and greed, which is idolatry.

Galatians 5:19 The acts of the flesh are obvious: sexual immorality, impurity and debauchery; 20 idolatry and witchcraft; hatred, discord, jealousy, fits of rage, selfish ambition, dissensions, factions 21 and envy; drunkenness, orgies, and the like. I warn you, as I did before, that those who live like this will not inherit the kingdom of God.

James 1:2 Consider it pure joy, my brothers and sisters, whenever you face trials of many kinds, 3 because you know that the testing of your faith produces perseverance.

Proverbs 10:28 The prospect of the righteous is joy, but the hopes of the wicked come to nothing.

Proverbs 16:20 Whoever gives heed to instruction prospers, and blessed is the one who trusts in the LORD.

17 Since man's natural instincts lead him to sin, all men are sinners; and all sinners go to hell. If everyone goes to hell, then you will meet all your friends there. Heaven must be populated with some rather strange creatures if they all lived for was to go to a place where they can strum harps for eternity. — hell

Matthew 13:48 When it was full, the fishermen pulled it up on the shore. Then they sat down and collected the good fish in baskets, but threw the bad away. 49 This is how it will be at the end of the age. The angels will come

and separate the wicked from the righteous 50 and throw them into the blazing furnace, where there will be weeping and gnashing of teeth.

Revelation 20:14 Then death and Hades were thrown into the lake of fire. The lake of fire is the second death.

Revelation 19:20 But the beast was captured, and with it the false prophet who had performed the signs on its behalf. With these signs he had deluded those who had received the mark of the beast and worshiped its image. The two of them were thrown alive into the fiery lake of burning sulfur.

Matthew 25:41 "Then he will say to those on his left, 'Depart from me, you who are cursed, into the eternal fire prepared for the devil and his angels.

Revelation 21:8 But the cowardly, the unbelieving, the vile, the murderers, the sexually immoral, those who practice magic arts, the idolaters and all liars—they will be consigned to the fiery lake of burning sulfur. This is the second death."

Matthew 25:46 "Then they will go away to eternal punishment, but the righteous to eternal life."

Mark 9:47 And if your eye causes you to stumble, pluck it out. It is better for you to enter the kingdom of God with one eye than to have two eyes and be thrown into hell, 48 where "'the worms that eat them do not die, and the fire is not quenched.'

18   Today, as always, man needs to enjoy himself   indulgence
here and now, instead of waiting for his rewards in heaven. So, why not have a religion based on indulgence? Certainly, it is consistent with the nature of the beast. We are no longer supplicating weaklings trembling before an unmerciful "God" who cares not whether we live or die. We are self-respecting, prideful people - we are Satanists!

2 Timothy 3:1 But mark this: There will be terrible times in the last days. 2 People will be lovers of themselves, lovers of money, boastful, proud, abusive, disobedient to their parents, ungrateful, unholy, 3 without love, unforgiving, slanderous, without self-control, brutal, not lovers of the good, 4 treacherous, rash, conceited, lovers of pleasure rather than lovers of God— 5 having a form of godliness but denying its power. Have nothing to do with such people. 6 They are the kind who worm their way into homes and gain control over gullible women, who are loaded down with sins and are swayed by all kinds of evil desires, 7 always learning but never able to come to a knowledge of the truth. 8 Just as Jannes and Jambres opposed Moses, so also these teachers oppose the truth. They are men of depraved minds, who, as far as the faith is concerned, are rejected. 9 But they will not get very far because, as in the case of those men, their folly will be clear to everyone.

Proverbs 25:16 If you find honey, eat just enough—too much of it, and you will vomit.

Proverbs 23:21 for drunkards and gluttons become poor, and drowsiness clothes them in rags.

19	Love is one of the most intense emotions felt by man; another is hate. Forcing yourself to feel indiscriminate love is very unnatural. If you try to love everyone you only lessen your feelings for those who deserve your love. Repressed hatred can lead to many physical and emotional ailments. By learning to release your hatred towards those who deserve it, you cleanse yourself of these malignant emotions and need not take your pent-up hatred out on your loved ones.	love vs hate

Matthew 5:43 "You have heard that it was said, 'Love your neighbor and hate your enemy.' 44 But I tell you, love your enemies and pray for those who persecute you, 45 that you may be children of your Father in heaven. He causes his sun to rise on the evil and the good, and sends rain on the righteous and the

unrighteous. 46 If you love those who love you, what reward will you get? Are not even the tax collectors doing that? 47 And if you greet only your own people, what are you doing more than others? Do not even pagans do that? 48 Be perfect, therefore, as your heavenly Father is perfect.

Luke 6:27 "But to you who are listening I say: Love your enemies, do good to those who hate you, 28 bless those who curse you, pray for those who mistreat you. 29 If someone slaps you on one cheek, turn to them the other also. If someone takes your coat, do not withhold your shirt from them. 30 Give to everyone who asks you, and if anyone takes what belongs to you, do not demand it back. 31 Do to others as you would have them do to you. 32 "If you love those who love you, what credit is that to you? Even sinners love those who love them. 33 And if you do good to those who are good to you, what credit is that to you? Even sinners do that. 34 And if you lend to those from whom you expect repayment, what credit is that to you? Even sinners lend to sinners, expecting to be repaid in full. 35 But love your enemies, do good to them, and lend to them without expecting to get anything back. Then your reward will be great, and you will be children of the Most High, because he is kind to the ungrateful and wicked. 36 Be merciful, just as your Father is merciful.37 "Do not judge, and you will not be judged. Do not condemn, and you will not be condemned. Forgive, and you will be forgiven. 38 Give, and it will be given to you. A good measure, pressed down, shaken together and running over, will be poured into your lap. For with the measure you use, it will be measured to you."

20 Satanism condones any type of sexual activity which properly satisfies your individual desires - be it heterosexual, homosexual, bisexual, or even asexual, if you choose. Satanism also sanctions any fetish or deviation which will   sexual desires

enhance your sex-life, so long as it involves no one who does not wish to be involved.

Matthew 5:28 But I tell you that anyone who looks at a woman lustfully has already committed adultery with her in his heart.

1 John 2:16 For everything in the world—the lust of the flesh, the lust of the eyes, and the pride of life—comes not from the Father but from the world. 17 The world and its desires pass away, but whoever does the will of God lives forever. 18 Dear children, this is the last hour; and as you have heard that the antichrist is coming, even now many antichrists have come. This is how we know it is the last hour.

2 Corinthians 12:21 I am afraid that when I come again my God will humble me before you, and I will be grieved over many who have sinned earlier and have not repented of the impurity, sexual sin and debauchery in which they have indulged.

1 Corinthians 6:18 Flee from sexual immorality. All other sins a person commits are outside the body, but whoever sins sexually, sins against their own body. 19 Do you not know that your bodies are temples of the Holy Spirit, who is in you, whom you have received from God? You are not your own; 20 you were bought at a price. Therefore honor God with your bodies.

21 Satanism encourages its followers to indulge in their natural desires. Only by doing so can you be a completely satisfied person with no frustrations which can be harmful to yourself and others around you. Therefore, the most simplified description of the Satanic belief is: Indulgence instead of Abstinence   indulgence

Matthew 23:25 "Woe to you, teachers of the law and Pharisees, you hypocrites! You clean the outside of the cup and dish, but inside they are full of greed and self-indulgence. 26 Blind Pharisee! First clean the inside of the cup and dish, and then the outside also will be clean. 27 "Woe to you, teachers of the law and Pharisees, you hypocrites! You are like whitewashed tombs, which look beautiful on the outside but on the inside are full of the bones of the dead and everything unclean. 28 In the same way, on the outside you appear to people as righteous but on the inside you are full of hypocrisy and wickedness.

Romans 8:7 The mind governed by the flesh is hostile to God; it does not submit to God's law, nor can it do so. 8 Those who are in the realm of the flesh cannot please God. 9 You, however, are not in the realm of the flesh but are in the realm of the Spirit, if indeed the Spirit of God lives in you. And if anyone does not have the Spirit of Christ, they do not belong to Christ.

22   The use of a human sacrifice in a Satanic ritual does not imply that the sacrifice is slaughtered "to appease the gods". Symbolically, the victim is destroyed through the working of a hex or curse, which in turn leads to the physical, mental or emotional destruction of the "sacrifice" in ways and means not attributable to the magician. The only time a Satanist would perform a human sacrifice would be if it were to serve a twofold purpose; that being to release the magician's wrath in the throwing of a curse, and more important, to dispose of a totally obnoxious and deserving individual.   *human sacrifice*

Deuteronomy 18:10 Let no one be found among you who sacrifices their son or daughter in the fire, who practices divination or sorcery, interprets omens, engages in witchcraft, 11 or casts spells, or who is a medium or spiritist or who consults the dead.

Romans 3:25 God presented Christ as a sacrifice of atonement, through the shedding of his blood—to be received by faith. He did this to demonstrate his righteousness, because in his forbearance he had left the sins committed beforehand unpunished—26 he did it to demonstrate his righteousness at the present time, so as to be just and the one who justifies those who have faith in Jesus.

23 Anyone who says "we must try to understand"   enemies
those who make life miserable for those   persecution
undeserving of misery is aiding and abetting a
social cancer! The apologists for these rabid
humans deserve any clobberings they get at the
hands of their charges! Mad dogs are destroyed,
and they need help far more than the human
who conveniently made froths at the mouth
when irrational behavior is in order! It is easy to
say, "So what! - these people are insecure, so
they can't hurt me." But the fact remains -given
the opportunity they would destroy you!
Therefore, you have every right to
(symbolically) destroy them, and if your curse
provokes their actual annihilation, rejoice that
you have been instrumental in ridding the world
of a pest!

Luke 6:27 "But to you who are listening I say: Love your enemies, do good to those who hate you, 28 bless those who curse you, pray for those who mistreat you. 29 If someone slaps you on one cheek, turn to them the other also. If someone takes your coat, do not withhold your shirt from them. 30 Give to everyone who asks you, and if anyone takes what belongs to you, do not demand it back. 31 Do to others as you would have them do to you.

Matthew 5:11 "Blessed are you when people insult you, persecute you and falsely say all kinds of evil against you because of me. 12 Rejoice and be glad, because great is your reward in heaven, for in the same way they persecuted the prophets who were before you.

Proverbs 25:21 If your enemy is hungry, give him food to eat; if he is thirsty, give him water to drink. 22 In doing this, you will heap burning coals on his head, and the LORD will reward you.

24 THE highest of all holidays in the Satanic   birthday
religion is the date of one's own birth. This is in   true god
direct contradiction to the holy of holy days of
other religions, which deify a particular god
who has been created in an anthropomorphic

form of their own image, thereby showing that the ego is not really buried. The Satanist feels: "Why not really be honest and if you are going to create a god in your image, why not create that god as yourself." Every man is a god if he chooses to recognize himself as one.

1 Corinthians 8:4 So then, about eating food sacrificed to idols: We know that "An idol is nothing at all in the world" and that "There is no God but one." 5 For even if there are so-called gods, whether in heaven or on earth (as indeed there are many "gods" and many "lords"), 6 yet for us there is but one God, the Father, from whom all things came and for whom we live; and there is but one Lord, Jesus Christ, through whom all

Mark 12:29 "The most important one," answered Jesus, "is this: 'Hear, O Israel: The Lord our God, the Lord is one. 30 Love the Lord your God with all your heart and with all your soul and with all your mind and with all your strength.' 31 The second is this: 'Love your neighbor as yourself.' There is no commandment greater than these." 32 "Well said, teacher," the man replied. "You are right in saying that God is one and there is no other but him. 33 To love him with all your heart, with all your understanding and with all your strength, and to love your neighbor as yourself is more important than all burnt offerings and sacrifices." 34 When Jesus saw that he had answered wisely, he said to him, "You are not far from the kingdom of God." And from then on no one dared ask him any more questions.

Nehemiah 9:6 You alone are the Lord. You made the heavens, even the highest heavens, and all their starry host, the earth and all that is on it, the seas and all that is in them. You give life to everything, and the multitudes of heaven worship you.

Isaiah 43:10 "You are my witnesses," declares the LORD, "and my servant whom I have chosen, so that you may know and believe

me and understand that I am he. Before me no
god was formed, nor will there be one after me.
11 I, even I, am the LORD, and apart from me
there is no savior.

25 Ritual magic consists of the performance of a formal ceremony, taking place, at least in part, within the confines of an area set aside for such purposes and at a specific time. Its main function is to isolate the otherwise dissipated adrenal and other emotionally induced energy, and convert it into a dynamically transmittable force. It is purely an emotional, rather than intellectual, act. Any and all intellectual activity must take place before the ceremony, not during it. This type of magic is sometimes known as "Greater Magic". ritual magic

Galatians 5:19 The acts of the flesh are obvious: sexual immorality, impurity and debauchery; 20 idolatry and witchcraft; hatred, discord, jealousy, fits of rage, selfish ambition, dissensions, factions 21 and envy; drunkenness, orgies, and the like. I warn you, as I did before, that those who live like this will not inherit the kingdom of God.

Revelation 21:8 But the cowardly, the unbelieving, the vile, the murderers, the sexually immoral, those who practice magic arts, the idolaters and all liars—they will be consigned to the fiery lake of burning sulfur. This is the second death."

Isaiah 8:19 When someone tells you to consult mediums and spiritists, who whisper and mutter, should not a people inquire of their God? Why consult the dead on behalf of the living? 20 Consult God's instruction and the testimony of warning. If anyone does not speak according to this word, they have no light of dawn.

Malachi 3:5 "So I will come to put you on trial. I will be quick to testify against sorcerers, adulterers and perjurers, against those who defraud laborers of their wages, who oppress the widows and the fatherless, and deprive the

foreigners among you of justice, but do not fear me," says the Lord Almighty.

Deuteronomy 18:10 Let no one be found among you who sacrifices their son or daughter in the fire, who practices divination or sorcery, interprets omens, engages in witchcraft, 11 or casts spells, or who is a medium or spiritist or who consults the dead. 12 Anyone who does these things is detestable to the Lord; because of these same detestable practices the Lord your God will drive out those nations before you.

The real witches were rarely executed, or even brought to trial, as they were proficient in the art of enchantment and could charm the men and save their own lives. Most of the real witches were sleeping with the inquisitors. This is the origin of the word "glamour". The antiquated meaning of glamour is witchcraft.

witchcraft

Revelation 21:8 But the cowardly, the unbelieving, the vile, the murderers, the sexually immoral, those who practice magic arts, the idolaters and all liars—they will be consigned to the fiery lake of burning sulfur. This is the second death."

2 Chronicles 33: Manasseh was twelve years old when he became king, and he reigned in Jerusalem fifty-five years. 2 He did evil in the eyes of the Lord, following the detestable practices of the nations the Lord had driven out before the Israelites. 3 He rebuilt the high places his father Hezekiah had demolished; he also erected altars to the Baals and made Asherah poles. He bowed down to all the starry hosts and worshiped them. 4 He built altars in the temple of the Lord, of which the Lord had said, "My Name will remain in Jerusalem forever." 5 In both courts of the temple of the Lord, he built altars to all the starry hosts. 6 He sacrificed his children in the fire in the Valley of Ben Hinnom, practiced divination and witchcraft, sought omens, and consulted mediums and spiritists. He did much evil in the eyes of the Lord, arousing his anger.

Deuteronomy 18:10 Let no one be found among you who sacrifices their son or daughter in the fire, who practices divination or sorcery, interprets omens, engages in witchcraft, 11 or casts spells, or who is a medium or spiritist or who consults the dead. 12 Anyone who does these things is detestable to the Lord; because of these same detestable practices the Lord your God will drive out those nations before you. 13 You must be blameless before the Lord your God.

The Three Types of Satanic Ritual

27 The first of these we shall call a sex ritual. A sex ritual is what is commonly known as a love charm or spell. The purpose in performing such a ritual is to create desire on the part of the person whom you desire, or to summon a sex partner to fulfill your desires. If you have no specific person or type of person in mind strong enough to cause direct sexual feeling   lust

1 Corinthians 6:18 Flee from sexual immorality. All other sins a person commits are outside the body, but whoever sins sexually, sins against their own body.

1 Peter 2:11 Dear friends, I urge you, as foreigners and exiles, to abstain from sinful desires, which wage war against your soul. 12 Live such good lives among the pagans that, though they accuse you of doing wrong, they may see your good deeds and glorify God on the day he visits us.

28 The second type of ritual is of a compassionate nature. The compassion, or sentiment, ritual is performed for the purpose of helping others, or helping oneself. Health, domestic happiness, business activities, material success, and scholastic prowess are but a few of the situations covered in a compassion ritual. It might be said that this form of ceremony could fall into the realm of genuine charity, bearing in mind that "charity begins at home".   helping

1 John 3:17 If anyone has material possessions and sees a brother or sister in need

but has no pity on them, how can the love of God be in that person? 18 Dear children, let us not love with words or speech but with actions and in truth. 19 This is how we know that we belong to the truth and how we set our hearts at rest in his presence: 20 If our hearts condemn us, we know that God is greater than our hearts, and he knows everything.

Matthew 25:35 For I was hungry and you gave me something to eat, I was thirsty and you gave me something to drink, I was a stranger and you invited me in, 36 I needed clothes and you clothed me, I was sick and you looked after me, I was in prison and you came to visit me.'

Acts 20:35 In everything I did, I showed you that by this kind of hard work we must help the weak, remembering the words the Lord Jesus himself said: 'It is more blessed to give than to receive.' "

Leviticus 25:35 "'If any of your fellow Israelites become poor and are unable to support themselves among you, help them as you would a foreigner and stranger, so they can continue to live among you.

28 The third motivating force is that of destruction.   curse
This is a ceremony used for anger, annoyance, disdain, contempt, or just plain hate. It is known as a hex, curse, or destroying agent.

Luke 6:28 bless those who curse you, pray for those who mistreat you.

Matthew 5:21 "You have heard that it was said to the people long ago, 'You shall not murder, and anyone who murders will be subject to judgment.' 22 But I tell you that anyone who is angry with a brother or sister will be subject to judgment. Again, anyone who says to a brother or sister, 'Raca,' is answerable to the court. And anyone who says, 'You fool!' will be in danger of the fire of hell.

James 3:9 With the tongue we praise our Lord and Father, and with it we curse human beings, who have been made in God's likeness. 10 Out of the same mouth come praise and cursing. My brothers and sisters, this should not be. 11 Can both fresh water and salt water flow from the same spring? 12 My brothers and sisters, can a fig tree bear olives, or a grapevine bear figs? Neither can a salt spring produce fresh water. 13 Who is wise and understanding among you? Let them show it by their good life, by deeds done in the humility that comes from wisdom.

29   Concerning Destruction: Be certain you DO NOT care if the intended victim lives or dies, before you throw your curse, and having caused their destruction, revel, rather than feel remorse.   victim

Matthew 5:43 "You have heard that it was said, 'Love your neighbor and hate your enemy.' 44 But I tell you, love your enemies and pray for those who persecute you, 45 that you may be children of your Father in heaven. He causes his sun to rise on the evil and the good, and sends rain on the righteous and the unrighteous.

Romans 12:14 Bless those who persecute you; bless and do not curse. 15 Rejoice with those who rejoice; mourn with those who mourn. 16 Live in harmony with one another. Do not be proud, but be willing to associate with people of low position. Do not be conceited. 17 Do not repay anyone evil for evil. Be careful to do what is right in the eyes of everyone. 18 If it is possible, as far as it depends on you, live at peace with everyone. 19 Do not take revenge, my dear friends, but leave room for God's wrath, for it is written: "It is mine to avenge; I will repay," says the Lord. 20 On the contrary: "If your enemy is hungry, feed him; if he is thirsty, give him something to drink. In doing this, you will heap burning coals on his head." 21 Do not be overcome by evil, but overcome evil with good.

The Ingredients Used In The Performance Of Satanic Magic

30   A. Desire - THE first ingredient in the performance of a ritual is desire, otherwise known as motivation, temptation, or emotional   ritual desire

persuasion. If you do not truly desire any end result, you should not attempt to perform a working. There is no such thing as a "practice" working, and the only way that a magician could do "tricks" such as moving inanimate objects, would be to have a strong emotional need to do so. It is true that if the magician wishes to gain power through impressing others with his feats of magic, he must produce tangible proof of his ability. The Satanic concept of magic, however, fails to find gratification in the proving of magical prowess.

Proverbs 16:1 To humans belong the plans of the heart, but from the LORD comes the proper answer of the tongue. 2 All a person's ways seem pure to them, but motives are weighed by the LORD. 3 Commit to the LORD whatever you do, and he will establish your plans. 4 The LORD works out everything to its proper end— even the wicked for a day of disaster. 5 The LORD detests all the proud of heart. Be sure of this: They will not go unpunished. 6 Through love and faithfulness sin is atoned for; through the fear of the LORD evil is avoided. 7 When the LORD takes pleasure in anyone's way, he causes their enemies to make peace with them. 8 Better a little with righteousness than much gain with injustice. 9 In their hearts humans plan their course, but the LORD establishes their steps.

31 B. Timing - It is to be emphasized that the magician must be at his peak of efficiency, as he represents the "sending" factor when he performs his ritual. Traditionally speaking, witches and sorcerers are night people, and understandably so. What better schedule on which to live, for the sending of thoughts towards unsuspecting sleepers! If only people were aware of the thoughts injected into their minds while they slept! The dream state is the birthplace of much of the future. Great thoughts are manifest upon awakening, and the mind that retains, in conscious form, these thoughts, shall

ritual timing

produce much.

Mark 1:15 "The time has come," he said. "The kingdom of God has come near. Repent and believe the good news!"

1 Timothy 4:1 The Spirit clearly says that in later times some will abandon the faith and follow deceiving spirits and things taught by demons. 2 Such teachings come through hypocritical liars, whose consciences have been seared as with a hot iron. 3 They forbid people to marry and order them to abstain from certain foods, which God created to be received with thanksgiving by those who believe and who know the truth. 4 For everything God created is good, and nothing is to be rejected if it is received with thanksgiving, 5 because it is consecrated by the word of God and prayer.

32 Should the fearful ask, "Is there no defense against such witchery?" it must be answered thus -"Yes, there is protection. You must never sleep, never daydream, never be without a vital thought, and never have an open mind. Then you shall be protected from the forces of magic."   magic defence

Ephesians 6:10 Finally, be strong in the Lord and in his mighty power. 11 Put on the full armor of God, so that you can take your stand against the devil's schemes. 12 For our struggle is not against flesh and blood, but against the rulers, against the authorities, against the powers of this dark world and against the spiritual forces of evil in the heavenly realms. 13 Therefore put on the full armor of God, so that when the day of evil comes, you may be able to stand your ground, and after you have done everything, to stand. 14 Stand firm then, with the belt of truth buckled around your waist, with the breastplate of righteousness in place, 15 and with your feet fitted with the readiness that comes from the gospel of peace. 16 In addition to all this, take up the shield of faith, with which you can extinguish all the flaming arrows of the evil one. 17 Take the helmet of salvation and the sword of the Spirit, which is the word of God. 18 And pray in the Spirit on all occasions with all kinds of prayers and requests. With this in mind, be alert and always keep on praying for all the Lord's people.

33   C. Imagery - If you have material desires, you must gaze upon images of them – surround yourself with the smells and sounds conducive to them - create a lodestone which will attract the situation or thing that you wish! To insure the destruction of an enemy, you must destroy them by proxy! They must be shot, stabbed, sickened, burned, smashed, drowned, or rent in the most vividly convincing manner! It is easy to see why the religions of the right-hand path frown upon the creation of "graven images". The imagery used by the sorcerer is a working mechanism for material reality, which is totally opposed to esoteric spirituality.   *magic imagery enemies*

Matthew 5:44 But I tell you, love your enemies and pray for those who persecute you, 45 that you may be children of your Father in heaven. He causes his sun to rise on the evil and the good, and sends rain on the righteous and the unrighteous.

Luke 6:35 But love your enemies, do good to them, and lend to them without expecting to get anything back. Then your reward will be great, and you will be children of the Most High, because he is kind to the ungrateful and wicked.

1 Peter 3:9 Do not repay evil with evil or insult with insult. On the contrary, repay evil with blessing, because to this you were called so that you may inherit a blessing.

34   D. Direction- The purpose of the ritual is to FREE the magician from thoughts that would consume him, were he to dwell upon them constantly. Contemplation, daydreaming and constant scheming burns up emotional energy that could be gathered together in a dynamically usable force; not to mention the fact that normal productivity is severely depleted by such consuming anxiety.   *mental peace*

Philippians 4:6 Do not be anxious about anything, but in every situation, by prayer and petition, with thanksgiving, present your requests to God. 7 And the peace of God, which transcends all understanding, will guard your hearts and your minds in Christ Jesus.

John 16:33 "I have told you these things, so that in me you may have peace. In this world you will have trouble. But take heart! I have overcome the world."

Hebrews 12:11 No discipline seems pleasant at the time, but painful. Later on, however, it produces a harvest of righteousness and peace for those who have been trained by it. 12 Therefore, strengthen your feeble arms and weak knees. 13 "Make level paths for your feet," so that the lame may not be disabled, but rather healed. 14 Make every effort to live in peace with everyone and to be holy; without holiness no one will see the Lord.

Psalm 4:8 In peace I will lie down and sleep, for you alone, LORD, make me dwell in safety.

35 E. The Balance Factor - The aspiring witch who nature deludes herself into thinking that a powerful enough working will always succeed, despite a magical imbalance, is forgetting one essential rule: Magic Is Like Nature Itself, And Success In Magic Requires Working In Harmony With Nature, Not Against It.

Romans 1:20 For since the creation of the world God's invisible qualities—his eternal power and divine nature—have been clearly seen, being understood from what has been made, so that people are without excuse.

Job 12:7 "But ask the animals, and they will teach you, or the birds in the sky, and they will tell you; 8 or speak to the earth, and it will teach you, or let the fish in the sea inform you. 9 Which of all these does not know that the hand of the LORD has done this? 10 In his hand is the life of every creature and the breath of all mankind.

Job 37:14 "Listen to this, Job; stop and

consider God's wonders. 15 Do you know how God controls the clouds and makes his lightning flash? 16 Do you know how the clouds hang poised, those wonders of him who has perfect knowledge?

Revelation 4:11 "You are worthy, our Lord and God, to receive glory and honor and power, for you created all things, and by your will they were created and have their being."

The Satanic Ritual

36 To Summon One For Lustful Purpose Or Establish A Sexually Gratifying Situation Leave the area of the altar and remove yourself to that place, either in the same room or without, that will be most conducive to the working of the respective ritual. Then, fashion whatever imagery you possibly can that will parallel in as exact a way possible the situation towards which you strive. Remember, you have five senses to utilize, so do not feel you must limit your imagery to one. lust

1 Thessalonians 4:3 It is God's will that you should be sanctified: that you should avoid sexual immorality; 4 that each of you should learn to control your own body in a way that is holy and honorable, 5 not in passionate lust like the pagans, who do not know God; 6 and that in this matter no one should wrong or take advantage of a brother or sister. The Lord will punish all those who commit such sins, as we told you and warned you before.

Colossians 3:2 Set your minds on things above, not on earthly things. 3 For you died, and your life is now hidden with Christ in God. 4 When Christ, who is your life, appears, then you also will appear with him in glory. 5 Put to death, therefore, whatever belongs to your earthly nature: sexual immorality, impurity, lust, evil desires and greed, which is idolatry.

37 To Insure Help Or Success For One Who Has Your Sympathy Or Compassion (Including Yourself) Remain in close proximity of the altar and with as vivid a mental image as possible of intentions

the person you wish to help (or intense self-pity), state your desire in your own terms. Should your emotions be genuine enough, they will be accompanied the shedding of tears, which should be allowed to flow without restraint.

Matthew 7:13 "Enter through the narrow gate. For wide is the gate and broad is the road that leads to destruction, and many enter through it. 14 But small is the gate and narrow the road that leads to life, and only a few find it. 15 "Watch out for false prophets. They come to you in sheep's clothing, but inwardly they are ferocious wolves.

Ephesians 3:10 His intent was that now, through the church, the manifold wisdom of God should be made known to the rulers and authorities in the heavenly realms, 11 according to his eternal purpose that he accomplished in Christ Jesus our Lord.

Proverbs 16:2 All a person's ways seem pure to them, but motives are weighed by the Lord.

38   To Cause The Destruction Of An Enemy   enemies
Remain in the area of the altar unless imagery is more easily obtained in another spot, such as in the vicinity of the victim. Producing the image of the victim, proceed to inflict the destruction upon the effigy in the manner of your choice.

Luke 6:27 "But to you who are listening I say: Love your enemies, do good to those who hate you, 28 bless those who curse you, pray for those who mistreat you. 29 If someone slaps you on one cheek, turn to them the other also. If someone takes your coat, do not withhold your shirt from them. 30 Give to everyone who asks you, and if anyone takes what belongs to you, do not demand it back.

James 4:4 You adulterous people, don't you know that friendship with the world means enmity against God? Therefore, anyone who chooses to be a friend of the world becomes an enemy of God.

Luke 12:2 There is nothing concealed that will

not be disclosed, or hidden that will not be made known. 3 What you have said in the dark will be heard in the daylight, and what you have whispered in the ear in the inner rooms will be proclaimed from the roofs.

Psalm 103:8 The Lord is compassionate and gracious, slow to anger, abounding in love.

Psalm 37:1 Do not fret because of those who are evil or be envious of those who do wrong; 2 for like the grass they will soon wither, like green plants they will soon die away. 3 Trust in the LORD and do good; dwell in the land and enjoy safe pasture. 4 Take delight in the LORD, and he will give you the desires of your heart. 5 Commit your way to the LORD; trust in him and he will do this: 6 He will make your righteous reward shine like the dawn, your vindication like the noonday sun.

39 Black is chosen for the attire in the ritual chamber because it is symbolic of the Powers of Darkness. Sexually appealing clothing is worn by women for the purpose of stimulating the emotions of the male participants, and thereby intensifying the outpouring of adrenal or bioelectrical energy which will insure a more powerful working. — immodesty

1 Timothy 2:9 I also want the women to dress modestly, with decency and propriety, adorning themselves, not with elaborate hairstyles or gold or pearls or expensive clothes, 10 but with good deeds, appropriate for women who profess to worship God.

1 Corinthians 6:19 Do you not know that your bodies are temples of the Holy Spirit, who is in you, whom you have received from God? You are not your own; 20 you were bought at a price. Therefore honor God with your bodies.

1 Peter 3:3 Your beauty should not come from outward adornment, such as elaborate hairstyles and the wearing of gold jewelry or fine clothes. 4 Rather, it should be that of your inner self, the unfading beauty of a gentle and quiet spirit, which is of great worth in God's

sight. 5 For this is the way the holy women of the past who put their hope in God used to adorn themselves. They submitted themselves to their own husbands,

40 Satanism is a religion of the flesh, rather than of the spirit; therefore, an altar of flesh is used in Satanic ceremonies. The purpose of an altar is to serve as a focal point towards which all attention is focused during a ceremony. A nude woman is used as the altar in Satanic rituals because woman is the natural passive receptor, and represents the earth mother. — altar

Galatians 5:16 So I say, walk by the Spirit, and you will not gratify the desires of the flesh. 17 For the flesh desires what is contrary to the Spirit, and the Spirit what is contrary to the flesh. They are in conflict with each other, so that you are not to do whatever you want.

Romans 8:5 Those who live according to the flesh have their minds set on what the flesh desires; but those who live in accordance with the Spirit have their minds set on what the Spirit desires.

Magick In Theory And Practice by The Master Therion Aleister Crowley
Introduction

1 Magic is the Highest, most Absolute, and most Divine Knowledge of Natural Philosophy, advanced in its works and wonderful operations by a right understanding of the inward and occult virtue of things; so that true Agents being applied to proper Patients, strange and admirable effects will thereby be produced. Whence magicians are profound and diligent searchers into Nature; they, because of their skill, know how to anticipate an effect, the which to the vulgar shall seem to be a miracle. — knowledge

Colossians 2:2 My goal is that they may be encouraged in heart and united in love, so that

they may have the full riches of complete understanding, in order that they may know the mystery of God, namely, Christ, 3 in whom are hidden all the treasures of wisdom and knowledge.

2 Timothy 3:16 All Scripture is God-breathed and is useful for teaching, rebuking, correcting and training in righteousness, 17 so that the servant of God may be thoroughly equipped for every good work.

Proverbs 1:7 7 The fear of the LORD is the beginning of knowledge, but fools despise wisdom and instruction.

2 Every man has a right to fulfil his own will without being afraid that it may interfere with that of others; for if he is in his proper place, it is the fault of others if they interfere with him. (Illustration: If a man like Napoleon were actually appointed by destiny to control Europe, he should not be blamed for exercising his rights. To oppose him would be an error. Any one so doing would have made a mistake as to his own destiny, except in so far as it might be necessary for him to learn to lessons of defeat.   man's will

1 John 5:14 This is the confidence we have in approaching God: that if we ask anything according to his will, he hears us.

John 1:12 Yet to all who did receive him, to those who believed in his name, he gave the right to become children of God— 13 children born not of natural descent, nor of human decision or a husband's will, but born of God.

Proverbs 19:21 Many are the plans in a person's heart, but it is the LORD's purpose that prevails.

Proverbs 16:1 To humans belong the plans of the heart, but from the LORD comes the proper answer of the tongue.

The Principles Of Ritual

3 For example, God is above sex; and therefore neither man nor woman as such can be said fully to understand, much less to represent, God. It is therefore incumbent on the male   masculine vs feminine

magician to cultivate those female virtues in which he is deficient, and this task he must of course accomplish without in any way impairing his virility.

Galatians 3:28 There is neither Jew nor Gentile, neither slave nor free, nor is there male and female, for you are all one in Christ Jesus.

1 Corinthians 11:12 For as woman came from man, so also man is born of woman. But everything comes from God.

1 Peter 3:7 Husbands, in the same way be considerate as you live with your wives, and treat them with respect as the weaker partner and as heirs with you of the gracious gift of life, so that nothing will hinder your prayers.

Genesis 1:27 So God created mankind in his own image, in the image of God he created them; male and female he created them.

The Formulae Of The Elemental Weapons

4   Now in order to invoke any being, it is said by Hermes Trismegistus that the magi employ three methods. The first, for the vulgar, is that of supplication. In this the crude objective theory is assumed as true. There is a god named A, whom you, B, proceed to petition, in exactly the same sense as a boy might ask his father for pocket-money. The second method involves a little more subtlety, inasmuch as the magician endeavours to harmonize himself with the nature of the god, and to a certain extent exalts himself, in the course of the ceremony; but the third method is the only one worthy of our consideration. This consists of a real identification of the magician and the god.   invocation prayer

Matthew 6:9 "This, then, is how you should pray: " 'Our Father in heaven, hallowed be your name, 10 your kingdom come, your will be done, on earth as it is in heaven. 11 Give us today our daily bread. 12 And forgive us our debts, as we also have forgiven our debtors. 13 And lead us not into temptation, but deliver us from the evil one. '

Mark 11:22 "Have faith in God," Jesus

answered. 23 "Truly I tell you, if anyone says to this mountain, 'Go, throw yourself into the sea,' and does not doubt in their heart but believes that what they say will happen, it will be done for them. 24 Therefore I tell you, whatever you ask for in prayer, believe that you have received it, and it will be yours.

Romans 8:26 In the same way, the Spirit helps us in our weakness. We do not know what we ought to pray for, but the Spirit himself intercedes for us through wordless groans. 27 And he who searches our hearts knows the mind of the Spirit, because the Spirit intercedes for God's people in accordance with the will of God.

James 5:13 Is anyone among you in trouble? Let them pray. Is anyone happy? Let them sing songs of praise. 14 Is anyone among you sick? Let them call the elders of the church to pray over them and anoint them with oil in the name of the Lord. 15 And the prayer offered in faith will make the sick person well; the Lord will raise them up. If they have sinned, they will be forgiven. 16 Therefore confess your sins to each other and pray for each other so that you may be healed. The prayer of a righteous person is powerful and effective.

Psalm 145:18 The LORD is near to all who call on him, to all who call on him in truth.

5   The Egyptian Gods are so complete in their nature, so perfectly spiritual and yet so perfectly material, that this one invocation is sufficient. The God bethinks him that the spirit of Mercury should now appear to the magician; and it is so. This Egyptian formula is therefore to be preferred to the Hierarchical formula of the Hebrews with its tedious prayers, conjurations, and curses.   false gods paganism

Judges 2:12 They forsook the Lord, the God of their ancestors, who had brought them out of Egypt. They followed and worshiped various gods of the peoples around them. They aroused the Lord's anger 13 because they forsook him

and served Baal and the Ashtoreths.

1 Samuel 12:10 They cried out to the Lord and said, 'We have sinned; we have forsaken the Lord and served the Baals and the Ashtoreths. But now deliver us from the hands of our enemies, and we will serve you.'

Judges 2:10 After that whole generation had been gathered to their ancestors, another generation grew up who knew neither the Lord nor what he had done for Israel. 11 Then the Israelites did evil in the eyes of the Lord and served the Baals. 12 They forsook the Lord, the God of their ancestors, who had brought them out of Egypt. They followed and worshiped various gods of the peoples around them. They aroused the Lord's anger 13 because they forsook him and served Baal and the Ashtoreths.

6   With this understanding, we may rehabilitate the Hebrew system of invocations. The mind is the great enemy; so, by invoking enthusiastically a person whom we know not to exist, we are rebuking that mind. Yet we should not refrain altogether from philosophising in the light of the Holy Qabalah. We should accept the Magical Hierarchy as a more or less convenient classification of the facts of the Universe as they are known to us; and as our knowledge and understanding of those facts increase, so should we endeavour to adjust our idea of what we mean by any symbol.   *mind as enemy Kabbalah*

John 1:1 In the beginning was the Word, and the Word was with God, and the Word was God. 2 He was with God in the beginning. 3 Through him all things were made; without him nothing was made that has been made.

John 14:6 Jesus answered, "I am the way and the truth and the life. No one comes to the Father except through me.

Colossians 1:15 The Son is the image of the invisible God, the firstborn over all creation. 16 For in him all things were created: things in heaven and on earth, visible and invisible,

whether thrones or powers or rulers or authorities; all things have been created through him and for him. 17 He is before all things, and in him all things hold together.
   Romans 15:4 For everything that was written in the past was written to teach us, so that through the endurance taught in the Scriptures and the encouragement they provide we might have hope.

The Formula of I.A.O.

7   The doctrine of resurrection as vulgarly understood is false and absurd. It is not even "Scriptural". St. Paul does not identify the glorified body which rises with the mortal body which dies. On the contrary, he repeatedly insists on the distinction. The same is true of a magical ceremony. The magician who is destroyed by absorption in the Godhead is really destroyed. The miserable mortal automaton remains in the Circle.   Resurrection of Christ

Ephesians 1:17 I keep asking that the God of our Lord Jesus Christ, the glorious Father, may give you the Spirit of wisdom and revelation, so that you may know him better. 18 I pray that the eyes of your heart may be enlightened in order that you may know the hope to which he has called you, the riches of his glorious inheritance in his holy people, 19 and his incomparably great power for us who believe. That power is the same as the mighty strength 20 he exerted when he raised Christ from the dead and seated him at his right hand in the heavenly realms, 21 far above all rule and authority, power and dominion, and every name that is invoked, not only in the present age but also in the one to come.

1 Peter 1:3 Praise be to the God and Father of our Lord Jesus Christ! In his great mercy he has given us new birth into a living hope through the resurrection of Jesus Christ from the dead, 4 and into an inheritance that can never perish, spoil or fade. This inheritance is kept in heaven for you, 5 who through faith are shielded by God's power until the coming of the salvation that is ready to be revealed in the last time.

Philippians 3:7 But whatever were gains to me I now consider loss for the sake of Christ. 8 What is more, I consider everything a loss because of the surpassing worth of knowing Christ Jesus my Lord, for whose sake I have lost all things. I consider them garbage, that I may gain Christ 9 and be found in him, not having a righteousness of my own that comes from the law, but that which is through faith in Christ— the righteousness that comes from God on the basis of faith. 10 I want to know Christ—yes, to know the power of his resurrection and participation in his sufferings, becoming like him in his death, 11 and so, somehow, attaining to the resurrection from the dead.

8	The exalted "Devil" (also the "other" secret Eye) by the formula of the Initiation of Horus elsewhere described in detail. This "Devil" is called Satan or Shaitan, and regarded with horror by people who are ignorant of his formula, and, imagining themselves to be evil, accuse Nature herself of their own phantasmal crime. Satan is Saturn, Set, Abrasax, Adad, Adonis, Attis, Adam, Adonai, etc. The most serious charge against him is that he is the Sun in the South. The Ancient Initiates, dwelling as they did in lands whose blood was the water of the Nile or the Euphrates, connected the South with life-withering heat, and cursed that quarter where the solar darts were deadliest.	names of Satan

2 Corinthians 6:15 What harmony is there between Christ and Belial? Or what does a believer have in common with an unbeliever?

Isaiah 14:12 How you have fallen from heaven, morning star, son of the dawn! You have been cast down to the earth, you who once laid low the nations!

Revelation 12:9 The great dragon was hurled down—that ancient serpent called the devil, or Satan, who leads the whole world astray. He was hurled to the earth, and his angels with him.

Matthew 10:25 It is enough for students to be like their teachers, and servants like their masters. If the head of the house has been called Beelzebul, how much more the members of his household!

Revelation 13:1 The dragon stood on the shore of the sea. And I saw a beast coming out of the sea. It had ten horns and seven heads, with ten crowns on its horns, and on each head a blasphemous name. 2 The beast I saw resembled a leopard, but had feet like those of a bear and a mouth like that of a lion. The dragon gave the beast his power and his throne and great authority. 3 One of the heads of the beast seemed to have had a fatal wound, but the fatal wound had been healed. The whole world was filled with wonder and followed the beast. 4 People worshiped the dragon because he had given authority to the beast, and they also worshiped the beast and asked, "Who is like the beast? Who can wage war against it?" 5 The beast was given a mouth to utter proud words and blasphemies and to exercise its authority for forty-two months. 6 It opened its mouth to blaspheme God, and to slander his name and his dwelling place and those who live in heaven. 7 It was given power to wage war against God's holy people and to conquer them. And it was given authority over every tribe, people, language and nation. 8 All inhabitants of the earth will worship the beast—all whose names have not been written in the Lamb's book of life, the Lamb who was slain from the creation of the world.

9 Whoever has ears, let them hear.
10 "If anyone is to go into captivity,
    into captivity they will go.
If anyone is to be killed with the sword,
    with the sword they will be killed."
This calls for patient endurance and faithfulness on the part of God's people. The

Beast out of the Earth 11 Then I saw a second beast, coming out of the earth. It had two horns like a lamb, but it spoke like a dragon. 12 It exercised all the authority of the first beast on its behalf, and made the earth and its inhabitants worship the first beast, whose fatal wound had been healed. 13 And it performed great signs, even causing fire to come down from heaven to the earth in full view of the people. 14 Because of the signs it was given power to perform on behalf of the first beast, it deceived the inhabitants of the earth. It ordered them to set up an image in honor of the beast who was wounded by the sword and yet lived. 15 The second beast was given power to give breath to the image of the first beast, so that the image could speak and cause all who refused to worship the image to be killed. 16 It also forced all people, great and small, rich and poor, free and slave, to receive a mark on their right hands or on their foreheads, 17 so that they could not buy or sell unless they had the mark, which is the name of the beast or the number of its name. 18 This calls for wisdom. Let the person who has insight calculate the number of the beast, for it is the number of a man. That number is 666.

9   These antitheses are real only as a statement of relation; they are the conventions of an arbitrary device for representing our ideas in a pluralistic symbolism based on duality. "Good" must be defined in terms of human ideals and instincts.   good defined

Matthew 19:16 Just then a man came up to Jesus and asked, "Teacher, what good thing must I do to get eternal life?" 17 "Why do you ask me about what is good?" Jesus replied. "There is only One who is good. If you want to enter life, keep the commandments." 18 "Which ones?" he inquired. Jesus replied, " 'You shall not murder, you shall not commit adultery, you shall not steal, you shall not give false testimony, 19 honor your father and mother,' and 'love your neighbor as yourself.'"

Romans 8:28 And we know that in all things God works for the good of those who love him, who have been called according to his purpose.

Isaiah 5:20 Woe to those who call evil good and good evil, who put darkness for light and light for darkness, who put bitter for sweet and sweet for bitter.

Psalm 107:1 Give thanks to the LORD, for he is good; his love endures forever.

Psalm 16:2 I say to the LORD, "You are my Lord; apart from you I have no good thing."

The Magical Memory

10 There is no more important task than the exploration of one's previous incarnations. It has been objected to reincarnation that the population of this planet has been increasing rapidly. Were do the new souls come from? It is not necessary to invent theories about other planets; it is enough to say that the earth is passing through a period when human units are being built up from the elements with increased frequency.   reincarnation

Hebrews 9:27 Just as people are destined to die once, and after that to face judgment, 28 so Christ was sacrificed once to take away the sins of many; and he will appear a second time, not to bear sin, but to bring salvation to those who are waiting for him.

John 11:25 Jesus said to her, "I am the resurrection and the life. The one who believes in me will live, even though they die; 26 and whoever lives by believing in me will never die. Do you believe this?" 27 "Yes, Lord," she replied, "I believe that you are the Messiah, the Son of God, who is to come into the world."

Revelation 20:11 Then I saw a great white throne and him who was seated on it. The earth and the heavens fled from his presence, and there was no place for them. 12 And I saw the dead, great and small, standing before the throne, and books were opened. Another book was opened, which is the book of life. The dead were judged according to what they had done as recorded in the books.

Job 14:10 But a man dies and is laid low; he breathes his last and is no more. 11 As the water of a lake dries up or a riverbed becomes parched and dry, 12 so he lies down and does not rise; till the heavens are no more, people will not awake or be roused from their sleep.

11	One's life may represent the full possibilities of a certain partial Karma. One may have devoted one's incarnation to discharging the liabilities of one part of one's previous character. For instance, one might devote a lifetime to settling the bill run up by Napoleon for causing unnecessary suffering, with the object of starting afresh, clear of debt, in a life devoted to reaping the reward of the Corsican's invaluable services to the race.	karma

Galatians 6:7 Do not be deceived: God cannot be mocked. A man reaps what he sows. 8 Whoever sows to please their flesh, from the flesh will reap destruction; whoever sows to please the Spirit, from the Spirit will reap eternal life.

2 Corinthians 5:10 For we must all appear before the judgment seat of Christ, so that each of us may receive what is due us for the things done while in the body, whether good or bad.

James 3:18 Peacemakers who sow in peace reap a harvest of righteousness.

12	Genuine recollections almost invariably explain oneself to oneself. Suppose, for example, that you feel an instinctive aversion to some particular kind of wine. Try as you will, you can find no reason for your idiosyncrasy. Suppose, then, that when you explore some previous incarnation, you remember that you died by a poison administered in a wine of that character, your aversion is explained by the proverb, "A burnt child dreads the fire." It may be objected that in such a case your libido has created a phantasm of itself in the manner which Freud has explained. The criticism is just, but its value is reduced if it should happen that you were not	bad memories

aware of its existence until your Magical Memory attracted your attention to it. In fact, the essence of the test consists in this: that your memory notifies you of something which is the logical conclusion of the premises postulated by the past.

2 Corinthians 5:17 Therefore, if anyone is in Christ, the new creation has come: The old has gone, the new is here!

John 9:1 As he went along, he saw a man blind from birth. 2 His disciples asked him, "Rabbi, who sinned, this man or his parents, that he was born blind?" 3 "Neither this man nor his parents sinned," said Jesus, "but this happened so that the works of God might be displayed in him. 4 As long as it is day, we must do the works of him who sent me. Night is coming, when no one can work. 5 While I am in the world, I am the light of the world."

Isaiah 43:18 "Forget the former things; do not dwell on the past. 19 See, I am doing a new thing! Now it springs up; do you not perceive it? I am making a way in the wilderness and streams in the wasteland.

13 No scientific hypothesis can adduce stronger evidence evidence of its validity than the confirmation of its predictions by experimental evidence. The objective can always be expressed in subjective symbols if necessary. The controversy is ultimately unmeaning. However we interpret the evidence, its relative truth depends in its internal coherence. We may therefore say that any magical recollection is genuine if it gives the explanation of our external or internal conditions. Anything which throws light upon the Universe, anything which reveals us to ourselves, should be welcome in this world of riddles.

Matthew 18:16 But if they will not listen, take one or two others along, so that 'every matter may be established by the testimony of two or three witnesses.'

1 Timothy 5:19 Do not entertain an

accusation against an elder unless it is brought by two or three witnesses. 20 But those elders who are sinning you are to reprove before everyone, so that the others may take warning.

Exodus 23:1 "Do not spread false reports. Do not help a guilty person by being a malicious witness.

Of Equilibrium

14 "Before there was equilibrium, countenance beheld not countenance." The full significance of this aphorism is an Arcanum of the grade of Ipsissimus. It may, however, be partially apprehended by study of Liber Aleph, and the Book of the Law and the Commentaries thereon. It explains Existence. So sayeth the holiest of the Books of the ancient Qabalah.

balance

Revelation 6:5 When the Lamb opened the third seal, I heard the third living creature say, "Come!" I looked, and there before me was a black horse! Its rider was holding a pair of scales in his hand.

2 Peter 3:17 Therefore, dear friends, since you have been forewarned, be on your guard so that you may not be carried away by the error of the lawless and fall from your secure position.

1 Corinthians 10:No temptation has overtaken you except what is common to mankind. And God is faithful; he will not let you be tempted beyond what you can bear. But when you are tempted, he will also provide a way out so that you can endure it.

Ecclesiastes 3:1 There is a time for everything, and a season for every activity under the heavens: 2 a time to be born and a time to die, a time to plant and a time to uproot, 3 a time to kill and a time to heal, a time to tear down and a time to build, 4 a time to weep and a time to laugh, a time to mourn and a time to dance, 5 a time to scatter stones and a time to gather them, a time to embrace and a time to refrain from embracing, 6 a time to search and a time to give up, a time to keep and a time to throw away, 7 a time to tear and a time to mend, a time to be silent and a time to speak, 8 a time to love and a time to hate, a time for war and a time for peace.

Proverbs 11:1 The Lord detests dishonest scales, but accurate weights find favor with him.

Leviticus 19:36 Use honest scales and honest weights, an honest ephah and an honest hin. I am the Lord your God, who brought you out of Egypt.

15 As our record extends into the past, the evidence of its truth is cumulative. Every incarnation that we remember must increase our comprehension of ourselves as we are. Each accession of knowledge must indicate with unmistakable accuracy the solution of some enigma which is propounded by the Sphynx of our own unknown birth-city, Thebes. The complicated situation in which we find ourselves is composed of elements; and no element of it came out of nothing. Newton's First Law applies to every plane of thought. The theory of evolution is omniform.   truth

1 John 4:6 We are from God, and whoever knows God listens to us; but whoever is not from God does not listen to us. This is how we recognize the Spirit of truth and the spirit of falsehood.

John 8:31 To the Jews who had believed him, Jesus said, "If you hold to my teaching, you are really my disciples. 32 Then you will know the truth, and the truth will set you free."

Philippians 4:8 Finally, brothers and sisters, whatever is true, whatever is noble, whatever is right, whatever is pure, whatever is lovely, whatever is admirable—if anything is excellent or praiseworthy—think about such things. 9 Whatever you have learned or received or heard from me, or seen in me—put it into practice. And the God of peace will be with you.

Psalms 119:30 I have chosen the way of faithfulness; I have set my heart on your laws.

Of Silence And Secrecy: and of the Barbarous Names of Evocation

16 At a n***** [Deleted due to Racist term used by Crowley] camp meeting in the "United" States of America, devotees were worked up to such a pitch of excitement that the whole assembly developed a furious form of hysteria. The comparatively intelligible cries of "Glory" and "Hallelujah" no longer expressed the situation. Somebody screamed out "Ta-ra-ra-boom-de-ay!", and this was taken up by the whole meeting and yelled continuously, until reaction set in. The affair got into the papers, and some particularly bright disciple of John Stuart Mill, logician and economist, thought that these words, having set one set of fools crazy, might do the same to all the other fools in the world. He accordingly wrote a song, and produced the desired result. This is the most notorious example of recent times of the power exerted by a barbarous name of evocation. — racism

Galatians 3:28 There is neither Jew nor Gentile, neither slave nor free, nor is there male and female, for you are all one in Christ Jesus.

Romans 2:8 But for those who are self-seeking and who reject the truth and follow evil, there will be wrath and anger. 9 There will be trouble and distress for every human being who does evil: first for the Jew, then for the Gentile; 10 but glory, honor and peace for everyone who does good: first for the Jew, then for the Gentile. 11 For God does not show favoritism.

Genesis 1:26 Then God said, "Let us make mankind in our image, in our likeness, so that they may rule over the fish in the sea and the birds in the sky, over the livestock and all the wild animals, and over all the creatures that move along the ground." 27 So God created mankind in his own image, in the image of God he created them; male and female he created them.

Leviticus 19:34 The foreigner residing among you must be treated as your native-born. Love

them as yourself, for you were foreigners in Egypt. I am the Lord your God.

17 Magick recognizes frankly that truth is relative, subjective, and apparent   relativism

Colossians 2:8 See to it that no one takes you captive through hollow and deceptive philosophy, which depends on human tradition and the elemental spiritual forces of this world rather than on Christ.

Romans 8:7 The mind governed by the flesh is hostile to God; it does not submit to God's law, nor can it do so.

Proverbs 14:12 There is a way that appears to be right, but in the end it leads to death.

Isaiah 5:20 Woe to those who call evil good and good evil, who put darkness for light and light for darkness, who put bitter for sweet and sweet for bitter. 21 Woe to those who are wise in their own eyes and clever in their own sight.

Of the Gestures

18 Attitudes are of two Kinds: natural and artificial. Of the first kind, prostration is the obvious example. It comes natural to man (poor creature!) to throw himself to the ground in the presence of the object of his adoration.<<The Magician must eschew prostration, or even the "bending of the knee in supplication", as infamous and ignominious, an abdication of his sovereignty.>>   pride / humility

James 4:8 Come near to God and he will come near to you. Wash your hands, you sinners, and purify your hearts, you double-minded. 9 Grieve, mourn and wail. Change your laughter to mourning and your joy to gloom. 10 Humble yourselves before the Lord, and he will lift you up.

Philippians 2:3 Do nothing out of selfish ambition or vain conceit. Rather, in humility value others above yourselves, 4 not looking to your own interests but each of you to the interests of the others.

Galatians 6:4 Each one should test their own actions. Then they can take pride in themselves

alone, without comparing themselves to someone else, 5 for each one should carry their own load.

Isaiah 2:12 The LORD Almighty has a day in store for all the proud and lofty, for all that is exalted (and they will be humbled),

Jeremiah 9:23 This is what the LORD says: "Let not the wise boast of their wisdom or the strong boast of their strength or the rich boast of their riches, 24 but let the one who boasts boast about this: that they have the understanding to know me, that I am the LORD, who exercises kindness, justice and righteousness on earth, for in these I delight," declares the LORD. 25 "The days are coming," declares the LORD, "when I will punish all who are circumcised only in the flesh—

19 With practice, giddiness is altogether conquered; exhaustion then takes its place and the enemy of Will. It is through the mutual destruction of these antagonisms in the mental and moral being of the magician that Samadhi is begotten.

ecstacy
samadhi

Revelation 1:10 On the Lord's Day I was in the Spirit, and I heard behind me a loud voice like a trumpet, 11 which said: "Write on a scroll what you see and send it to the seven churches: to Ephesus, Smyrna, Pergamum, Thyatira, Sardis, Philadelphia and Laodicea." 12 I turned around to see the voice that was speaking to me. And when I turned I saw seven golden lampstands, 13 and among the lampstands was someone like a son of man, dressed in a robe reaching down to his feet and with a golden sash around his chest. 14 The hair on his head was white like wool, as white as snow, and his eyes were like blazing fire.

2 Timothy 3:16 All Scripture is God-breathed and is useful for teaching, rebuking, correcting and training in righteousness, 17 so that the servant of God may be thoroughly equipped for every good work.

Daniel 2:19 During the night the mystery was

revealed to Daniel in a vision. Then Daniel praised the God of heaven 20 and said: "Praise be to the name of God for ever and ever; wisdom and power are his. 21 He changes times and seasons; he deposes kings and raises up others. He gives wisdom to the wise and knowledge to the discerning.

Ezekiel 11:24 The Spirit lifted me up and brought me to the exiles in Babylonia in the vision given by the Spirit of God. Then the vision I had seen went up from me, 25 and I told the exiles everything the Lord had shown me.

Of Our Lady Babalon and of the Beast Whereon She Rideth

20   The essential magical work, apart from any particular operation, is the proper formation of the Magical Being or Body of Light....Therefore, although he may be able to penetrate the utmost recesses of the heavens, or conduct vigorous combats with the most unpronounceable demons of the pit, it may be impossible for him to do as much as knock a vase from a mantelpiece. His magical body is composed of matter too tenuous to affect directly the gross matter of which illusions such as tables and chairs are made.   heaven

John 3:5 Jesus answered, "Very truly I tell you, no one can enter the kingdom of God unless they are born of water and the Spirit. 6 Flesh gives birth to flesh, but the Spirit gives birth to spirit. 7 You should not be surprised at my saying, 'You must be born again.' 8 The wind blows wherever it pleases. You hear its sound, but you cannot tell where it comes from or where it is going. So it is with everyone born of the Spirit."

John 14:2 My Father's house has many rooms; if that were not so, would I have told you that I am going there to prepare a place for you? 3 And if I go and prepare a place for you, I will come back and take you to be with me that you also may be where I am.

Philippians 3:20 But our citizenship is in

heaven. And we eagerly await a Savior from there, the Lord Jesus Christ, 21 who, by the power that enables him to bring everything under his control, will transform our lowly bodies so that they will be like his glorious body.

Acts 1:11 "Men of Galilee," they said, "why do you stand here looking into the sky? This same Jesus, who has been taken from you into heaven, will come back in the same way you have seen him go into heaven."

Matthew 18:15 "If your brother or sister sins, go and point out their fault, just between the two of you. If they listen to you, you have won them over. 16 But if they will not listen, take one or two others along, so that 'every matter may be established by the testimony of two or three witnesses.' 17 If they still refuse to listen, tell it to the church; and if they refuse to listen even to the church, treat them as you would a pagan or a tax collector. 18 "Truly I tell you, whatever you bind on earth will be bound in heaven, and whatever you loose on earth will be loosed in heaven.

1 Corinthians 15:40 There are also heavenly bodies and there are earthly bodies; but the splendor of the heavenly bodies is one kind, and the splendor of the earthly bodies is another. 41 The sun has one kind of splendor, the moon another and the stars another; and star differs from star in splendor. 42 So will it be with the resurrection of the dead. The body that is sown is perishable, it is raised imperishable; 43 it is sown in dishonor, it is raised in glory; it is sown in weakness, it is raised in power; 44 it is sown a natural body, it is raised a spiritual body. If there is a natural body, there is also a spiritual body. 45 So it is written: "The first man Adam became a living being"; the last Adam, a life-giving spirit. 46 The spiritual did not come first, but the natural, and after that the spiritual. 47 The first man was of the dust of the earth; the second man is of heaven. 48 As was the earthly man, so are those who are of the earth; and as is the heavenly man, so also are those who are of heaven. 49 And just as we have borne the image of the earthly man, so shall we bear the image of the heavenly man.

Of the Bloody Sacrifice

21	Enough has now been said to show that the bloody sacrifice has from time immemorial been the most considered part of Magick. The ethics of the thing appear to have concerned no one; nor, to tell the truth, need they do so.	blood sacrifice

Hebrews 9:14 How much more, then, will the blood of Christ, who through the eternal Spirit offered himself unblemished to God, cleanse our consciences from acts that lead to death, so that we may serve the living God!

22	The blood is the life. This simple statement is explained by the Hindus by saying that the blood is the principal vehicle of vital Prana.<<Prana or force" is often used as a generic term for all kinds of subtle energy. The prana of the body is only one of its "vayus". Vayu means air or spirit. The idea is that all bodily forces are manifestations of the finer forces of the more real body, this real body being a subtle and invisible thing.>>	lifeforce prana

John 6:63 The Spirit gives life; the flesh counts for nothing. The words I have spoken to you—they are full of the Spirit and life.

1 Corinthians 15:22 For as in Adam all die, so in Christ all will be made alive.

23	Sexual intercourse creates a link between its exponents, and therefore a responsibility.>> For the highest spiritual working one must accordingly choose that victim which contains the greatest and purest force. A male child of perfect innocence and high intelligence<<It appears from the Magical Records of Frater Perdurabo that He made this particular sacrifice on an average about 150 times every year between 1912 e.v. and 1928 e.v. Contrast J.K.Huyman's "La-Bas", where a perverted form of Magic of an analogous order is	sexual intercourse human sacrifice

234

described.

Revelation 21:8 But the cowardly, the unbelieving, the vile, the murderers, the sexually immoral, those who practice magic arts, the idolaters and all liars—they will be consigned to the fiery lake of burning sulfur. This is the second death."

Matthew 26:52 "Put your sword back in its place," Jesus said to him, "for all who draw the sword will die by the sword. 53 Do you think I cannot call on my Father, and he will at once put at my disposal more than twelve legions of angels? 54 But how then would the Scriptures be fulfilled that say it must happen in this way?"

Deuteronomy 5:17 "You shall not murder.

Exodus 23:7 Have nothing to do with a false charge and do not put an innocent or honest person to death, for I will not acquit the guilty.

Leviticus 24:17 "'Anyone who takes the life of a human being is to be put to death.

Of the Banishings: and of the Purifications

24 A man who is normally an "allround good sort" vices often becomes intolerable when he gets rid of his collection of vices; he is swept into monomania by the spiritual pride which had been previously restrained by countervailing passions.

Colossians 3:5 Put to death, therefore, whatever belongs to your earthly nature: sexual immorality, impurity, lust, evil desires and greed, which is idolatry.

1 Corinthians 6:18 Flee from sexual immorality. All other sins a person commits are outside the body, but whoever sins sexually, sins against their own body. 19 Do you not know that your bodies are temples of the Holy Spirit, who is in you, whom you have received from God? You are not your own; 20 you were bought at a price. Therefore honor God with your bodies.

Matthew 5:30 And if your right hand causes you to stumble, cut it off and throw it away. It is better for you to lose one part of your body than for your whole body to go into hell.

Romans 13:12 The night is nearly over; the day is almost here. So let us put aside the deeds of darkness and put on the armor of light. 13 Let us behave decently, as in the daytime, not in carousing and drunkenness, not in sexual immorality and debauchery, not in dissension and jealousy. 14 Rather, clothe yourselves with the Lord Jesus Christ, and do not think about how to gratify the desires of the flesh

Galatians 5:17 For the flesh desires what is contrary to the Spirit, and the Spirit what is contrary to the flesh. They are in conflict with each other, so that you are not to do whatever you want.

1 Thessalonians 4:3 It is God's will that you should be sanctified: that you should avoid sexual immorality; 4 that each of you should learn to control your own body in a way that is holy and honorable, 5 not in passionate lust like the pagans, who do not know God; 6 and that in this matter no one should wrong or take advantage of a brother or sister.[b] The Lord will punish all those who commit such sins, as we told you and warned you before.

25 The formula is as follows. "Do what thou wilt shall be the whole of the Law." "What is thy Will?" "It is my will to eat and drink" "To what end?" "That my body may be fortified thereby." "To what end?" "That I may accomplish the Great Work." "Love is the law, love under will." "Fall to!" This may be adapted as a monologue. One may also add the inquiry "What is the Great Work?" and answer appropriately, when it seems useful to specify the nature of the Operation in progress at the time. The point is to seize every occasion of bringing every available force to bear upon the objective of the assault.

The Great Work

John 6:28 Then they asked him, "What must we do to do the works God requires?" 29 Jesus answered, "The work of God is this: to believe in the one he has sent."

John 9:4 As long as it is day, we must do the works of him who sent me. Night is coming, when no one can work.

Philippians 2:12 Therefore, my dear friends, as you have always obeyed—not only in my presence, but now much more in my absence—continue to work out your salvation with fear and trembling, 13 for it is God who works in you to will and to act in order to fulfill his good purpose.

1 Corinthians 1:27 But God chose the foolish things of the world to shame the wise; God chose the weak things of the world to shame the strong. 28 God chose the lowly things of this world and the despised things—and the things that are not—to nullify the things that are, 29 so that no one may boast before him.

Deuteronomy 7:9 Know therefore that the Lord your God is God; he is the faithful God, keeping his covenant of love to a thousand generations of those who love him and keep his commandments. 10 But those who hate him he will repay to their face by destruction; he will not be slow to repay to their face those who hate him. 11 Therefore, take care to follow the commands, decrees and laws I give you today.

26 The cleansed and consecrated Magician takes his cleansed and consecrated instruments into that cleansed and consecrated place, and there proceeds to repeat that double ceremony in the ceremony itself, which has these same two main parts.   cleansing

1 John 1:9 9 If we confess our sins, he is faithful and just and will forgive us our sins and purify us from all unrighteousness.

Titus 3:4 But when the kindness and love of God our Savior appeared, 5 he saved us, not because of righteous things we had done, but because of his mercy. He saved us through the washing of rebirth and renewal by the Holy Spirit, 6 whom he poured out on us generously through Jesus Christ our Savior, 7 so that, having been justified by his grace, we might become heirs having the hope of eternal life.

2 Corinthians 7:1 Therefore, since we have these promises, dear friends, let us purify ourselves from everything that contaminates body and spirit, perfecting holiness out of reverence for God. 2 Make room for us in your hearts. We have wronged no one, we have corrupted no one, we have exploited no one. 3 I do not say this to condemn you; I have said before that you have such a place in our hearts that we would live or die with you. 4 I have spoken to you with great frankness; I take great pride in you. I am greatly encouraged; in all our troubles my joy knows no bounds.

Psalm 51:10 Create in me a pure heart, O God, and renew a steadfast spirit within me.

Of the Consecrations: with an account of the Nature and Nurture of the Magical Link

27   Consecration is the active dedication of a thing   consecration
to a single purpose. Banishing prevents its use for any other purpose, but it remains inert until consecrated. Purification is performed by water, and banishing by air, whose weapon is the sword. Consecration is performed by fire, usually symbolised by the holy lamp.<<The general conception is that the three active elements co-operate to affect earth; but earth itself may be employed as an instrument. Its function is solidification. The use of the Pentacle is indeed very necessary in some types of operation, especially those whose object involves manifestation in matter, and the fixation in (more or less) permanent form of the subtle forces of Nature.>>

Romans 12:1 Therefore, I urge you, brothers and sisters, in view of God's mercy, to offer your bodies as a living sacrifice, holy and pleasing to God—this is your true and proper worship. 2 Do not conform to the pattern of this world, but be transformed by the renewing of your mind. Then you will be able to test and approve what God's will is—his good, pleasing and perfect will.

1 Peter 2:9 But you are a chosen people, a royal priesthood, a holy nation, God's special possession, that you may declare the praises of him who called you out of darkness into his wonderful light.

1 Peter 3:15 But in your hearts revere Christ as Lord. Always be prepared to give an answer to everyone who asks you to give the reason for the hope that you have. But do this with gentleness and respect, 16 keeping a clear conscience, so that those who speak maliciously against your good behavior in Christ may be ashamed of their slander. 17 For it is better, if it is God's will, to suffer for doing good than for doing evil.

Exodus 13:2 "Consecrate to me every firstborn male. The first offspring of every womb among the Israelites belongs to me, whether human or animal."

Isaiah 1:16 Wash and make yourselves clean. Take your evil deeds out of my sight; stop doing wrong. 17 Learn to do right; seek justice. Defend the oppressed. Take up the cause of the fatherless; plead the case of the widow. 18 "Come now, let us settle the matter," says the LORD. "Though your sins are like scarlet, they shall be as white as snow; though they are red as crimson, they shall be like wool. 19 If you are willing and obedient, you will eat the good things of the land; 20 but if you resist and rebel, you will be devoured by the sword." For the mouth of the LORD has spoken.

Numbers 11:18 "Tell the people: 'Consecrate yourselves in preparation for tomorrow, when you will eat meat. The Lord heard you when you wailed, "If only we had meat to eat! We were better off in Egypt!" Now the Lord will give you meat, and you will eat it.

28   What does the Magician do? He applies himself   exorcist
to invoke a God, and this God compels the
appearance of a spirit whose function is to
perform the Will of the magician at the moment.

There is no trace of what may be called machinery in the method. The exorcist hardly takes the pains of preparing a material basis for the spirit to incarnate except the bare connection of himself with his sigil.

Mark 16:16 Whoever believes and is baptized will be saved, but whoever does not believe will be condemned. 17 And these signs will accompany those who believe: In my name they will drive out demons; they will speak in new tongues; 18 they will pick up snakes with their hands; and when they drink deadly poison, it will not hurt them at all; they will place their hands on sick people, and they will get well."

Luke 4:33 In the synagogue there was a man possessed by a demon, an impure spirit. He cried out at the top of his voice, 34 "Go away! What do you want with us, Jesus of Nazareth? Have you come to destroy us? I know who you are—the Holy One of God!" 35 "Be quiet!" Jesus said sternly. "Come out of him!" Then the demon threw the man down before them all and came out without injuring him. 36 All the people were amazed and said to each other, "What words these are! With authority and power he gives orders to impure spirits and they come out!"

Acts 19:13 Some Jews who went around driving out evil spirits tried to invoke the name of the Lord Jesus over those who were demon-possessed. They would say, "In the name of the Jesus whom Paul preaches, I command you to come out." 14 Seven sons of Sceva, a Jewish chief priest, were doing this. 15 One day the evil spirit answered them, "Jesus I know, and Paul I know about, but who are you?" 16 Then the man who had the evil spirit jumped on them and overpowered them all. He gave them such a beating that they ran out of the house naked and bleeding. 17 When this became known to the Jews and Greeks living in Ephesus, they were all seized with fear, and the name of the Lord Jesus was held in high honor. 18 Many of those who believed now came and openly confessed what they had done. 19 A number who had practiced sorcery brought their scrolls together and burned them publicly. When they calculated the value of the scrolls, the total came to fifty thousand drachmas. 20 In this way the word of the Lord spread widely and grew in power.

29 The same may be said of witches, who appear   idols to have been wiser than the thaumaturgists who despised them. They at least made waxen images --- identified by baptism --- of the people they wished to control. They at least used appropriate bases for Magical manifestations, such as blood and other vehicles of animal force, with those of vegetable virtue such as herbs. They were also careful to put their bewitched products into actual contact --- material or astral --- with their victims. The classical exorcists, on the contrary, for all their learning, were careless about this essential condition. They acted as stupidly as people who should write business letters and omit to post them.

1 John 5:19 We know that we are children of God, and that the whole world is under the control of the evil one. 20 We know also that the Son of God has come and has given us understanding, so that we may know him who is true. And we are in him who is true by being in his Son Jesus Christ. He is the true God and eternal life.

Romans 1:21 For although they knew God, they neither glorified him as God nor gave thanks to him, but their thinking became futile and their foolish hearts were darkened. 22 Although they claimed to be wise, they became fools 23 and exchanged the glory of the immortal God for images made to look like a mortal human being and birds and animals and reptiles.

Psalm 115:4 But their idols are silver and gold, made by human hands. 5 They have mouths, but cannot speak, eyes, but cannot see.

6 They have ears, but cannot hear, noses, but cannot smell. 7 They have hands, but cannot feel, feet, but cannot walk, nor can they utter a sound with their throats. 8 Those who make them will be like them, and so will all who trust in them.

Exodus 20:3 "You shall have no other gods before me. 4 "You shall not make for yourself an image in the form of anything in heaven above or on the earth beneath or in the waters below. 5 You shall not bow down to them or worship them; for I, the Lord your God, am a jealous God, punishing the children for the sin of the parents to the third and fourth generation of those who hate me, 6 but showing love to a thousand generations of those who love me and keep my commandments.

Jonah 2:8 "Those who cling to worthless idols turn away from God's love for them. 9 But I, with shouts of grateful praise, will sacrifice to you. What I have vowed I will make good. I will say, 'Salvation comes from the LORD.' "

30 If one will the death of a sinner, it is not sufficient to hate him, even if we grant that the vibrations of thought, when sufficiently powerful and pure, may modify the Astral light sufficiently to impress its intention to a certain extent on such people as happen to be sensitive. It is much surer to use one's mind and muscle in service of that hate by devising and making a dagger, and then applying the dagger to the heart of one's enemy. One must give one's hate a bodily form of the same order as that which one's enemy has taken for his manifestation.   enemy hatred

Luke 6:27 "But to you who are listening I say: Love your enemies, do good to those who hate you, 28 bless those who curse you, pray for those who mistreat you. 29 If someone slaps you on one cheek, turn to them the other also. If someone takes your coat, do not withhold your shirt from them. 30 Give to everyone who asks you, and if anyone takes what belongs to you, do not demand it back.

Romans 12:18 If it is possible, as far as it depends on you, live at peace with everyone. 19 Do not take revenge, my dear friends, but leave room for God's wrath, for it is written: "It is mine to avenge; I will repay," says the Lord. 20 On the contrary: "If your enemy is hungry, feed him; if he is thirsty, give him something to drink. In doing this, you will heap burning coals on his head."

Matthew 5:43 "You have heard that it was said, 'Love your neighbor and hate your enemy.' 44 But I tell you, love your enemies and pray for those who persecute you, 45 that you may be children of your Father in heaven. He causes his sun to rise on the evil and the good, and sends rain on the righteous and the unrighteous.

1 Peter 3:9 Do not repay evil with evil or insult with insult. On the contrary, repay evil with blessing, because to this you were called so that you may inherit a blessing.

Proverbs 24:17 Do not gloat when your enemy falls; when they stumble, do not let your heart rejoice, 18 or the LORD will see and disapprove and turn his wrath away from them.

Psalms 37:1 Do not fret because of those who are evil or be envious of those who do wrong; 2 for like the grass they will soon wither, like green plants they will soon die away. 3 Trust in the LORD and do good; dwell in the land and enjoy safe pasture. 4 Take delight in the LORD, and he will give you the desires of your heart. 5 Commit your way to the LORD; trust in him and he will do this: 6 He will make your righteous reward shine like the dawn, your vindication like the noonday sun.

31 Remember that Magick includes all acts soever. Anything may serve as a Magical weapon. To impose one's Will on a nation, for instance, one's talisman may be a newspaper, one's triangle a church, or one's circle a Club. To win a woman, one's pantacle may be a necklace; to discover a treasure, one's wand may be a

weapons

dramatist's pen, or one's incantation a popular song.

2 Corinthians 10:4 The weapons we fight with are not the weapons of the world. On the contrary, they have divine power to demolish strongholds. 5 We demolish arguments and every pretension that sets itself up against the knowledge of God, and we take captive every thought to make it obedient to Christ.

Ephesians 6:10 Finally, be strong in the Lord and in his mighty power. 11 Put on the full armor of God, so that you can take your stand against the devil's schemes. 12 For our struggle is not against flesh and blood, but against the rulers, against the authorities, against the powers of this dark world and against the spiritual forces of evil in the heavenly realms. 13 Therefore put on the full armor of God, so that when the day of evil comes, you may be able to stand your ground, and after you have done everything, to stand.

Ephesians 6:17 Take the helmet of salvation and the sword of the Spirit, which is the word of God. 18 And pray in the Spirit on all occasions with all kinds of prayers and requests. With this in mind, be alert and always keep on praying for all the Lord's people.

32 Again, a sorcerer might happen to possess an object belonging magically to a rich man, such as a compromising letter, which is really as much part of him as his liver; he may then master the will of that man by intimidating his mind. His power to publish the letter is as effective as if he could injure the man's body directly. These "natural" cases may be transposed into subtler terms; for instance, one might master another man, even a stranger, by sheer concentration of will, ceremonially or otherwise wrought up to the requisite potential. But in one way or another that will must be made to impinge on the man; by the normal means of contact if possible, if not, by attacking some sensitive spot in his subconscious revenge
dominance

sensorium.

Matthew 20:25 Jesus called them together and said, "You know that the rulers of the Gentiles lord it over them, and their high officials exercise authority over them. 26 Not so with you. Instead, whoever wants to become great among you must be your servant, 27 and whoever wants to be first must be your slave— 28 just as the Son of Man did not come to be served, but to serve, and to give his life as a ransom for many.

Romans 16:17 I urge you, brothers and sisters, to watch out for those who cause divisions and put obstacles in your way that are contrary to the teaching you have learned. Keep away from them. 18 For such people are not serving our Lord Christ, but their own appetites. By smooth talk and flattery they deceive the minds of naive people.

Ephesians 6:9 And masters, treat your slaves in the same way. Do not threaten them, since you know that he who is both their Master and yours is in heaven, and there is no favoritism with him.

Philippians 2:3 Do nothing out of selfish ambition or vain conceit. Rather, in humility value others above yourselves, 4 not looking to your own interests but each of you to the interests of the others.

Proverbs 31:Speak up and judge fairly; defend the rights of the poor and needy.

Of the Oath

33 The third operation in any magical ceremony is the oath or proclamation. The Magician, armed and ready, stands in the centre of the Circle, and strikes once upon the bell as if to call the attention of the Universe. He then declares "who he is", reciting his magical history by the proclamation of the grades which he has attained, giving the signs and words of those grades.<<This is not merely to prove himself a person in authority. It is to trace the chain of causes that have let to the present position, so   karma

that the operation is seen as karma.>>

John 3:36 Whoever believes in the Son has eternal life, but whoever rejects the Son will not see life, for God's wrath remains on them.

Matthew 25:40 "The King will reply, 'Truly I tell you, whatever you did for one of the least of these brothers and sisters of mine, you did for me.' 41 "Then he will say to those on his left, 'Depart from me, you who are cursed, into the eternal fire prepared for the devil and his angels. 42 For I was hungry and you gave me nothing to eat, I was thirsty and you gave me nothing to drink, 43 I was a stranger and you did not invite me in, I needed clothes and you did not clothe me, I was sick and in prison and you did not look after me.' 44 "They also will answer, 'Lord, when did we see you hungry or thirsty or a stranger or needing clothes or sick or in prison, and did not help you?' 45 "He will reply, 'Truly I tell you, whatever you did not do for one of the least of these, you did not do for me.' 46 "Then they will go away to eternal punishment, but the righteous to eternal life."

1 John 1:9 If we confess our sins, he is faithful and just and will forgive us our sins and purify us from all unrighteousness.

34 The Oath is the foundation of all Work in Magick, as it is an affirmation of the Will. An Oath binds the Magician for ever.   oaths

Matthew 23:16 "Woe to you, blind guides! You say, 'If anyone swears by the temple, it means nothing; but anyone who swears by the gold of the temple is bound by that oath.' 17 You blind fools! Which is greater: the gold, or the temple that makes the gold sacred? 18 You also say, 'If anyone swears by the altar, it means nothing; but anyone who swears by the gift on the altar is bound by that oath.' 19 You blind men! Which is greater: the gift, or the altar that makes the gift sacred? 20 Therefore, anyone who swears by the altar swears by it and by everything on it. 21 And anyone who swears by the temple swears by it and by the one who dwells in it. 22 And anyone who swears by heaven swears by God's throne and by the one who sits on it.

Matthew 5:33 "Again, you have heard that it was said to the people long ago, 'Do not break your oath, but fulfill to the Lord the vows you have made.' 34 But I tell you, do not swear an oath at all: either by heaven, for it is God's throne; 35 or by the earth, for it is his footstool; or by Jerusalem, for it is the city of the Great King. 36 And do not swear by your head, for you cannot make even one hair white or black. 37 All you need to say is simply 'Yes' or 'No'; anything beyond this comes from the evil one.

James 5:12 Above all, my brothers and sisters, do not swear—not by heaven or by earth or by anything else. All you need to say is a simple "Yes" or "No." Otherwise you will be condemned.

Joshua 9:20 This is what will do to them: We will let them live, so that God's wrath will not fall on us for breaking the oath we swore to them."

Leviticus 5:4 or if anyone thoughtlessly takes an oath to do anything, whether good or evil (in any matter one might carelessly swear about) even though they are unaware of it, but then they learn of it and realize their guilt— 5 when anyone becomes aware that they are guilty in any of these matters, they must confess in what way they have sinned.

35   In Magick, likewise, the Adept who is sworn to   angels attain to the Knowledge and Conversation of his Holy Guardian Angel may in his grosser days have been expert as a Healer, to find that he is now incapable of any such work. He will probably be puzzled, and wonder whether he has lost all his power. Yet the cause may be no more than that the Wisdom of his Angel depreciates the interference of ignorant kindliness with diseases which may have been sent to the sufferer for a purpose profoundly important to his welfare.

Hebrews 1:13 To which of the angels did God ever say, "Sit at my right hand until I make your enemies a footstool for your feet? 14 Are not all angels ministering spirits sent to serve those who will inherit salvation?

Revelation 12:7 Then war broke out in heaven. Michael and his angels fought against the dragon, and the dragon and his angels fought back. 8 But he was not strong enough, and they lost their place in heaven. 9 The great dragon was hurled down—that ancient serpent called the devil, or Satan, who leads the whole world astray. He was hurled to the earth, and his angels with him.

Revelation 22:8 I, John, am the one who heard and saw these things. And when I had heard and seen them, I fell down to worship at the feet of the angel who had been showing them to me. 9 But he said to me, "Don't do that! I am a fellow servant with you and with your fellow prophets and with all who keep the words of this scroll. Worship God!"

Job 4:15 A spirit glided past my face, and the hair on my body stood on end. 16 It stopped, but I could not tell what it was. A form stood before my eyes, and I heard a hushed voice: 17 'Can a mortal be more righteous than God? Can even a strong man be more pure than his Maker? 18 If God places no trust in his servants, if he charges his angels with error, 19 how much more those who live in houses of clay, whose foundations are in the dust, who are crushed more readily than a moth!

Isaiah 6:1 In the year that King Uzziah died, I saw the Lord, high and exalted, seated on a throne; and the train of his robe filled the temple. 2 Above him were seraphim, each with six wings: With two wings they covered their faces, with two they covered their feet, and with two they were flying. 3 And they were calling to one another: "Holy, holy, holy is the LORD Almighty; the whole earth is full of his glory."

Of the Invocation

36   The Magician addresses a direct petition to the   prayer
Being invoked. But the secret of success in
invocation has not hitherto been disclosed. It is
an exceedingly simple one. It is practically of
no importance whatever that the invocation
should be "right". There are a thousand different
ways of compassing the end proposed, so far as
external things are concerned. The whole secret
may be summarised in these four words:
"Enflame thyself in praying."<<This is
Qabalistically expressed in the old Formula:
Domine noster, audi tuo servo! kyrie Christe! O
Christe!>> The mind must be exalted until it
loses consciousness of self.

Romans 8:26 In the same way, the Spirit helps us in our weakness. We do not know what we ought to pray for, but the Spirit himself intercedes for us through wordless groans. 27 And he who searches our hearts knows the mind of the Spirit, because the Spirit intercedes for God's people in accordance with the will of God.

Ephesians 6:18 And pray in the Spirit on all occasions with all kinds of prayers and requests. With this in mind, be alert and always keep on praying for all the Lord's people. 19 Pray also for me, that whenever I speak, words may be given me so that I will fearlessly make known the mystery of the gospel, 20 for which I am an ambassador in chains. Pray that I may declare it fearlessly, as I should.

Philippians 4:6 Do not be anxious about anything, but in every situation, by prayer and petition, with thanksgiving, present your requests to God. 7 And the peace of God, which transcends all understanding, will guard your hearts and your minds in Christ Jesus.

James 5:13 Is anyone among you in trouble? Let them pray. Is anyone happy? Let them sing songs of praise. 14 Is anyone among you sick? Let them call the elders of the church to pray over them and anoint them with oil in the name of the Lord. 15 And the prayer offered in faith will make the sick person well; the Lord will raise them up. If they have sinned, they will be forgiven. 16 Therefore confess your sins to each other and pray for each other so that you may be healed. The prayer of a righteous person is powerful and effective.

Psalm 17:1 Hear me, LORD, my plea is just; listen to my cry. Hear my prayer— it does not rise from deceitful lips.

Psalm 34:17 The righteous cry out, and the LORD hears them; he delivers them from all their troubles.

Psalm 66:18 If I had cherished sin in my heart, the Lord would not have listened; 19 but God has surely listened and has heard my prayer. 20 Praise be to God, who has not rejected my prayer or withheld his love from me!

37   Beside these open methods thee are also a number of mental methods of Invocation ... The third is the assumption of the form of the God --- by transmuting the astral body into His shape. This last method is really essential to all proper invocation, and cannot be too sedulously practised.   false gods
invocation

1 John 5:21 Dear children, keep yourselves from idols.

Revelation 9:20 The rest of mankind who were not killed by these plagues still did not repent of the work of their hands; they did not stop worshiping demons, and idols of gold, silver, bronze, stone and wood—idols that cannot see or hear or walk. 21 Nor did they repent of their murders, their magic arts, their sexual immorality or their thefts.

1 Corinthians 10:7 Do not be idolaters, as some of them were; as it is written: "The people sat down to eat and drink and got up to indulge in revelry." 8 We should not commit sexual immorality, as some of them did—and in one day twenty-three thousand of them died. 9 We should not test Christ, as some of them did— and were killed by snakes.

1 Corinthians 10:20 No, but the sacrifices of pagans are offered to demons, not to God, and I do not want you to be participants with demons.

Jonah 2:8 "Those who cling to worthless idols turn away from God's love for them.

Leviticus 19:4 "'Do not turn to idols or make metal gods for yourselves. I am the Lord your God.

Of the Charge to The Spirit With Some Account of the Constraints and Curses Occasionally Necessary

38   On the appearance of the spirit, or the spirits manifestation of the force in the talisman which is being consecrated, it is necessary to bind it by an Oath or Charge. A spirit should be made to lay its hand visibly on the weapon by whose might it has been evoked, and to "swear obedience and faith to Him that liveth and triumpheth, that regneth above him in His palaces as the Balance of Righteousness and Truth" by the names used in the evocation.

1 Corinthians 10:21 You cannot drink the cup of the Lord and the cup of demons too; you cannot have a part in both the Lord's table and the table of demons.

1 Timothy 4:1 The Spirit clearly says that in later times some will abandon the faith and follow deceiving spirits and things taught by demons. 2 Such teachings come through hypocritical liars, whose consciences have been seared as with a hot iron.

Luke 8:1 After this, Jesus traveled about from one town and village to another, proclaiming the good news of the kingdom of God. The Twelve were with him, 2 and also some women who had been cured of evil spirits and diseases: Mary (called Magdalene) from whom seven demons had come out;

Isaiah 8:19 When someone tells you to consult mediums and spiritists, who whisper and mutter, should not a people inquire of their God? Why consult the dead on behalf of the living?

39   Now, there are a great many talismans in this   talismans
world which are being left lying about in a most
reprehensibly careless manner. Such are the
objects of popular adoration, as ikons, and idols.
But, it is actually true that a great deal of real
magical Force is locked up in such things;
consequently, by destroying these sacred
symbols, you can overcome magically the
people who adore them.

1 Corinthians 6:19 Do you not know that your bodies are temples of the Holy Spirit, who is in you, whom you have received from God? You are not your own; 20 you were bought at a price. Therefore honor God with your bodies.

Ezekiel 13:18 and say, 'This is what the Sovereign Lord says: Woe to the women who sew magic charms on all their wrists and make veils of various lengths for their heads in order to ensnare people. Will you ensnare the lives of my people but preserve your own? 19 You have profaned me among my people for a few handfuls of barley and scraps of bread. By lying to my people, who listen to lies, you have killed those who should not have died and have spared those who should not live. 20 "'Therefore this is what the Sovereign Lord says: I am against your magic charms with which you ensnare people like birds and I will tear them from your arms; I will set free the people that you ensnare like birds. 21 I will tear off your veils and save my people from your hands, and they will no longer fall prey to your power. Then you will know that I am the Lord.

2 Kings 23:24 Furthermore, Josiah got rid of the mediums and spiritists, the household gods, the idols and all the other detestable things seen in Judah and Jerusalem. This he did to fulfill the requirements of the law written in the book that Hilkiah the priest had discovered in the temple of the Lord.

40   It is not at all irrational to fight for one's flag,   money
provided that the flag is an object which really
means something to somebody. Similarly, with

the most widely spread and most devotedly worshipped talisman of all, money, you can evidently break the magical will of a worshipper of money by taking his money away from him, or by destroying its value in some way or another. But, in the case of money, general experience tells us that there is very little of it lying about loose. In this case, above all, people have recognised its talismanic virtue, that is to say, its power as an instrument of the will.

Mark 10:21 Jesus looked at him and loved him. "One thing you lack," he said. "Go, sell everything you have and give to the poor, and you will have treasure in heaven. Then come, follow me."

Matthew 6:24 "No one can serve two masters. Either you will hate the one and love the other, or you will be devoted to the one and despise the other. You cannot serve both God and money. 25 "Therefore I tell you, do not worry about your life, what you will eat or drink; or about your body, what you will wear. Is not life more than food, and the body more than clothes?

1 Peter 5:2 Be shepherds of God's flock that is under your care, watching over them—not because you must, but because you are willing, as God wants you to be; not pursuing dishonest gain, but eager to serve; 3 not lording it over those entrusted to you, but being examples to the flock.

Jeremiah 9:23 This is what the LORD says: "Let not the wise boast of their wisdom or the strong boast of their strength or the rich boast of their riches, 24 but let the one who boasts boast about this: that they have the understanding to know me, that I am the LORD, who exercises kindness, justice and righteousness on earth, for in these I delight," declares the LORD.

Proverbs 16:16 How much better to get wisdom than gold, to get insight rather than silver!

Of the License to Depart

41   It is as foolish to do Magick without method, as if it were anything else. To do Magick without keeping a record is like trying to run a business without bookkeeping. There are a great many people who quite misunderstand the nature of Magick. They have an idea that it is something vague and unreal, instead of being, as it is, a direct means of coming into contact with reality.   reality

Colossians 2:18 Do not let anyone who delights in false humility and the worship of angels disqualify you. Such a person also goes into great detail about what they have seen; they are puffed up with idle notions by their unspiritual mind. 19 They have lost connection with the head, from whom the whole body, supported and held together by its ligaments and sinews, grows as God causes it to grow. 20 Since you died with Christ to the elemental spiritual forces of this world, why, as though you still belonged to the world, do you submit to its rules: 21 "Do not handle! Do not taste! Do not touch!"? 22 These rules, which have to do with things that are all destined to perish with use, are based on merely human commands and teachings.

Hebrews 9:24 For Christ did not enter a sanctuary made with human hands that was only a copy of the true one; he entered heaven itself, now to appear for us in God's presence.

Romans 1:25 They exchanged the truth about God for a lie, and worshiped and served created things rather than the Creator—who is forever praised. Amen.

Of Clairvoyance and the Body of Light

42   There is no such thing as truth in the perceptible universe; every idea when analysed is found to contain a contradiction. It is quite useless (except as a temporary expedient) to set up one class of ideas against another as being "more real". The advance of man towards God is not necessarily an advance towards truth.   truth

John 1:14 The Word became flesh and made his dwelling among us. We have seen his glory, the glory of the one and only Son, who came from the Father, full of grace and truth.

Ephesians 4:20 That, however, is not the way of life you learned 21 when you heard about Christ and were taught in him in accordance with the truth that is in Jesus.

John 14:16 And I will ask the Father, and he will give you another advocate to help you and be with you forever—17 the Spirit of truth. The world cannot accept him, because it neither sees him nor knows him. But you know him, for he lives with you and will be in you.

Psalms 119:160 All your words are true; all your righteous laws are eternal.

43 Develop the body of Light until it is just as real to you as your other body, teach it to travel to any desired symbol, and enable it to perform all necessary Rites and Invocations. In short, educate it. Ultimately, the relation of that body with your own must be exceedingly intimate; but before this harmonizing takes place, you should begin by a careful differentiation. The first thing to do, therefore, is to get the body outside your own. To avoid muddling the two, you begin by imagining a shape resembling yourself standing in front of you. Do not say: "Oh, it's only imagination!" The time to test that is later on, when you have secured a fairly clear mental image of such a body. Try to imagine how your own body would look if you were standing in its place; try to transfer your consciousness to the Body of Light.

light

John 8:12 When Jesus spoke again to the people, he said, "I am the light of the world. Whoever follows me will never walk in darkness, but will have the light of life."

1 John 1:5 This is the message we have heard from him and declare to you: God is light; in him there is no darkness at all. 6 If we claim to have fellowship with him and yet walk in the darkness, we lie and do not live out the truth. 7

But if we walk in the light, as he is in the light, we have fellowship with one another, and the blood of Jesus, his Son, purifies us from all sin.

Ephesians 5:8 For you were once darkness, but now you are light in the Lord. Live as children of light 9 (for the fruit of the light consists in all goodness, righteousness and truth) 10 and find out what pleases the Lord.

Psalm 119:105 Your word is a lamp for my feet, a light on my path.

Genesis 1:3 And God said, "Let there be light," and there was light.

44   You may also try "rising on the planes". With a little practice, especially if you have a good Guru, you ought to be able to slip in and out of your astral body as easily as you slip in and out of a dressing-gown.   guru
spiritual
guide

John 16:13 But when he, the Spirit of truth, comes, he will guide you into all the truth. He will not speak on his own; he will speak only what he hears, and he will tell you what is yet to come.

John 14:26 But the Advocate, the Holy Spirit, whom the Father will send in my name, will teach you all things and will remind you of everything I have said to you.

1 Chronicles 10:13 Saul died because he was unfaithful to the Lord; he did not keep the word of the Lord and even consulted a medium for guidance, 14 and did not inquire of the Lord. So the Lord put him to death and turned the kingdom over to David son of Jesse.

Leviticus 19:31 "'Do not turn to mediums or seek out spiritists, for you will be defiled by them. I am the Lord your God.

Psalm 119:105 Your word is a lamp for my feet, a light on my path.

45   To sum up, the first task is to separate the astral form from the physical body, the second to develop the powers of the astral body, in particular those of sight, travel, and interpretation; third, to unify the two bodies without muddling them. This being   astral body
soul

accomplished, the magician is fitted to deal with the invisible.

Matthew 10:28 Do not be afraid of those who kill the body but cannot kill the soul. Rather, be afraid of the One who can destroy both soul and body in hell.

Matthew 22:35 One of them, an expert in the law, tested him with this question: 36 "Teacher, which is the greatest commandment in the Law?" 37 Jesus replied: "'Love the Lord your God with all your heart and with all your soul and with all your mind.'

1 Peter 1:22 Now that you have purified yourselves by obeying the truth so that you have sincere love for each other, love one another deeply, from the heart.

Psalm 42:2 My soul thirsts for God, for the living God. When can I go and meet with God? 3 My tears have been my food day and night, while people say to me all day long, "Where is your God?" 4 These things I remember as I pour out my soul: how I used to go to the house of God under the protection of the Mighty One with shouts of joy and praise among the festive throng. 5 Why, my soul, are you downcast? Why so disturbed within me? Put your hope in God, for I will yet praise him, my Savior and my God. 6 My soul is downcast within me; therefore I will remember you from the land of the Jordan, the heights of Hermon— from Mount Mizar.

46 There are also planes corresponding to various religions past and present, all of which have their peculiar unity.   religions

Acts 17:24 "The God who made the world and everything in it is the Lord of heaven and earth and does not live in temples built by human hands. 25 And he is not served by human hands, as if he needed anything. Rather, he himself gives everyone life and breath and everything else. 26 From one man he made all the nations, that they should inhabit the whole earth; and he marked out their appointed times in history and the boundaries of their lands. 27 God did this so that they would seek him and perhaps reach out for him and find him, though he is not far from any one of us. 28 'For in him we live and move and have our being.' As some of your own poets have said, 'We are his offspring.' 29 "Therefore since we are God's offspring, we should not think that the divine being is like gold or silver or stone—an image made by human design and skill.

Mark 16:14 Later Jesus appeared to the Eleven as they were eating; he rebuked them for their lack of faith and their stubborn refusal to believe those who had seen him after he had risen. 15 He said to them, "Go into all the world and preach the gospel to all creation. 16 Whoever believes and is baptized will be saved, but whoever does not believe will be condemned.

47 Theism is "obscurum per obscurius." A male star is built up from the centre outwards; a female from the circumference inwards. This is what is meant when we say that woman has no soul. It explains fully the difference between the sexes.>> The true God is man. In man are all things hidden.   man as god

Galatians 6:3 If anyone thinks they are something when they are not, they deceive themselves. 4 Each one should test their own actions. Then they can take pride in themselves alone, without comparing themselves to someone else, 5 for each one should carry their own load.

John 17:3 Now this is eternal life: that they know you, the only true God, and Jesus Christ, whom you have sent.

Matthew 28:19 Therefore go and make disciples of all nations, baptizing them in the name of the Father and of the Son and of the Holy Spirit, 20 and teaching them to obey everything I have commanded you. And surely I am with you always, to the very end of the age."

48 Thus, it is necessary that the technique of   light

Magick should be perfected. The Body of Light must be rendered capable of going everywhere and doing everything. It is, therefore, always the question of drill which is of importance. You have got to go out Rising on the Planes every day of your life, year after year. You are not to be disheartened by failure, or too much encouraged by success, in any one practice or set of practices. What you are doing is what will be of real value to you in the end; and that is, developing a character, creating a Karma, which will give you the power to do your will.

karma

John 8:12 When Jesus spoke again to the people, he said, "I am the light of the world. Whoever follows me will never walk in darkness, but will have the light of life."

Matthew 7:2 For in the same way you judge others, you will be judged, and with the measure you use, it will be measured to you.

1 John 1:5 This is the message we have heard from him and declare to you: God is light; in him there is no darkness at all. 6 If we claim to have fellowship with him and yet walk in the darkness, we lie and do not live out the truth. 7 But if we walk in the light, as he is in the light, we have fellowship with one another, and the blood of Jesus, his Son, purifies us from all sin. 8 If we claim to be without sin, we deceive ourselves and the truth is not in us. 9 If we confess our sins, he is faithful and just and will forgive us our sins and purify us from all unrighteousness.

James 2:12 Speak and act as those who are going to be judged by the law that gives freedom, 13 because judgment without mercy will be shown to anyone who has not been merciful. Mercy triumphs over judgment.

Matthew 5:15 Neither do people light a lamp and put it under a bowl. Instead they put it on its stand, and it gives light to everyone in the house. 16 In the same way, let your light shine before others, that they may see your good deeds and glorify your Father in heaven.

Proverbs 5:22 The evil deeds of the wicked ensnare them; the cords of their sins hold them fast.

49   Divination is so important a branch of Magick as almost to demand a separate treatise.   divination

Deuteronomy 18:10 Let no one be found among you who sacrifices their son or daughter in the fire, who practices divination or sorcery, interprets omens, engages in witchcraft, 11 or casts spells, or who is a medium or spiritist or who consults the dead.

2 Kings 17:17 They sacrificed their sons and daughters in the fire. They practiced divination and sought omens and sold themselves to do evil in the eyes of the Lord, arousing his anger.

Jeremiah 27:9 So do not listen to your prophets, your diviners, your interpreters of dreams, your mediums or your sorcerers who tell you, 'You will not serve the king of Babylon.'

50   Care must be taken to employ none but spirits who are fit for the purpose, not only by reason of their capacity to supply information, but for their sympathy with the personality of the Magician. Any attempt to coerce unwilling spirits is dangerous. They obey from fear; their fear makes them flatter, and tell amiable falsehoods.   ghosts

Matthew 25:41 "Then he will say to those on his left, 'Depart from me, you who are cursed, into the eternal fire prepared for the devil and his angels.

2 Corinthians 11:14 And no wonder, for Satan himself masquerades as an angel of light. 15 It is not surprising, then, if his servants also masquerade as servants of righteousness. Their end will be what their actions deserve.

Isaiah 8:19 When someone tells you to consult mediums and spiritists, who whisper and mutter, should not a people inquire of their God? Why consult the dead on behalf of the living?

Leviticus 19:31 "'Do not turn to mediums or

seek out spiritists, for you will be defiled by them. I am the Lord your God.

Of the Eucharist and of the Art Of Alchemy

51 One of the simplest and most complete of Magick ceremonies is the Eucharist. It consists in taking common things, transmuting them into things divine, and consuming them. So far, it is a type of every magick ceremony, for the reabsorption of the force is a kind of consumption; but it has a more restricted application, as follows. Take a substance<<This may be of composite character.>> symbolic of the whole course of nature, make it God, and consume it. There are many ways of doing this; but they may easily be classified according to the number of the elements of which the sacrament is composed. The highest form of the Eucharist is that in which the Element consecrated is One.

eucharist

Luke 22:19 And he took bread, gave thanks and broke it, and gave it to them, saying, "This is my body given for you; do this in remembrance of me." 20 In the same way, after the supper he took the cup, saying, "This cup is the new covenant in my blood, which is poured out for you.

1 Corinthians 11:26 For whenever you eat this bread and drink this cup, you proclaim the Lord's death until he comes.

Matthew 26:26 While they were eating, Jesus took bread, and when he had given thanks, he broke it and gave it to his disciples, saying, "Take and eat; this is my body." 27 Then he took a cup, and when he had given thanks, he gave it to them, saying, "Drink from it, all of you. 28 This is my blood of the covenant, which is poured out for many for the forgiveness of sins. 29 I tell you, I will not drink from this fruit of the vine from now on until that day when I drink it new with you in my Father's kingdom."

John 6:55 For my flesh is real food and my blood is real drink. 56 Whoever eats my flesh and drinks my blood remains in me, and I in them. 57 Just as the living Father sent me and I live because of the Father, so the one who feeds on me will live because of me. 58 This is the bread that came down from heaven. Your ancestors ate manna and died, but whoever feeds on this bread will live forever." 59 He said this while teaching in the synagogue in Capernaum.

1 Corinthians 10:16 Is not the cup of thanksgiving for which we give thanks a participation in the blood of Christ? And is not the bread that we break a participation in the body of Christ? 17 Because there is one loaf, we, who are many, are one body, for we all share the one loaf.

52 The Magician takes an idea, purifies it, intensifies it by invoking into it the inspiration of his soul. It is no longer a scrawl scratched on a sheep-skin, but a word of Truth, imperishable, mighty to prevail throughout the sphere of its purport. The evocation of a spirit is precisely similar in essence. The exorcist takes dead material substances of a nature sympathetic to the being whom he intends to invoke. He banishes all impurities therefrom, prevents all interference therewith, and proceeds to give life to the subtle substance thus prepared by instilling his soul.

exorcism

Matthew 8:28 When he arrived at the other side in the region of the Gadarenes, two demon-possessed men coming from the tombs met him. They were so violent that no one could pass that way. 29 "What do you want with us, Son of God?" they shouted. "Have you come here to torture us before the appointed time?" 30 Some distance from them a large herd of pigs was feeding. 31 The demons begged Jesus, "If you drive us out, send us into the herd of pigs." 32 He said to them, "Go!" So they came out and went into the pigs, and the whole herd rushed down the steep bank into the lake and died in the water. 33 Those tending the pigs ran off, went into the town and reported all this, including what had happened to the demon-possessed men. 34 Then the whole town went out to meet Jesus. And when they saw him, they pleaded with him to leave their region.

Mark 16:16 Whoever believes and is baptized will be saved, but whoever does not believe will be condemned. 17 And these signs will accompany those who believe: In my name they will drive out demons; they will speak in new tongues; 18 they will pick up snakes with their hands; and when they drink deadly poison, it will not hurt them at all; they will place their hands on sick people, and they will get well."

Ephesians 6:10 Finally, be strong in the Lord and in his mighty power. 11 Put on the full armor of God, so that you can take your stand against the devil's schemes. 12 For our struggle is not against flesh and blood, but against the rulers, against the authorities, against the powers of this dark world and against the spiritual forces of evil in the heavenly realms. 13 Therefore put on the full armor of God, so that when the day of evil comes, you may be able to stand your ground, and after you have done everything, to stand. 14 Stand firm then, with the belt of truth buckled around your waist, with the breastplate of righteousness in place, 15 and with your feet fitted with the readiness that comes from the gospel of peace. 16 In addition to all this, take up the shield of faith, with which you can extinguish all the flaming arrows of the evil one. 17 Take the helmet of salvation and the sword of the Spirit, which is the word of God. 18 And pray in the Spirit on all occasions with all kinds of prayers and requests. With this in mind, be alert and always keep on praying for all the Lord's people.

53	the vehemence proper to the pure gas. We may summarize this thesis by saying that Alchemy includes as many possible operations as there are original ideas inherent in nature. Alchemy resembles evocation in its selection of appropriate material bases for the manifestation	alchemy

of the Will; but differs from it in proceeding without personification, or the intervention of alien planes.<<Some alchemists may object to this statement. I prefer to express no final opinion on the matter.>> It may be more closely compared with Initiation; for the effective element of the Product is of the essence of its own nature, and inherent therein; the Work similarly consists in isolating it from its accretions.

Revelation 21:8 But the cowardly, the unbelieving, the vile, the murderers, the sexually immoral, those who practice magic arts, the idolaters and all liars—they will be consigned to the fiery lake of burning sulfur. This is the second death."

Colossians 2:8 See to it that no one takes you captive through hollow and deceptive philosophy, which depends on human tradition and the elemental spiritual forces of this world rather than on Christ.

Deuteronomy 18:10 Let no one be found among you who sacrifices their son or daughter in the fire, who practices divination or sorcery, interprets omens, engages in witchcraft, 11 or casts spells, or who is a medium or spiritist or who consults the dead. 12 Anyone who does these things is detestable to the Lord; because of these same detestable practices the Lord your God will drive out those nations before you.

Of Black Magic of the Main Types of the Operations of Magick Art and of the Powers of the Sphinx

54 There are, of course, entirely black forms of magic. To him who has not given every drop of his blood for the cup of BABALON all magic power is dangerous. There are even more debased and evil forms, things in themselves black. Such is the use of spiritual force to material ends. Christian Scientists, Mental Healers, Professional Diviners, Psychics and the like, are all "ipso facto" Black Magicians. They exchange gold for dross. They sell their higher

Christian Scientists Mental healers

powers for gross and temporary benefit.

James 5:14 Is anyone among you sick? Let them call the elders of the church to pray over them and anoint them with oil in the name of the Lord. 15 And the prayer offered in faith will make the sick person well; the Lord will raise them up. If they have sinned, they will be forgiven.

Matthew 8:1 When Jesus came down from the mountainside, large crowds followed him. 2 A man with leprosy came and knelt before him and said, "Lord, if you are willing, you can make me clean." 3 Jesus reached out his hand and touched the man. "I am willing," he said. "Be clean!" Immediately he was cleansed of his leprosy.

Jeremiah 30:17 But I will restore you to health and heal your wounds,' declares the LORD, 'because you are called an outcast, Zion for whom no one cares.'

Psalm 30:2 LORD my God, I called to you for help, and you healed me.

55 This serpent, SATAN, is not the enemy of Man, but He who made Gods of our race, knowing Good and Evil; He bade "Know Thyself!" and taught Initiation. He is "the Devil" of the Book of Thoth, and His emblem is BAPHOMET, the Androgyne who is the hieroglyph of arcane perfection. The number of His Atu is XV, which is Yod He, the Monogram of the Eternal, the Father one with the Mother, the Virgin Seed one with all-containing Space. He is therefore Life, and Love. Satan

John 8:42 Jesus said to them, "If God were your Father, you would love me, for I have come here from God. I have not come on my own; God sent me. 43 Why is my language not clear to you? Because you are unable to hear what I say. 44 You belong to your father, the devil, and you want to carry out your father's desires. He was a murderer from the beginning, not holding to the truth, for there is no truth in him. When he lies, he speaks his native language, for he is a liar and the father of lies.

Revelation 20:1 And I saw an angel coming down out of heaven, having the key to the Abyss and holding in his hand a great chain. 2 He seized the dragon, that ancient serpent, who is the devil, or Satan, and bound him for a thousand years. 3 He threw him into the Abyss, and locked and sealed it over him, to keep him from deceiving the nations anymore until the thousand years were ended. After that, he must be set free for a short time.

Luke 22:1 Now the Festival of Unleavened Bread, called the Passover, was approaching, 2 and the chief priests and the teachers of the law were looking for some way to get rid of Jesus, for they were afraid of the people. 3 Then Satan entered Judas, called Iscariot, one of the Twelve. 4 And Judas went to the chief priests and the officers of the temple guard and discussed with them how he might betray Jesus. 5 They were delighted and agreed to give him money. 6 He consented, and watched for an opportunity to hand Jesus over to them when no crowd was present.

Isaiah 14:12 How you have fallen from heaven, morning star, son of the dawn! You have been cast down to the earth, you who once laid low the nations!

56 It is, however, always easy to call up the demons, for they are always calling you; and you have only to step down to their level and fraternize with them. They will tear you in pieces at their leisure. Not at once; they will wait until you have wholly broken the link between you and your Holy Guardian Angel before they pounce, lest at the last moment you escape. Anthony of Padua and (in our own times) "Macgregor" Mathers are examples of such victims. Nevertheless, every magician must firmly extend his empire to the depth of hell. "My adepts stand upright, their heads above the heavens, their feet below the hells."

Rev 17:14 They will wage war against the

demons
empire

Lamb, but the Lamb will triumph over them because he is Lord of lords and King of kings—and with him will be his called, chosen and faithful followers." 15 Then the angel said to me, "The waters you saw, where the prostitute sits, are peoples, multitudes, nations and languages. 16 The beast and the ten horns you saw will hate the prostitute. They will bring her to ruin and leave her naked; they will eat her flesh and burn her with fire. 17 For God has put it into their hearts to accomplish his purpose by agreeing to hand over to the beast their royal authority, until God's words are fulfilled. 18 The woman you saw is the great city that rules over the kings of the earth."

2 Sam 7:23 And who is like your people Israel—the one nation on earth that God went out to redeem as a people for himself, and to make a name for himself, and to perform great and awesome wonders by driving out nations and their gods from before your people, whom you redeemed from Egypt?

Dan 1:17 To these four young men God gave knowledge and understanding of all kinds of literature and learning. And Daniel could understand visions and dreams of all kinds. 18 At the end of the time set by the king to bring them into his service, the chief official presented them to Nebuchadnezzar. 19 The king talked with them, and he found none equal to Daniel, Hananiah, Mishael and Azariah; so they entered the king's service. 20 In every matter of wisdom and understanding about which the king questioned them, he found them ten times better than all the magicians and enchanters in his whole kingdom.

57	The operations of Magick art are difficult to classify, as they merge into each other, owing to the essential unity of their method and result. We may mention:....2. Consecrations of talismans in which a live spirit is bound into "dead" matter and vivifies the same.	talismans

Isaiah 3:18 In that day the Lord will snatch

away their finery: the bangles and headbands and crescent necklaces, 19 the earrings and bracelets and veils, 20 the headdresses and anklets and sashes, the perfume bottles and charms, 21 the signet rings and nose rings, 22 the fine robes and the capes and cloaks, the purses 23 and mirrors, and the linen garments and tiaras and shawls.

Ezekiel 13:18 and say, 'This is what the Sovereign Lord says: Woe to the women who sew magic charms on all their wrists and make veils of various lengths for their heads in order to ensnare people. Will you ensnare the lives of my people but preserve your own? 19 You have profaned me among my people for a few handfuls of barley and scraps of bread. By lying to my people, who listen to lies, you have killed those who should not have died and have spared those who should not live.

58   6. Works of destruction, which may be done in many different ways. One may fascinate and bend to one's will a person who has of his own right the power to destroy. One may employ spirits or talismans. The more powerful magicians of the last few centuries have employed books.   destruction building

1 Thessalonians 5:11 Therefore encourage one another and build each other up, just as in fact you are doing.

1 Corinthians 3:9 For we are co-workers in God's service; you are God's field, God's building. 10 By the grace God has given me, I laid a foundation as a wise builder, and someone else is building on it. But each one should build with care. 11 For no one can lay any foundation other than the one already laid, which is Jesus Christ. 12 If anyone builds on this foundation using gold, silver, costly stones, wood, hay or straw, 13 their work will be shown for what it is, because the Day will bring it to light. It will be revealed with fire, and the fire will test the quality of each person's work. 14 If what has been built survives, the builder will receive a reward. 15 If it is burned up, the builder will suffer loss but yet will be saved— even though only as one escaping through the flames.

Ephesians 2:19 Consequently, you are no longer foreigners and strangers, but fellow citizens with God's people and also members of his household, 20 built on the foundation of the apostles and prophets, with Christ Jesus himself as the chief cornerstone. 21 In him the whole building is joined together and rises to become a holy temple in the Lord. 22 And in him you too are being built together to become a dwelling in which God lives by his Spirit.

Proverbs 24:3 By wisdom a house is built, and through understanding it is established; 4 through knowledge its rooms are filled with rare and beautiful treasures.

59 Necromancy is of sufficient importance to demand a section to itself. It is justifiable in some exceptional cases. Suppose the magician fail to obtain access to living Teachers, or should he need some especial piece of knowledge which he has reason to believe died with some teacher of the past, it may be useful to evoke the "shade" of such a one, or read the "Akasic record" of his mind. — necromancy

1 John 4:1 Dear friends, do not believe every spirit, but test the spirits to see whether they are from God, because many false prophets have gone out into the world. 2 This is how you can recognize the Spirit of God: Every spirit that acknowledges that Jesus Christ has come in the flesh is from God, 3 but every spirit that does not acknowledge Jesus is not from God. This is the spirit of the antichrist, which you have heard is coming and even now is already in the world.

Rev 21:8 But the cowardly, the unbelieving, the vile, the murderers, the sexually immoral, those who practice magic arts, the idolaters and all liars—they will be consigned to the fiery lake of burning sulfur. This is the second

death."

Leviticus 19:31 "'Do not turn to mediums or seek out spiritists, for you will be defiled by them. I am the Lord your God.

Isaiah 8:19 When someone tells you to consult mediums and spiritists, who whisper and mutter, should not a people inquire of their God? Why consult the dead on behalf of the living? 20 Consult God's instruction and the testimony of warning. If anyone does not speak according to this word, they have no light of dawn. 21 Distressed and hungry, they will roam through the land; when they are famished, they will become enraged and, looking upward, will curse their king and their God.

60 This technique of Yoga is the most important detail of all our work. The MASTER THERION has been himself somewhat to blame in representing this technique as of value simply because it leads to the great rewards, such as Samadhi. He would have been wiser to base His teaching solely on the ground of evolution. But probably He thought of the words of the poet: "You dangle a carrot in front of her nose, And she goes wherever the carrot goes." samadhi yoga

1 John 4:13 This is how we know that we live in him and he in us: He has given us of his Spirit. 14 And we have seen and testify that the Father has sent his Son to be the Savior of the world. 15 If anyone acknowledges that Jesus is the Son of God, God lives in them and they in God.

1 Corinthians 6:17 But whoever is united with the Lord is one with him in spirit.

Romans 8:9 You, however, are not in the realm of the flesh but are in the realm of the Spirit, if indeed the Spirit of God lives in you. And if anyone does not have the Spirit of Christ, they do not belong to Christ.

Romans 6:5 For if we have been united with him in a death like his, we will certainly also be united with him in a resurrection like his.

1 Corinthians 6:19 Do you not know that your

bodies are temples of the Holy Spirit, who is in you, whom you have received from God? You are not your own; 20 you were bought at a price. Therefore honor God with your bodies.

Acts 2:38 Peter replied, "Repent and be baptized, every one of you, in the name of Jesus Christ for the forgiveness of your sins. And you will receive the gift of the Holy Spirit. 39 The promise is for you and your children and for all who are far off—for all whom the Lord our God will call." 40 With many other words he warned them; and he pleaded with them, "Save yourselves from this corrupt generation."

Subject Index

A

acausal, 107, 168
achievement, 70, 110
adept, 171
adeptship, 133
aeonic, 181
afterlife, 16, 62, 188
alchemy, 263
altar, 215
America, 145
amoral, 54
angels, 247
anti-christian, 106
anti-Christian, 170
antimatter, 169
arrogance, 119, 163
artist, 13
aryan race, 36
astral body, 256
atheism, 138
authority, 20, 166
ayranism, 35

B

bad memories, 225
balance, 227
baptism, 18
beauty, 13
birthday, 201
black magic, 79
black mass, 74
blasphemy, 138
blood, 23
blood sacrifice, 234
book, 70
building, 268
business, 12, 13, 49, 186, 189, 190

C

carnal nature, 182
catharsis, 149
celebrity, 13
ceremony, 27
chalice, 24
challenges, 98
chanting, 21
chants, 32
chaos, 44, 85, 144
charity, 183
Christian Scientists, 264
civilization, 131
cleansing, 237
communion, 45
communion hosts, 74
competition, 11, 12
compromise, 102
consecration, 238
correcting, 8
create, 64, 68
creation, 142
creed, 18
crime, 20
cross, 18
crystals, 18, 43, 81
culling, 49, 91, 105, 165, 177
curse, 206
cursing, 42

D

dark gods, 44, 77, 114, 169
dark side, 99
death, 174
deceiver, 42
defiance, 21, 37, 38, 52, 65, 112
delusions, 30
demonic possession, 83, 123, 124
demons, 26, 266
desires, 17, 71, 124

destiny, 60, 68, 136, 153
destruction, 268
development, 61
devil, 18
dichotomy, 151
discipleship, 133
disguise, 42
dissent, 118
divination, 260
divine presence, 63
dogma, 22
dominance, 244
drug dealing, 167

E

ecstacy, 231
ecstasy, 21
either or, 8
elections, 11
elite, 102
elitism, 161
emotionalism, 124
empathy, 171
empire, 266
enemies, 20, 40, 46, 186, 201, 210, 213
enemy, 16, 242
energies, 67, 156
energy, 45, 80, 94
enlightenment, 173
equality, 35
eucharist, 261
eunuchs, 186
evidence, 226
evil defined, 127
evolution, 14, 50, 121, 132, 180
excellence, 96, 157
exorcism, 262
exorcist, 239
experience, 50
expose evil, 8
extraversion vs introject, 125

F

false gods, 218
false gods, 43, 250
fame, 13
following, 51
following Jesus, 99
forgiveness, 193
free will, 136
freedom, 192
future, 29

G

gender, 13
ghosts, 260
goals, 13, 71
God's will, 22
gods, 37, 38, 93, 116
good vs evil, 151
gratification, 195
guru, 256

H

hatred, 29, 242
heaven, 33, 232
hell, 195
helping, 205
highest type, 101
history, 22, 87
Hitler, 152
holocaust, 36, 143
human sacrifice, 200, 234
humility, 13, 16, 190, 230

I

idolatry, 38
idols, 241
illegal activity, 128, 144
illusions, 13, 30
immodesty, 214
incitement of war, 130
individualism, 111, 162, 167

indulgence, 196, 199
initiation, 20, 73, 74
inner strength, 30
insight, 73
insight role, 158
insight roles, 181
insights, 58, 132
intentions, 212
invocation, 23, 217, 250
Islam, 148
isolation, 103
Israel, 34, 145

J

Jesus, 18, 75
jewelry, 115
judgment, 32
Jung, 78
justification, 23

K

Kabbalah, 219
karma, 225, 245, 258
knowledge, 68, 140, 158, 215

L

last days, 46
learning, 66
left hand path, 134
Left hand path, 137
life, 94
lifeforce, 234
light, 34, 255, 258
locus of control, 57
Lord's supper, 17, 25
love, 10, 11, 12
love one another, 185
love vs hate, 197
love your enemies, 187
lust, 39, 41, 47, 205, 212

M

magic, 17, 19
magic defence, 209
magic imagery, 210
magick, 78
man as god, 258
man's will, 22, 216
marketing, 25
Marxism, 179
masculine vs feminine, 216
materialism, 184
matrimony, 17
meeting, 25
membership, 25
mental darkness, 112
Mental healers, 264
mental peace, 210
mind as enemy, 219
money, 252
moon, 79
moral code, 52
morality, 53, 99
morals, 141
murder, 76

N

name, 24
names, 30
names of Satan, 221
National socialism, 179
nature, 211
nazarenes, 80
nazism, 34, 35, 147
Nazism, 180
necromancy, 269
neighbour, 12, 29
neither good nor evil, 108
new aeon, 95
new creation, 86
new individual, 150
new person, 49
non-believers, 16

O

oaths, 25, 246
obedience, 38
occult, 156
order, 44
other religions, 16

P

pacifism, 176
paganism, 218
partakers, 125
partner, 72
pathway, 121
persecution, 201
personal development, 112
personal growth, 55
personality, 13
pleasure, 17, 41, 140
pleasures, 28
politics, 129
possession, 114
potential, 56, 64
power, 23
praise, 16
prana, 234
prayer, 15, 17, 114, 192, 217, 249
presencing the dark, 176
pride, 28, 40, 51, 154, 230
prophesy, 147
psychology, 12, 14

R

racism, 35, 143
reality, 13, 254
reasoning, 160
rebellion, 52, 109, 118, 166
rebuking, 8
relativism, 230
religions, 257
religious sex, 43
renaming, 31
rest, 9

Resurrection of Christ, 220
revenge, 244
rewards, 59, 111
right hand path, 134
Right hand path, 137
ritual, 15, 17, 20, 23
ritual desire, 207
ritual magic, 203
ritual timing, 208
rituals, 31
ruler of the world, 42

S

sacrilege, 75
salt, 23
salvation, 18, 73
samadhi, 231, 270
Satan, 88, 139, 265
Satan is real, 84
Satanic morality, 164
seduction, 47
self-actualization, 27
self-awareness, 120
self-delusion, 118
self-development, 12
self-fulfillment, 26
self-insight, 165
self-knowledge, 28
servants of God, 24
sexual desires, 198
sexual intercourse, 234
singing, 21
sinister dialectic, 89
sinister temple, 113
sins, 195
society, 11, 12, 92
sorcery, 19, 78
soul, 49, 174, 256
spirit, 168
spirit of life, 122
spirits, 251
spiritual development, 104
spiritual growth, 59
spiritual guide, 256

stars, 36
strength, 16, 65
strength of character, 129
strong vs weak, 54
submission, 157
success, 9, 10, 11, 49, 55
survival, 14

T

talent, 90
talismans, 252, 267
tarot, 71, 155
teachings, 22
temple dedication, 19
temples, 75
temptation, 30, 36, 41
tests, 117
the cross, 184
the future, 95
The Great Work, 236
the strong, 9, 40
this life, 48
this world, 21
threats, 48
transmutation, 172
true god, 201
true king, 16
true success, 126
truth, 228, 254

U

understanding, 104

uniqueness, 104
unity, 24
universe, 82

V

vengeance, 33, 178, 184
vices, 235
victim, 207
victimization, 177
victims, 77, 105
victory, 9

W

war, 11
wars, 175
wasting life, 61
Way of life, 14
weakness, 189
weapons, 243
wisdom, 96, 97, 100, 110
witchcraft, 69, 204
works, 24
worldliness, 27
worldly pleasures, 58
worship, 15

Y

yoga, 270
youth, 16

www.ingramcontent.com/pod-product-compliance
Lightning Source LLC
Chambersburg PA
CBHW070131080526
44586CB00015B/1644